Freedom

from

Internal Spirits

Freedom

from

Internal Spirits

KIM MICHAELS

MORE TO LIFE PUBLISHING

www.morepublish.com

For foreign and translation rights,

contact info@ morepublish.com

ISBN: 978-87-93297-78-4

The information and insights in this book should not be considered as a form of therapy, advice, direction, diagnosis, and/or treatment of any kind. This information is not a substitute for medical, psychological, or other professional advice, counseling and care. All matters pertaining to your individual health should be supervised by a physician or appropriate health-care practitioner. No guarantee is made by the author or the publisher that the practices described in this book will yield successful results for anyone at any time. They are presented for informational purposes only, as the practice and proof rests with the individual.

For more information: *www.ascendedmasterlight.com and www.transcendencetoolbox.com*

CONTENTS

INTRODUCTION

This book is part of the series *The Path to Self-Mastery*. The purpose of the series is to give you a complete course for knowing and passing the mystical initiations of the seven spiritual rays. The books in the series form a progression, and it is recommended that you start by working through the books in the order they were released.

This book is the second in the series, with the first book being *The Power of Self*. The first book introduced many of the basic concepts about the spiritual path that you need in order to make the most efficient use of this and the following books. It is therefore recommended that you read *The Power of Self* before reading this and the succeeding books in the series.

The purpose of this book is to teach you about how we use our creative powers to create internal spirits that become part of our subconscious minds, almost like computer programs that take over our reactions to certain situations. These spirits serve a purpose for a time, but when it is time for us to rise to a higher level of the spiritual path, the spirits will actively work against our growth. Without being aware of such spirits and how to overcome them, it is difficult to rise beyond a certain level of spiritual growth.

This book is designed as a workbook in order to help you better integrate and apply the teachings. You will get the best results if you give the invocation that corresponds to the chapter you are studying (Chapter 3 through Chapter 21). It is recommended that you give a specific invocation once a day for nine days and then study part of the corresponding dictation before or after giving the invocation. Each evening, make calls to be taken to the Maha Chohan's retreat, located over Sri Lanka.

You give an invocation by reading it aloud, thereby invoking high-frequency spiritual energy. For more information about invocations and how to give them, please see the website: *www.transcendencetoolbox.com.* You can also purchase a recording of the invocations and give them along with the recording. The recording is available on *www.morepublish.com.*

In order to learn more about the ascended masters and how they give dictations, see the website *www.ascendedmaster-resources.com.* If you are not familiar with the concepts of the fall and of fallen beings, please read *Cosmology of Evil.* That book gives a profound yet easily understood explanation of why there are some beings who have no respect for the free will (or lives) of human beings. It explains why they are willing to do anything in order to control us or destroy those who will not be controlled.

1 | EXPRESSING YOUR CREATIVE POWERS

As explained in the Introduction, the first book in this series is *The Power of Self*. This chapter is a summary of the main ideas presented in that book. It is mainly given for people who have not yet read *The Power of Self*.

Matter = Energy

Right now, your self-awareness is focused in what is just one "pocket" in a much larger reality. This pocket if what we generally call "the material universe." What exactly is this universe? In 1905, Albert Einstein published the theory of relativity, best known for the formula $E=mc^2$. This formula proves that what we call "matter" is not a self-existing substance—in fact, it is a construct of our minds. In reality, matter is made from energy, and energy is a form of vibration.

The consequence is that matter is energy that vibrates within a certain spectrum. Yet there is an infinite continuum of vibrations, ranging from lower vibrations that we can detect with our physical senses, to vibrations so high that we cannot detect them with our senses or mechanical instruments. This means that there is a vast range of vibrations beyond what we call the material universe.

Human beings are generally aware of only a small pocket in the total spectrum of vibrations, yet this does not mean that the rest of the continuum is not real. In fact, if there was not a larger world beyond the material, the material world simply could not exist. This is even proven by Einstein's formula. We can divide with the same factor on both sides of the equal sign, which gives us this new formula:

$$\frac{E}{c^2} = \frac{m c^2}{c^2}$$

Since c^2 now appears twice on the right side, they cancel each other out and we end up with his final formula.

$$\frac{E}{c^2} = m$$

What this new formula tells us is that all matter, *m*, is truly created from a form of energy, E that vibrates at a very high level of vibration. Thus, the material universe is created from higher or finer energies that have been reduced in vibration by a very large reduction factor, namely the speed of light squared (*c^2*). In other words, what we call the material universe is made from higher energies, which we might call spiritual energies.

This means that the material world is not self-existing. In fact, the material world is not even existing as a separate unit. It only seems that way to us because with our present level of consciousness, we cannot perceive the higher vibrations. Yet this is not the only way we can perceive life.

Everything is Consciousness

Based on Einstein's theories, other physicists developed quantum mechanics, and they have proven that at the most fundamental level of matter, there is a form of consciousness. Our minds can interact with this consciousness, which means that our minds cannot be produced by the physical matter in the brain. Our minds must have existed before the brain. In fact, some physicists have concluded that the entire universe is a giant mind, rather than a giant machine. Meaning that consciousness is the fundamental reality.

This raises the question of how the very high vibrations were reduced to the level of the material universe? And the obvious answer for spiritually minded people is that this was done by spiritual beings in a higher realm. These beings are what in this series of books are called the "ascended masters." In reality, there is only one consciousness, one mind, namely that of the Creator. Yet this one mind has expressed itself as a hierarchy of spiritual beings, and they form a "chain of being" from the Creator to the lowest level of vibration, namely the material universe.

Who form the lowest level in this chain of being? Well, we human beings do. We are extensions of ascended masters in the lowest spiritual realm, the realm that is right above the material world in vibration. In fact, we have a part of our beings that permanently resides in the spiritual realm, and it is our higher self, also called the I AM Presence.

In reality, we are spiritual beings, and we have descended into the dense energies of the material realm where we have taken on bodies made from the energies of this realm. Yet our minds are still spiritual beings, which means we have the potential to become aware of who we are and where we came from. By attaining this awareness, we can also fulfill our original reason for coming here, namely to serve as co-creators.

The earth was created by a group of seven spiritual beings, called the Elohim. Yet they only created the earth from the outside, and they did not complete the work. We are co-creators, who are meant to finish the creation of the earth from the inside. When we unlock the full creative powers of the Self, we have two essential abilities. Our minds can serve as doorways for receiving spiritual light from a higher realm and then reducing it in vibration, so that it can be used to create in the material realm. Our minds also have the ability to formulate mental images and superimpose them upon the spiritual light whereby we can create physical structures.

Point-like Self-Awareness

If we are spiritual beings, why have most of us forgotten this fact and instead come to see ourselves as limited human beings? The explanation is that the earth is designed as an educational institution or laboratory, in which we can expand our awareness of who we are and the creative abilities we have. Thus, we do not descend into embodiment with the full awareness of what we are. Instead, we descend with a point-like self-awareness, which we are meant to gradually expand. This is how we grow in self-awareness, until we can pass the final exam in the schoolroom of earth and become ascended masters.

The core of your being is what the ascended masters call the "Conscious You." This is the seat of your imagination and free will. The Conscious You is not a separate being, but an extension of your spiritual self or I AM Presence. Thus, it has the ability to project itself into any situation in the material universe and experience it from the inside.

In order to project itself into a physical body, the Conscious You must first project itself into a "self" that is created from the energies of the material realm. Once the Conscious You is inside such a self, it will now look at life through the perception filter of the self. This explains why it is possible for us to forget our spiritual origin and come to believe we are limited, human beings. Once inside a material self, everything we "see" through that self confirms that we are limited material beings.

However, we can never quite forget that we came from somewhere outside the material world and the material self. That is why so many people have a longing for a higher world or a longing to understand the spiritual side of life. And forgetting about our spiritual origin is not wrong or a sin. In fact, we grow in self-awareness by going through this cycle or forgetting who we are and then gradually awakening to our true identity.

Your I AM Presence

You are here because the Conscious You was sent here by your I AM presence. The I AM Presence had two purposes for sending an extension of itself into the material realm.

One purpose was that it wanted to experience the material world from the inside, as this helps the Presence gain a valuable perspective on the spiritual world and who it is. This means that nothing you have experienced in this and past lifetimes is wasted. Even if you experienced a very unpleasant situation, your I AM Presence can learn from this by acknowledging:

"I am more than this." And you can transcend the experience – any experience – by awakening to the fact that you are the Conscious You and that you are pure awareness, which cannot be changed by anything on earth.

The second purpose is that the I AM Presence wants to expand its co-creative abilities, and it does so by expressing those powers through the Conscious You. Of course, this can happen fully only after the Conscious You awakens and comes to see itself as an open door for the I AM Presence. That is when you can express your full creative potential, which was described by Jesus when he said: "With men this is impossible, but with God all things are possible."

Jesus and other spiritual teachers came to show us our full creative potential. We cannot express that potential as long as we see ourselves as human beings. Yet by awakening to our true identity, we become the open doors that no man can shut. The purpose of this series of books is to help you develop the fullness of your co-creative powers. What exactly does that mean?

The seven spiritual rays

We earlier said that everything in the material universe is made from spiritual energies, whose vibration has been reduced. Einstein said this reduction factor is a mathematical constant, but in reality, there are seven such reduction factors. The ascended masters teach that there are seven spiritual rays that serve to reduce spiritual energy to the level of vibration where it can be used to construct what we see as matter objects.

There are a number of ascended masters who serve on each of the seven rays. The highest level is the level of the Elohim, and they are the beings who originally lowered the vibration of spiritual energy, until there was enough material to construct planet earth. They are still serving to send spiritual energy into the material realm, however now this happens largely through us.

The next level is the level of Archangels, who serve as a kind of intermediary or messenger between us and the spiritual realm. This is necessary because we have forgotten our spiritual origin and thus cannot use spiritual energy directly. The Archangels serve to provide us with energy, which can take the form of spiritual protection, healing and other qualities.

The next level is the level of the Chohans, which are the teachers for each spiritual ray. Their primary role is to meet us at our present level of consciousness and then seek to gradually awaken us to our true identity and creative potential. It is the seven Chohans who have sponsored this series of books, along with the Maha Chohan, who is the head teacher for all seven rays.

The key to self-mastery is to know the seven spiritual rays and to develop your co-creative abilities to their fullest. Each ray has certain positive qualities, and you express the creative power of a given ray through its positive qualities. For example, the First Ray is the ray of creative power and will, which means you seek to create something that benefits all people instead of only yourself as a separate being. When you do this, your creative expression will have only positive effects. The result being that your creative powers will be multiplied, and you will feel more and more free.

Each ray also has perversions. For example, the perversions of the First Ray are the desires to control others and force them into compliance. When you express your creative power through such lower desires and feelings, the result will be that the spiritual energy is lowered much further than when you express it through the positive qualities. This means your creative efforts will not be multiplied, and you will end up feeling less free.

The 144 levels of consciousness

The ascended masters teach that when a new self-aware being first descends into embodiment on earth, it descends at a certain level of consciousness. There are a total of 144 levels of consciousness that are possible on earth. When you reach the 144th level, you have mastered the lessons on earth, and you can ascend. If you descend to the lowest level, you can no longer embody on earth, and you will have to go to lower worlds than this planet.

A new lifestream first descends at the 48th level. It will descend into a protected learning environment where it is under the direct supervision of the seven Chohans. If it follows the outlined course, it will gradually raise its consciousness from the 48th to the 96th level of consciousness. In the process of doing this, it will learn to use each of the seven rays, until it masters all rays and can express them in a balanced manner. It can then move on to higher levels of learning beyond the 96th level.

It is, however, possible that a lifestream can decide to use its co-creative abilities for selfish purposes. This means it can go or fall below the 48th level of consciousness. This normally means that the lifestream will now lose direct contact with its spiritual teachers. Instead, it will have to learn by seeing how the material universe acts as a mirror, giving it the physical conditions that correspond to its level of consciousness. This is why most people on earth see life as a struggle where they are constantly in opposition to nature, other people or even

God. This is what the ascended masters call the School of Hard Knocks.

About this book

The purpose of this series of books is to offer people an outer reminder of the true inner path to self-mastery. The first book in the series, *The Power of Self*, offered a general introduction to the path, including more in-depth explanations of the concepts described above.

This book contains two parts. Part One contain a series of discourses given directly by the Maha Chohan, who as mentioned serves as the head teacher for all of the rays. This will give you valuable insights and tools for walking the path to self-mastery, and it will give you a good foundation for participating in the exercise in Part Two. It will also give you a good foundation for using each of the following books.

The second part of the book will give you a general introduction to the seven spiritual rays and the Chohans who serve as the spiritual teachers on those rays. It will also offer you a practical exercise where you learn to invoke the pure energies of the seven rays during a seven-month period.

The following books in the series will each be dedicated to one of the seven rays. As explained, you will need to use all of the seven rays in order to attain self-mastery and unlock your full creative powers. Thus, you will eventually need all of the following books. Yet it is possible that as you complete the seven-month course, you will get an intuitive sense that you are working specifically on one ray right now. Thus, you can, of course, go to the book for that ray instead of starting with the book for the First Ray.

Unless you have a strong sense that you are working on a specific ray, it is recommended that you start with the book on the First Ray and work your way through all the books in a linear fashion. This is the best way to rise towards the 96th level of consciousness. This is also the process that will work for you regardless of your present level of consciousness.

The entire series of books is designed so that anyone can make use of it, even people who are below the 48th level. Yet, of course, no book can do it all for you. The books are meant merely as conscious reminders, and if you truly take advantage of them, they will help you develop your inner contact with your I AM Presence and your ascended teachers. This will allow you to get intuitive guidance from within, guidance that will be personal and will go beyond what you can receive from any book.

What is a dictation?

The chapters in Part One were given as direct dictations from the Maha Chohan. In Part Two, each chapter contains a short dictation from the Chohan of that ray. A dictation is a form of communication from the ascended masters, given through a person who has been trained to receive these messages. In my case, I started doing this in 2002 and have since received over a thousand of these messages.

To receive a dictation, I attune my consciousness to the master and then feel how the master releases a stream of light and consciousness. I do not actually see or hear the words, but tune in to the stream, and then it is translated into words in my mind. Thus, I do not know what is being said until I hear myself speak the words. This means there is less risk that my consciousness interferes with or colors the message, as the only option I have is to stop the dictation.

This does not mean that the master can say anything he or she wants through me, as it is necessary for me to have some grasp of the concepts the master is talking about. A master could not, for example, give a meaningful message about nuclear physics through me because I do not know enough about the topic. So the translation of the master's message into words does depend on the concepts in my mind and how I use words. The principle is that the masters use what the messenger has in his or her consciousness and then multiplies it. This, of course, also means that the messages are easily understood by people from the same cultural background as the messenger. The messenger can be said to represent a certain group of people, and the messenger's consciousness translates the messages, so they are adapted to the consciousness of the recipients.

The purpose of a dictation is not simply to give a linear understanding that can be grasped with the outer mind. The masters embed many things in a dictation, first of all a stream of spiritual light that you can absorb. It is, in fact, this light more than the words that make dictations great tools for self-transcendence. If you are open, hearing or even reading a dictation can instantly shift your consciousness, especially if you already have an affinity with the master who is speaking.

You can indeed absorb the master's light by reading a dictation. Yet you will get a more powerful experience from listening to a recording of the dictation. In our online store (www.morepublish.com) you can purchase and download recordings of the dictations in this book.

2 | INTRODUCING THE MAHA CHOHAN

"Maha" means great, which signifies that the Maha Chohan is the leader or director of the seven chohans. The name Maha Chohan is actually the name of the spiritual office, and not an individual being. Thus, the office has over time been held by different individual masters. The current master holding the office has not revealed his individual ascended master name.

The master currently holding the office of the Maha Chohan was embodied as the Greek poet Homer, famous for bringing forth the Iliad and the Odyssey. These epic poems symbolize the journey we all make, as we confront the "monsters" of the subconscious mind and find our way home to oneness with the I AM Presence. In his last lifetime, the Maha Chohan was embodied as a humble shepherd, proving that ascended masters are not always embodied as prominent people from history. Which means the rest of us can ascend as well.

The Maha Chohan is the director of the Temple of Comfort, which is located in the etheric realm over the island of Sri Lanka. This temple is also the planetary focus for the energies of the Holy Spirit, and the Maha Chohan is the planetary representative of this spiritual force.

The Holy Spirit is an energy or movement that is created through the combined creative efforts of all beings who have raised their consciousness since the world of form was created. In other words, any time we express our creativity in a benevolent way, meaning a way aimed at raising all life, we tie in to the creative flow of the Holy Spirit, also called the River of Life.

This means that when our motives and intentions are pure, the Holy Spirit will magnify our creative efforts. We can also call to the Holy Spirit to help us see any elements in our being that are not pure. And we can invoke the all-transforming energies of the Holy Spirit in order to purify our four lower bodies of all imperfections. The reason why invoking the Holy Spirit is so effective is that it is formed by the creative efforts of all seven rays, meaning it combines the positive qualities of all seven rays in a perfectly balanced way.

One might therefore say that the Maha Chohan is the archetype of a being who has the perfect balance between the seven rays. When you encounter the Presence of the Maha Chohan, you are immediately struck by how different he is from the seven Chohans. An individual Chohan has attainment on all seven rays, but since the Chohan is the primary representative of one ray, he or she naturally radiates the qualities of that ray in greater measure.

The Maha Chohan has mastered all seven rays, combined with the Eighth Ray of Integration. Thus, experiencing his Presence can take two forms. If you are currently working on a specific ray, the Maha Chohan can adjust his appearance to radiate the qualities of that ray more strongly. Yet if you take a closer look, you will see that his Presence is constantly shifting or oscillating, so that he will not maintain the radiance of a specific ray for long. Instead, his Presence may visibly shift from radiating one color to radiating a rainbow of all seven colors.

In the Presence of the Maha Chohan, you quickly become aware of the sense of being completely enveloped in a very soothing and comforting energy. This is because the Maha Chohan is constantly attuned to the flow of the Holy Spirit, and thus he can see that any appearance on earth is ultimately unreal, and it is also in the process of constantly changing. You may come to the Maha Chohan with certain burdens or problems, but if you make an effort to still the outer mind and attune to his Presence, you will soon get the feeling that these problems can all be transcended.

You quickly realize that the Maha Chohan is so comforting because he has absolutely no trace of criticism, condemnation or judgment. How could he judge any human being, when he knows any appearance is temporary and will inevitably be changed by the magnetic pull of the Holy Spirit? In order to get a feel for this force, consider that we do not actually feel how the earth is constantly moving through space. Yet science has discovered that the entire universe is expanding, so our solar system is constantly being carried along this giant cosmic river. Obviously, no force on earth could possibly withstand or stop this cosmic movement. And likewise, no force in the human mind can stop the flow of the Holy Spirit.

Surely, we have free will, and thus we can close ourselves off, so that the Holy Spirit cannot flow through our individual beings. Yet our resistance of the Holy Spirit simply cannot last forever, for as the entire universe continues to move, it will become harder and harder for us to resist the flow. Thus, there will come a point, when our minds become so chaotic that we can no longer stand it, and we eventually surrender some of our resistance to the flow of the Spirit. Knowing this, the Maha Chohan has no need to criticize us, but he stands ever ready to help us let go of our resistance and surrender ourselves into the flow of the River of Life. The Maha Chohan seeks to help you know that you can give up any aspect of the separate self, and that when you do so, God will "remember your sins no more." Thus, he helps you see that there really is no problem to solve, and there is no need to compensate for any shortcomings, mistakes or imperfections.

You simply let go of the illusions, and you invoke the seven rays and the Holy Spirit to transmute all misqualified energies, and then you are free to again flow with the exhilarating, ever-transcending force with which the Maha Chohan is one. If you will let him, he will help you feel one with that force as well, which is when you will know that this feeling of oneness is worth surrendering all aspects of the outer self. For it truly is incomparable; it is the Pearl of Great Price, and the Maha Chohan finds no greater joy, than when he can bestow this Pearl upon students who have passed the initiations of the Holy Spirit. This ceremony takes place in the central hall of his retreat, which contains a powerful focus for the energies of the Holy Spirit.

3 | YOU ARE MORE THAN YOUR MIND

The Maha Chohan I AM. The Maha Chohan is the title I have, the name of the office I hold. It is not my name as an individual God-free being, but my name is not important, as my identity – individuality, characteristics – are not important for the office I hold.

Truly, when you hold this office, you are transcending the individuality and personality, as it can be seen from the vantage point of a being that is embodied on earth. You have left this separate self, this lower self behind. You have so integrated all of the seven spiritual rays that it is almost meaningless to talk about individuality, when you talk to and for human beings in embodiment.

You can indeed know me as an individual being. I do of course have individual characteristics, but you cannot know them through the perception filter of the separate self. You can know them only by transcending that perception filter, by coming into oneness with me. And of course, the same is true for each of the Chohans of the seven rays.

How to truly know a spiritual ray

How can you know a particular Chohan? How can you know a particular spiritual ray? Yes, we have given you certain characteristics, but if you focus your attention on those characteristics, they will actually become a hindrance to you knowing that ray. For the ray cannot be confined to the outer characteristics.

You can know a ray only by coming into oneness with it, into oneness with the Chohan or the Archangel or the Elohim of that ray. Then, when you come into oneness, you are not looking at a particular ray as you normally look at things on earth where you look as if you were a separate subject studying a separate object from a distance, seeking to know its characteristics from a distance.

Instead you have made use of the most basic ability that you have, the ability of the Conscious You to withdraw itself from its identification with the lower self and instead come into oneness with something greater than that lower self. And of course, when you come into oneness with a particular spiritual ray, or the Chohan of that ray, you are not looking at that ray from a distance. You are not looking at it as an object for study.

You are forgetting yourself as a separate subject studying something distant from yourself, separate from yourself, set apart from your self. Instead, you have blended your consciousness with the consciousness of the Chohan. Thus, you are not looking at the ray from the outside; you are looking at it from the inside. You see what life looks like from the perspective of that particular ray.

This is how you get to know that ray. This is how you get to know what life looks like seen through that ray. When you blend into oneness with the First Ray, then the First Ray no longer forms a veil. Do you see that as long as you are looking at the First Ray as a separate subject studying a distant object, you cannot see through the light of that ray? It forms a veil, and you cannot see through the veil; and thus you cannot see the spiritual realm, you see only the material realm.

Applying the rays

Although the material realm is made from the energies of the seven rays, they have been lowered in vibration to the point where they have taken on a density that actually hides that they are expressions of the seven rays. So you may look at a rock or a mountain, and you cannot see that this seemingly solid substance is actually made out of light. And it is not made out of only one kind of light, but a blending of all seven rays. And therefore, the mountain looks massive, looks solid, to you, and it obscures your vision.

Likewise, when you become aware that there are seven rays, they will at first seem like distant objects available for study. There is nothing wrong with taking the approach of studying the rays. However, as I said, it is possible for a spiritual student to focus so much on studying the outer characteristics of the rays that you fail to see the light itself. You fail to come into oneness with the light, being so focused on studying the outer characteristics.

You see, when you look at the spiritual rays from the perspective of an unenlightened human being, you will see them as seven veils that prevent you from seeing into the spiritual realm. You may realize – you may even have some intuitive experience – that there are energies beyond the material substance that you detect with your senses. But when you attempt to see beyond the veil of matter, you only see another veil, made up of the seven spiritual rays. So it is entirely possible to become so focused on studying these rays and their characteristics, studying an outer teaching that you either do not see the ray, or that you forget to go beyond study and strive for *gnosis*, meaning "oneness with."

Knowledge vs Gnosis

Most people on earth are looking through the filter of the outer self, based on the illusion of separation and the many dualistic polarities that spring from that separation from your source. What they are actually doing, when they are studying an object, is that they are projecting predefined images, beliefs, and opinions – predefined symbols – upon the object of study, even as scientists in the field of quantum physics have realized.

When you perceive through this filter, what you see is not the object in its pure form. What you see is a combination of the vibration of the object and the vibrations found in your own mind—your perception filter. You are projecting that perception filter upon the object. As long as you are projecting any mental image at the object, you do not actually see the object, you see a mirage—an image created as an interference pattern between what you are projecting out and the consciousness behind the object of study.

This is "knowledge" as the world calls it; linear, analytical knowledge. It is not wisdom; it is not *gnosis*. You know only how your own mind interacts with that object. This leads to the conclusion that your mind, the human mind, can become a closed system, for you cannot see beyond your own projections. Your own projections have created such a dense veil, such a dense mental box that you really do not even see that there is anything beyond the box. You think you have attained what, from a worldly perspective, may seem like ultimate knowledge, for you think you have managed to force the entire universe into your thought-system, your belief system, your mental box.

A Mind clouded with images

This is precisely the situation that all people have, when they come to the point of studying under the seven Chohans and the Maha Chohan. You do not come to us with a mind that is free, for if it was already free, you would not need us, would you?

You come to us with a mind that is clouded by these images of what you think the world is like, what you think God is like, what you think you are like. The question is how willing you are to let us, the Chohans, challenge your images, your beliefs, and your pet theories of what life is like. When the student is ready, the teacher appears. This is the universal law that guides the interaction between spiritual teachers, true teachers, and the students in embodiment. But how ready are you? This is the question to ponder.

You see, science has discovered a simple law, called the second law of thermodynamics, which states that in a closed system, there will be such contradictory forces that all of the structures of the system will eventually be broken down, until nothing is left. So when your mind becomes a closed system, you become subject to the second law of thermodynamics, which is what we have called the School of Hard Knocks. At that point, when your mind is closed, you are not ready for a spiritual teacher. None of the seven Chohans can do anything for you.

You may attract a spiritual teacher on earth who claims that he or she can do something for you. You may even attract teachers from beyond the material realm in one of the lower realms – whether it be the emotional or the mental – who claim they can do something for you. Some of them may even parade as ascended masters, but you see, the deeper reality is that no teacher can ever do anything for you. The teacher can only inspire you to do something for yourself, for the simple reason that the true path is a path of self-mastery. And thus, you must be the one who takes charge. I cannot master your mind for you! Only you can master your own mind.

How to be teachable

As long as you believe you can fit the universe or the ascended masters or God into your mental box, you are not reachable, you are not teachable for the Chohans. We must simply stand by and watch how you learn from the School of Hard Knocks where you might follow false teachers until you have had enough of it. Or you might become subject to the material realm where you learn only by seeing a physical outpicturing of the mental images you are projecting out. You might even go into a spiral of limiting your creative freedom more and more, until you feel you can no longer move and you finally cry out for deliverance, crying out that there must be more to life, there must be a different approach to life.

You see, even when you cry out for deliverance, we of the Chohans cannot necessarily help you. The essential ingredient, the essential characteristic, of a person who is ready for the teacher of the Chohans is that you have realized that you must question your own perception, you must question the way you look at life.

Thus, we might say that the very first step on the path that is offered by the Chohans is that you acknowledge your ignorance. You actually acknowledge that even though you may have great knowledge from a worldly perspective that knowledge has now formed a prison around your mind that is holding you back. The common conception of ignorance in the world is that there is something you do not know. And in a sense, this is true; there is something you do not know, but why do you not know it?

It is actually not because the container of your mind is empty that you do not know what you do not know. It is because the container of your mind is too full, so that you cannot see what is beyond the contents of the container of your mind. Thus, before you come to the point where the Chohans can do anything for you, you must have at least some subtle sense that you need to question or look beyond the contents of the container of your mind. You must dare to question at least some of your pet theories, some of your deeply held beliefs, some of the things you have taken for granted.

We of the Chohans fully understand that when you first come to this point, you are not ready to question every belief you have. If you were to question them all at once, you would end up in an identity crisis, feeling like you do not know who you are. For you have, of course, built a sense of identity based on your beliefs.

Clutching your ideas

We are not asking you to throw them all out at once. But we are asking you to be willing to look at some of them, and to be willing to let us, each of the Chohans, challenge some of your beliefs. If you are not willing to do this, then we cannot help you. If you clutch your ideas, as the Zen Buddhists say, then we must let you sit there, clutching your ideas, until there is some openness somewhere where you are now willing to look beyond some idea. Then we have something to work with, then the Chohans can go in and say: "Then question that idea." And we will use that as a starting point. Whatever you are willing to question, we will use it as a starting point, until you have questioned that idea and then become open to questioning another idea. Then, gradually, we can take you further and further, until you come to those pivotal ideas that define your sense of identity, and therefore are not even contents of the container of self but actually make up the walls of the container of self. That is when you begin to dis-identify yourself from your beliefs. You begin to realize that you are not your beliefs; you are more than your beliefs.

That is when you can become open to the idea that the "you" that you are is not the outer self—that is so defined by beliefs and experiences in this world. You are beyond this outer self, you are beyond the appearances of this world, and you are beyond the conditions in this world. That is when you can begin to realize that you have the ability to step outside of the lower self. Even if it is only for a split second in the beginning, you can experience a state of consciousness where you are looking at an object without looking through the perception filter of the separate self. And therefore, you are not projecting anything upon the object.

Suddenly, then, you can have a glimpse, even a short glimpse that you are experiencing the object as it is. That is when you begin the true process of knowledge, the true process of *gnosis*. As long as you are seeing an object through the perception filter of the separate self, you must see the object as separate from the self, and you cannot come into oneness with the object or the consciousness behind it. You cannot come into oneness with the Chohan of a given ray as long as you see – as long as you look at that ray – through the perception filter. Only when you step outside of that filter – and have a glimpse of how that Chohan really is, when you do not see the Chohan through a filter – that is when you begin to know the ray. Then you can build upon that, you can multiply the talents you have been given and you can come gradually into oneness with the ray. When you come into oneness with the First Ray and the Chohan of Master MORE, then that ray will no longer form a veil that will obscure your vision of the spiritual realm. Now, when you are in oneness with the First Ray, it does not obscure your vision, for you see through it.

> And thus you are one step closer to heaven,
> through oneness with one of the sacred seven.

A babbling brook

As you work your way up through the seven rays, you gain a clearer and clearer vision of the spiritual realm, the spiritual reality. Then you can begin to come into the oneness that takes you to the 96th level of consciousness where you now face the choice of whether you will continue to seek to raise up the separate self – even using the knowledge you have gained on the seven rays to do so – or whether you will step up to a higher vision and seek to raise all life where you begin to see that all life is your true self.

There is only one self. There is only one mind; there is only one consciousness. There is only one Spirit, and it is the Holy Spirit that is lifting up all life that is carrying all life along with it, as a river moving towards the ocean of infinity.

I will end this discourse by giving you the image that if you want to know the Holy Spirit – the One Spirit, the Creative Spirit, the River of Life – then, contemplate the image of a babbling brook. If there is one close to where you live, then go there. Lie down on the banks of the brook and listen. Otherwise I am sure you can find a recording somewhere of the sound of a babbling brook. Allow yourself to be still, allow yourself to listen to the sound.

There are two aspects to which I would call your attention. The first aspect is that the brook is constantly flowing. Contemplate the fact that you cannot stop the flow of the river. You cannot stop the water from flowing; it is flowing eternally, on-goingly, and it never stops.

You may think that your mind can come up with a scheme for damming the river, but the water would keep rising until it overflows the dam. No dam reaches into heaven, but the water will. So no matter what human beings might do to dam up the River of Life – which is what most worldly thought systems are aimed at doing – there will come a point where the water will overflow.

When you contemplate the ongoingness of the river, you can come to realize, you can see and experience, the absolute futility – the absolute vanity – of thinking you can stop the flow, you can dam the river, you can force it into a matrix where it will be stationary. The One Spirit, the Holy Spirit, will never fit into any matrix created by the separate mind! It will always go on, it will always transcend, and it will always flow.

If you want to move on, if you want to get out of your self-created prison, then you must be willing to flow. We of the Chohans are here to help you flow. We are not here to give you stationary knowledge of each of the seven rays, so that you can sit there and feel wiser and smarter than other people because you know about the spiritual rays and they do not. If that is how you look at the seven rays, then you are misunderstanding what the seven rays and the path is all about.

Turbulence in your life

We have no desire to see our students become the proud, who have spiritual pride of thinking they are superior to those who do not know the ascended masters. What point would it be for us, who are already free from the dualistic mind of the ego and have no desire to set ourselves apart or make ourselves better than others? In order to know us, you must be willing to flow with us, for we are constantly flowing. We are not stationary, and so contemplate this aspect of the river, the ongoingness, the ever-moving forward thrust of the river towards the ultimate goal of oneness with the ocean of self. Then move on to the second aspect.

Consider why the brook is babbling. It is because the river, the water in the river, is flowing over the rocks at the bottom of the stream bed. As the water passes over the rocks, it creates turbulence, and turbulence creates the sound.

Now then, these rocks in the brook are a symbol for the beliefs you have in the container of self, the beliefs that are based on duality, the mental images of seeing your self as a separate subject, studying a separate object.

This is what you need to discard. You need to be willing to allow us, the Chohans, to get you to look at each rock in the stream of your consciousness, to see it for what it is, see the dualistic illusions behind it. Then take it out, throw it away and say: "I no longer need this in the stream of my consciousness."

Then, as you walk up through the seven rays, through the 48th level of consciousness towards the 96th, you throw away more and more rocks, and what will happen? What will happen is that the stream of your consciousness becomes more and more quiet. There is no longer the turbulence in your mind.

In a sense, we could say that the River of Life is already flowing through your mind—or you would not be alive. You are resisting the flow, and that is why you cannot see. You cannot see beyond the turbulence created as the water of life flows over the rocks. And your mind is so chaotic, so filled with mental and emotional noise that you cannot see anything beyond the noise that is generated inside your mind.

As you throw out rock after rock, there is no longer the turbulence. There will come a point where you begin to lock in to the stillness behind the babbling of the brook, the babbling of the mind, the eternal ongoing babbling of the ego. That is when you can begin, as I said, to see without seeing through the perception filter of the separate self. That is pure seeing that is true seeing that is naked awareness, pure awareness.

Quieting the mind

The first goal I set before you is to make it your goal to quiet the mind, so that you may actually see things as they really are. So that you may see the seven rays and the Chohans as they really are; without projecting an image upon that which you want to know. Beyond that, there is the larger goal of coming into oneness, instead of seeing everything from a distance. This is the first installment I wish to give you. There is plenty here to contemplate, but there is certainly plenty to come.

I thank you for your attention up until this point in the river, but be aware that the moment you put your attention on a point in the river that point will move on. The water of life will move on. The rock may keep its position, and so if you focus on the rock, you will be a stationary object. And you will feel that life is flowing by you, as the water of life is rushing over you. But at some point, you can give up clinging to the rock and flow with the stream, and then you will no longer feel that you are left out, or that life is leaving you behind.

As long as you are willing to move with life, how can you be left behind? Only that which is stationary can be left behind.

I AM the Maha Chohan, and I AM forever moving, forever transcending, forever becoming MORE. I am not only *in* the River of Life; I *AM* the River of Life for planet earth.

4 | INVOKING GNOSIS

In the name I AM THAT I AM, Jesus Christ, I call to my I AM Presence to flow through the I Will Be Presence that I AM and give this invocation with full power. I call to beloved Elohim Hercules and Amazonia, Archangel Michael and Faith, Master MORE and the Maha Chohan to help me experience what gnosis is. Help me see and surrender all patterns that block my oneness with the Maha Chohan and my oneness with my I AM Presence, including ...

[Make personal calls]

Part 1

1. Maha Chohan, help me see beyond the perception filter of my separate self and know you as an individual being. Help me transcend my perception filter and come into oneness with you.

O Hercules Blue, we're one with your will,
all space in our beings with Blue Flame you fill,
a beacon that radiates light to the earth,
bringing about our planet's rebirth.

O Hercules Blue, all life you defend,
giving us power to always transcend,
in you the expansion of self has no end,
as we in God's infinite spirals ascend.

2. Maha Chohan, help me see that if I focus my attention on the characteristics of a Chohan or spiritual ray, they will actually become a hindrance to me knowing that Chohan or ray. For the Chohan or ray cannot be confined to outer characteristics.

O Hercules Blue, your wisdom so great,
within us a sense of knowing create,
a new frame of reference we suddenly gain,
for going beyond duality's pain.

O Hercules Blue, all life you defend,
giving us power to always transcend,
in you the expansion of self has no end,
as we in God's infinite spirals ascend.

3. Maha Chohan, help me see that I can know a ray only by coming into oneness with it, into oneness with the Chohan, Archangel or Elohim of that ray.

O Hercules Blue, we lovingly raise,
our voices in giving God infinite praise,
in feeling your flame, so clearly we see,
transcending the self is the true alchemy.

**O Hercules Blue, all life you defend,
giving us power to always transcend,
in you the expansion of self has no end,
as we in God's infinite spirals ascend.**

4. Maha Chohan, help me see that when I come into oneness, I am not looking at a particular ray as I normally look at things on earth, where I look as if I were a separate subject studying a separate object from a distance.

O Hercules Blue, all life now you heal,
enveloping all in your Blue-flame Seal,
we're grateful for playing a personal part,
In God's infinitely intricate work of art.

**O Hercules Blue, all life you defend,
giving us power to always transcend,
in you the expansion of self has no end,
as we in God's infinite spirals ascend.**

5. Maha Chohan, help me make use of the most basic ability I have, the ability of the Conscious You to withdraw itself from identification with the lower self and instead come into oneness with something greater than that lower self.

O Hercules Blue, your Temple of Light,
revealed to us all through our inner sight,
your power allows us to forge on until,
we pierce every veil and climb every hill.

**O Hercules Blue, all life you defend,
giving us power to always transcend,**

**in you the expansion of self has no end,
as we in God's infinite spirals ascend.**

6. Maha Chohan, help me see that when I come into oneness with a particular spiritual ray, or the Chohan of that ray, I am not looking at that ray from a distance. I am not looking at it as an object for study.

O Hercules Blue, I pledge now my life,
in helping this planet transcend human strife,
duality's lies are pierced by your light,
restoring the fullness of our inner sight.

**O Hercules Blue, all life you defend,
giving us power to always transcend,
in you the expansion of self has no end,
as we in God's infinite spirals ascend.**

7. Maha Chohan, help me forget myself as a separate subject studying something distant from myself, separate from myself, set apart from my self.

O Hercules Blue, we set all life free,
from the subtlest lies of duality,
the prince of this world no more has a bond,
for with you we go completely beyond.

**O Hercules Blue, all life you defend,
giving us power to always transcend,
in you the expansion of self has no end,
as we in God's infinite spirals ascend.**

8. Maha Chohan, help me blend my consciousness with the consciousness of the Chohan so I am not looking at the ray from the outside; I am looking at it from the inside. I see what life looks like from the perspective of that particular ray.

O Hercules Blue, in oneness with thee,
we open our hearts to your reality,
your electric-blue fire within us reveal,
our innermost longing for all that is real.

**O Hercules Blue, all life you defend,
giving us power to always transcend,
in you the expansion of self has no end,
as we in God's infinite spirals ascend.**

9. Maha Chohan, help me see that when I blend into oneness with any ray, then that ray no longer forms a veil. As long as I am looking at a ray as a separate subject studying a distant object, I cannot see through the light of that ray because it forms a veil.

O Hercules Blue, you fill every space,
with infinite Power and infinite Grace,
you embody the key to creativity,
the will to transcend into Infinity.

**O Hercules Blue, all life you defend,
giving us power to always transcend,
in you the expansion of self has no end,
as we in God's infinite spirals ascend.**

Part 2

1. Maha Chohan, help me see that the material realm is made from the energies of the seven rays, but they have been lowered in vibration and taken on a density that hides that they are expressions of the seven rays.

Michael Archangel, in your flame so blue,
there is no more night, there is only you.
In oneness with you, we're filled with your light,
what glorious wonder, revealed to our sight.

Michael Archangel, your Knowing so strong,
Michael Archangel, oh sweep us along.
Michael Archangel, we're singing your song,
Michael Archangel, with you we belong.

2. Maha Chohan, help me see that seemingly solid substances are actually made out of light, namely a blending of all seven rays.

Michael Archangel, protection you give,
within your blue shield, we ever shall live.
Sealed from all creatures, roaming the night,
we remain in your sphere, of electric blue light.

Michael Archangel, your Knowing so strong,
Michael Archangel, oh sweep us along.
Michael Archangel, we're singing your song,
Michael Archangel, with you we belong.

3. Maha Chohan, help me avoid focusing so much on studying the outer characteristics that I fail to see the light or come into oneness with the light.

> Michael Archangel, what power you bring,
> as millions of angels, praises will sing.
> Consuming the demons, of doubt and of fear,
> we know that your Presence, will always be near.

> **Michael Archangel, your Knowing so strong,**
> **Michael Archangel, oh sweep us along.**
> **Michael Archangel, we're singing your song,**
> **Michael Archangel, with you we belong.**

4. Maha Chohan, help me see that if I focus on outer characteristics, the spiritual rays form seven veils that prevent me from seeing into the spiritual realm. Help me strive for *gnosis*, meaning "oneness with."

> Michael Archangel, God's will is your love,
> you bring to us all, God's light from Above.
> God's will is to see, all life taking flight,
> transcendence of self, our most sacred right.

> **Michael Archangel, your Knowing so strong,**
> **Michael Archangel, oh sweep us along.**
> **Michael Archangel, we're singing your song,**
> **Michael Archangel, with you we belong.**

5. Maha Chohan, help me see that when I look through the filter of the outer self, based on the illusion of separation and the dualistic polarities, I am actually projecting predefined images, beliefs, and opinions upon the object of study.

Michael Archangel, you are the best friend,
from all worldly dangers you do us defend,
the devil no match for your power of light,
and therefore our souls can freely take flight.

Michael Archangel, your Knowing so strong,
Michael Archangel, oh sweep us along.
Michael Archangel, we're singing your song,
Michael Archangel, with you we belong.

6. Maha Chohan, help me see that when I perceive through this filter, what I see is not the object in its pure form. I see a combination of the vibration of the object and the vibrations found in my own mind—my perception filter.

Michael Archangel, as children we play,
we're bringing the earth into a new day,
we raise it from all of the patterns so old,
our planet's life story is by us retold.

Michael Archangel, your Knowing so strong,
Michael Archangel, oh sweep us along.
Michael Archangel, we're singing your song,
Michael Archangel, with you we belong.

7. Maha Chohan, help me see that as long as I am projecting any mental image at the object, I am not seeing the object. I see a mirage—an image created as an interference pattern between what I am projecting out and the consciousness behind the object.

Michael Archangel, God's power you show,
that you are invincible, this we do know,

you are undivided and thus can withstand,
anything coming from serpentine band.

Michael Archangel, your Knowing so strong,
Michael Archangel, oh sweep us along.
Michael Archangel, we're singing your song,
Michael Archangel, with you we belong.

8. Maha Chohan, help me see that although this is linear, analytical knowledge, it is not wisdom; it is not *gnosis*. I know only how my own mind interacts with that object.

Michael Archangel, come raise now the earth,
giving her thus a complete rebirth,
collective the mind that we do now raise,
for this we do give our infinite praise.

Michael Archangel, your Knowing so strong,
Michael Archangel, oh sweep us along.
Michael Archangel, we're singing your song,
Michael Archangel, with you we belong.

9. Maha Chohan, help me see that my mind can become a closed system, for I cannot see beyond my own projections. My own projections have created such a dense mental box that I do not see that there is something beyond the box.

Michael Archangel, the earth is now new,
covered in Blue-flame as the morning dew,
our planet now sparkles throughout all of space, .
as we are receiving your infinite Grace.

**Michael Archangel, your Knowing so strong,
Michael Archangel, oh sweep us along.
Michael Archangel, we're singing your song,
Michael Archangel, with you we belong.**

Part 3

1. Maha Chohan, help me see how this can make me think
I have attained what may seem like ultimate knowledge, for
I think I have managed to force the entire universe into my
thought-system, my belief system, my mental box.

Master MORE, come to the fore,
we will absorb your flame of MORE.
Master MORE, our will so strong,
our power centers cleared by song.

**Master MORE, your Sacred Heart,
from this we will no more depart,
we are forever in your flow,
of Diamond Will that you bestow.**

2. Maha Chohan, help me see that when I start studying under
the seven Chohans and you, I do not come with a mind that
is free, I come with a mind that is clouded by images of what
I think the world is like, what I think God is like, what I think
I am like.

Master MORE, your wisdom flows,
as our attunement ever grows.

Master MORE, we have a tie,
that helps us see through Serpent's lie.

Master MORE, your Sacred Heart,
from this we will no more depart,
we are forever in your flow,
of Diamond Will that you bestow.

3. Maha Chohan, I am willing to let you, the Chohans, challenge my images, my beliefs, and my pet theories of what life is like. I am determined to be ready for the teacher to appear.

Master MORE, your love so pink,
there is no purer love, we think.
Master MORE, you set us free,
from all conditionality.

Master MORE, your Sacred Heart,
from this we will no more depart,
we are forever in your flow,
of Diamond Will that you bestow.

4. Maha Chohan, help me see that when my mind becomes a closed system, I become subject to the second law of thermodynamics, the School of Hard Knocks. When my mind is closed, I am not ready for a spiritual teacher and none of the Chohans can do anything for me.

Master MORE, we will endure,
your discipline that makes us pure.
Master MORE, intentions true,
as we are always one with you.

**Master MORE, your Sacred Heart,
from this we will no more depart,
we are forever in your flow,
of Diamond Will that you bestow.**

5. Maha Chohan, help me see the deeper reality that no teacher can ever do anything for me. The teacher can only inspire me to do something for myself, for the simple reason that the true path is a path of self-mastery.

Master MORE, our vision raised,
the will of God is always praised.
Master MORE, creative will,
raising all life higher still.

**Master MORE, your Sacred Heart,
from this we will no more depart,
we are forever in your flow,
of Diamond Will that you bestow.**

6. Maha Chohan, help me see that I must be the one who takes charge. *You* cannot master *my* mind for me! Only *I* can master my own mind.

Master MORE, your peace is power,
the demons of war it will devour.
Master MORE, we serve all life,
our flames consuming war and strife.

**Master MORE, your Sacred Heart,
from this we will no more depart,
we are forever in your flow,
of Diamond Will that you bestow.**

7. Maha Chohan, help me see that as long as I believe I can fit the universe or the ascended masters into my mental box, I am not reachable, I am not teachable for the Chohans.

> Master MORE, we are so free,
> eternal bond from you we see.
> Master MORE, we find rebirth,
> in flow of your eternal mirth.
>
> **Master MORE, your Sacred Heart,**
> **from this we will no more depart,**
> **we are forever in your flow,**
> **of Diamond Will that you bestow.**

8. Maha Chohan, I am ready for the teacher of the Chohans because I am willing to question my own perception, I am willing to question the way I look at life.

> Master MORE, you balance all,
> the seven rays upon our call.
> Master MORE, forever MORE,
> we are the Spirit's open door.
>
> **Master MORE, your Sacred Heart,**
> **from this we will no more depart,**
> **we are forever in your flow,**
> **of Diamond Will that you bestow.**

9. Maha Chohan, I acknowledge my ignorance. I acknowledge that even though I may have great knowledge from a worldly perspective, that knowledge forms a prison around my mind that is holding me back.

Master MORE, your Presence here,
filling up the inner sphere.
Life is now a sacred flow,
God Power we on all bestow.

**Master MORE, your Sacred Heart,
from this we will no more depart,
we are forever in your flow,
of Diamond Will that you bestow.**

Part 4

1. Maha Chohan, help me see that the common conception of ignorance is that there is something we do not know. But why do we not know it?

Maha Chohan, I will to grow,
I feel the power of your flow.
Maha Chohan, the veil is rent,
creative will from heaven sent.

**O Holy Spirit, flow through me,
I am the open door for thee.
O mighty rushing stream of Light,
transcendence is my sacred right.**

2. Maha Chohan, help me see that it is not because the container of my mind is empty that I do not know. It is because the container of my mind is too full, so that I cannot see what is beyond the contents of my mind.

Maha Chohan, your wisdom streams,
awaken all from matter's dreams.
Maha Chohan, your balance bring,
let bells of integration ring.

**O Holy Spirit, flow through me,
I am the open door for thee.
O mighty rushing stream of Light,
transcendence is my sacred right.**

3. Maha Chohan, help me see that in order to come to the point where the Chohans can do anything for me, I must be willing to question and look beyond the contents of my mind.

Maha Chohan, love's mighty call,
the prison walls are shattered all.
Maha Chohan, set all life free
through unconditionality.

**O Holy Spirit, flow through me,
I am the open door for thee.
O mighty rushing stream of Light,
transcendence is my sacred right.**

4. Maha Chohan, I am willing to question my pet theories, my deeply held beliefs, the things I have taken for granted. I am willing to let the Chohans challenge some of my beliefs.

Maha Chohan, intentions pure,
all life is one, I know for sure.
Maha Chohan, I am awake,
surrender all for oneness' sake.

O Holy Spirit, flow through me,
I am the open door for thee.
O mighty rushing stream of Light,
transcendence is my sacred right.

5. Maha Chohan, help me start to question my ideas and gradually come to question the pivotal ideas that define my sense of identity, and therefore are not even contents of the container of self but make up the walls of the container of self.

Maha Chohan, help all men see,
through veils of unreality.
Maha Chohan, with single eye,
I know I am the greater "I."

O Holy Spirit, flow through me,
I am the open door for thee.
O mighty rushing stream of Light,
transcendence is my sacred right.

6. Maha Chohan, help me begin to dis-identify myself from my beliefs and realize that I am not my beliefs; I am more than my beliefs.

Maha Chohan, your peace I find,
Maitreya shows me to be kind.
Maha Chohan, all war will cease,
now flooding all with sacred peace.

O Holy Spirit, flow through me,
I am the open door for thee.
O mighty rushing stream of Light,
transcendence is my sacred right.

7. Maha Chohan, help me see that the "you" that I am is not
the outer self—that is so defined by beliefs and experiences
in this world. I am beyond this outer self, I am beyond the
appearances and the conditions in this world.

> Maha Chohan, you balance all,
> the seven rays upon my call.
> Maha Chohan, all life is free,
> transcending for eternity.

> **O Holy Spirit, flow through me,**
> **I am the open door for thee.**
> **O mighty rushing stream of Light,**
> **transcendence is my sacred right.**

8. Maha Chohan, help me begin to realize that I have the ability
to step outside of the lower self. Help me experience a state of
consciousness where I am looking at an object without looking through the perception filter of the separate self. I am not
projecting anything upon the object.

> Maha Chohan, your sacred Flame,
> what beauty in your blessed name.
> Maha Chohan, what rushing flow,
> the Spirit one with life below.

> **O Holy Spirit, flow through me,**
> **I am the open door for thee.**
> **O mighty rushing stream of Light,**
> **transcendence is my sacred right.**

9. Maha Chohan, help me have a glimpse that I am experiencing the object as it is. Help me begin the true process of knowledge, the true process of *gnosis*.

> Maha Chohan, your Presence here,
> filling up the inner sphere.
> Life is now a sacred flow,
> God Wisdom we on all bestow.

> **O Holy Spirit, flow through me,**
> **I am the open door for thee.**
> **O mighty rushing stream of Light,**
> **transcendence is my sacred right.**

Sealing:

In the name of the Divine Mother, I fully accept that the power of these calls is used to set free the Ma-ter light, so it can outpicture the perfect vision of Christ for my own life, for all people and for the planet. In the name I AM THAT I AM, it is done! Amen.

5 | THE TWO TYPES OF SPIRITS

I AM the Maha Chohan. In this chapter we will consider the question: What is the Holy Spirit, the One Spirit, the River of Life?

You know the teaching we have given [See *The Power of Self*], of how the Creator first manifested a void by withdrawing itself into a singularity, then projecting itself out as the first sphere. And after the first sphere ascended, it became the foundation for creating the second sphere, and so on until the sphere in which you live, in which the material universe is found. What you need to understand here is this: God has not singled-handedly created the world of form.

The Creator has not sat there as the almighty, remote Creator and created the world of form, so to speak, from the outside. Creation is a two-fold process; it is a process whereby the One Creator creates individual self-aware extensions of itself, sends them into the latest sphere, and then they co-create the world of form from the inside, forming a figure-eight flow with the Creator.

And thus, what we see is that these self-aware extensions of the Creator create, essentially, in the same way as the Creator creates. For what exactly is it that the Creator creates, when it creates an extension of itself? What is the Creator?

How Spirit creates

The Creator is Spirit. How does Spirit create? You look at this process from the vantage point of the material universe where you have — for a variety of reasons that we need not go into here — been conditioned, programmed, to see the material universe as being separate from Spirit. You have the subtle image in your minds that God is a Spirit, but God created a world of form that is not Spirit that is separated from Spirit.

This is highly inaccurate, and it is non-constructive for your spiritual growth. Surely, we of the ascended masters understand full well that there are levels of consciousness, and that there are some levels of consciousness where you are simply not ready to grasp the truth that I will give you here. So we understand that there are people who need to hold on to the image that matter and Spirit are separate. For this is the only way they can have the experience that they desire to have; the experience of being separate, disconnected beings. Of course, the Law of Free Will must be allowed to outplay itself, so that they can have that experience until they have had enough of it.

Yet the deeper truth that I wish to reveal to those who are ready, those who have ears to hear and eyes to see, is that Spirit cannot create something that is separate from Spirit. Spirit cannot create something that is not Spirit. So, how does Spirit create? By creating spirit.

The Creator itself is beyond form, as you can conceive of form from inside the world of form. Yet in order to create the world of form, the Creator does not create a form that is separate from itself. The Creator, which is Spirit, can create a form in only one way, namely by creating a spirit, a spirit that is created in two distinct elements or phases.

First, the Creator must envision a matrix, a form, a geometric shape, which is what Saint Germain calls a symbol. Then, the Creator allows the stream of its own Being, consciousness and Spirit to flow through the matrix. This matrix then becomes animated by the Creator's Spirit, and therefore becomes a spirit that has a distinct form. This spirit is now charged with the task of maintaining that form.

Spirits and self-awareness

Now then, as you look at life from inside the material sphere, you are used to thinking in terms of inanimate matter and animate life forms. This is comparable – with some latitude for not taking things literally – to what the Creator does. The Creator creates inanimate forms that are upheld by a spirit that has consciousness but does not have self-awareness. Then, the Creator creates co-creators, who also have a form and therefore also started out as a matrix in the Creator's mind endowed by Spirit, endowed by a portion of Spirit so concentrated, so intensified that it makes them self-aware. So we now have spirits with awareness but no self-awareness, and Spirits with self-awareness.

Thus, you see a very important distinction. An "inanimate" spirit, so to speak, cannot transcend the basic matrix according to which it was created. It cannot consciously and deliberately transcend itself, recreate itself, redefine itself. This does not mean that the spirit cannot evolve; it can indeed evolve as you conceive of evolution in nature. It can evolve within the parameters set by its original matrix, which means that it can become more of that matrix. It can gather to itself energy, even consciousness, and therefore it can grow in power, in sophistication. But it cannot change itself deliberately and consciously.

In a sense, it cannot bring forth something that is new in a revolutionary or transcendental way. Yet a self-aware "animate" Spirit, a co-creator, does indeed have the ability to step back, look at itself and decide that it wants to be something different than what it is right now. And therefore, it can remake itself, recreate itself, transcend itself.

This means something profound. The co-creative Spirit has the same ability as the Creator, which is to formulate a matrix in its mind and to direct the stream of its consciousness through the matrix. Thus, a co-creative Spirit can create form, a new form not seen before. The inanimate spirit does not have the ability to envision or imagine something beyond its own matrix. It has enough consciousness to know that it exists that it wants to survive and that it wants to grow by gathering to itself more energy, more consciousness, and it can even expand itself within the matrix that defines it.

A co-creative Spirit can envision, imagine, a new matrix. But of course, there are limitations to what a co-creative Spirit can envision, and the limitations are set by the matrix that defines the co-creative Spirit. So you see, there are two phases in the evolution, the growth, of a co-creative Spirit. The first phase is that you are focused on creating forms, and the second phase is that you realize that in order to create forms that are completely new, you need to recreate yourself.

Recreating yourself as a Spirit

This then ties in with the teaching we have given about the 144 levels of consciousness that are possible on earth *[See The Power of Self]*. We have explained that when a new lifestream – what I call a co-creative Spirit – first takes embodiment on earth, it starts out at the 48th level of consciousness. The lifestream then goes through the process that we describe as the Path of the Seven Veils where it learns about and expands its co-creative abilities by using the seven spiritual rays whereby it rises to the 96th level of awareness.

This is the phase where you are exploring your co-creative abilities, your ability to create form. And in doing so, you are also expanding your self-awareness, but you are not in most cases doing this fully consciously. Your self-awareness, your sense of self, is being expanded through the experiences you have of interacting with the material universe, by you co-creating—formulating a matrix in your mind, animating it with consciousness, sending it out, projecting it out, and then seeing how the Ma-ter light takes on the form of the image.

But there comes a point, when you reach the 96th level where it is absolutely essential for you, if you are to grow beyond that level that you step back, look at yourself and come to an essential realization. So far, you have co-created and done exactly what you were meant to do. You have co-created within the parameters set by the original matrix that was defined by your spiritual parents and which is embedded in your I AM Presence. Yet it is now time to fully attune your mind to that matrix but also realize that the next phase of your path is to consciously and deliberately expand and recreate that matrix. For this is truly what the Path of Christhood is all about.

A Self that is ready to ascend

I give this teaching because in today's age there are many people who have already gone through these phases of learning
to use their co-creative abilities on the seven rays. They have
done this in past lifetimes, and they have gathered a consider-
able momentum, a co-creative momentum, on the seven rays.
You now see that our aim is to give you a series of books – one
by each Chohan – in order to facilitate the process whereby
co-creators can learn to use – consciously and deliberately –
the qualities of the seven rays.

One aspect of the purpose we have for this series is indeed
to help co-creators navigate the process of growing from the
48th to the 96th level of consciousness. Another purpose we
have is to help those who have gone below the 48th level come
back up above the 48th level, and continue the process from
where they left off, so that they can come more quickly to the
96th level.

But the reason why I give this teaching as the first in the
series is indeed that I want to make sure that those who have in
past lives gone though the process of learning about the seven
rays, can follow the teachings from the Chohans, but follow
them on a higher level than those who are still beneath the 96th
level of consciousness. You can then realize that your purpose
is not only to co-create through the seven rays but also to actually co-create the matrix that defines your "self," your sense
of self, so that you may do this consciously and deliberately;
not being so focused on creating forms, but being focused on
creating a Self that is ready to ascend.

But, before you ascend, you are ready to express yourself in
the material realm in a way that is not focused on creating specific forms or specific experiences for your Self. But instead, it
is focused on raising the consciousness – raising the awareness

of the whole, raising the collective consciousness — by challenging the spirits that make up that collective consciousness. And exactly how the collective consciousness is made up by spirits, will be the topic of my next discourse.

6 | INVOKING AWARENESS OF CO-CREATION

In the name I AM THAT I AM, Jesus Christ, I call to my I AM Presence to flow through the I Will Be Presence that I AM and give this invocation with full power. I call to beloved Elohim Apollo and Lumina, Archangel Jophiel and Christine, Lanto and the Maha Chohan to help me become more aware of my co-creative abilities. Help me see and surrender all patterns that block my oneness with the Maha Chohan and my oneness with my I AM Presence, including ...

[Make personal calls]

Part 1

1. Maha Chohan, help me see that as long as I am seeing an object through the perception filter of the separate self, I must see the object as separate from the

self, and I cannot come into oneness with the object or the consciousness behind it.

> Beloved Apollo, with your second ray,
> you open our eyes to see a new day,
> We see through duality's lies and deceit,
> transcending the mindset producing defeat.

> **Beloved Apollo, thou Elohim Gold,**
> **your radiant light our eyes now behold,**
> **as pages of wisdom you gently unfold,**
> **our planet is free from all that is old.**

2. Maha Chohan, help me see that I cannot come into oneness with the Chohan of a given ray as long as I look at that ray through my perception filter. Help me step outside of that filter and have a glimpse of how the Chohan really is.

> Beloved Apollo, in your flame we know,
> that your living wisdom is always a flow,
> in your light we see our own highest will,
> immersed in the stream that never stands still.

> **Beloved Apollo, thou Elohim Gold,**
> **your radiant light our eyes now behold,**
> **as pages of wisdom you gently unfold,**
> **our planet is free from all that is old.**

3. Maha Chohan, help me gradually come into oneness with the First Ray and the Chohan of Master MORE, so that the ray will no longer form a veil that will obscure my vision. Help me gradually do this for all of the rays.

Beloved Apollo, your light makes it clear,
why we have taken embodiment here,
exposing all lies causing the fall,
you help us reclaim the oneness of all.

**Beloved Apollo, thou Elohim Gold,
your radiant light our eyes now behold,
as pages of wisdom you gently unfold,
our planet is free from all that is old.**

4. Maha Chohan, help me see that there is only one self. There is only one mind; there is only one consciousness. There is only one Spirit, and it is the Holy Spirit that is lifting up all life, that is carrying all life along with it, as a river moving towards the ocean of infinity.

Beloved Apollo, exposing all lies,
we hereby surrender all ego-based ties,
we know our perception is truly the key,
to transcending the serpentine duality.

**Beloved Apollo, thou Elohim Gold,
your radiant light our eyes now behold,
as pages of wisdom you gently unfold,
our planet is free from all that is old.**

5. Maha Chohan, help me see that the One Spirit, the Holy Spirit, will never fit into any matrix created by the separate mind! It will always go on, it will always transcend and it will always flow.

Beloved Apollo, we heed now your call,
drawing us into Wisdom's Great Hall,

working to raise our own cosmic sphere,
together we form the tip of the spear.

**Beloved Apollo, thou Elohim Gold,
your radiant light our eyes now behold,
as pages of wisdom you gently unfold,
our planet is free from all that is old.**

6. Maha Chohan, I want to move on, I want to get out of my self-created prison and I am willing to flow. I see that the Chohans are here to help me flow, not to give me stationary knowledge of each of the seven rays.

Beloved Apollo, your wisdom so clear,
in oneness with you, no serpent we fear,
the beam in our eye we willingly see,
we're free from the serpent's own duality.

**Beloved Apollo, thou Elohim Gold,
your radiant light our eyes now behold,
as pages of wisdom you gently unfold,
our planet is free from all that is old.**

7. Maha Chohan, help me see that in order to know the Chohans, I must be willing to flow with you, for you are constantly flowing.

Beloved Apollo, you help us to see
through your knowing eyes we truly are free,
we willingly stand in your piercing gaze,
empowered, we exit duality's maze.

Beloved Apollo, thou Elohim Gold,
your radiant light our eyes now behold,
as pages of wisdom you gently unfold,
our planet is free from all that is old.

8. Maha Chohan, I am willing to allow you, the Chohans, to help me look at each rock in the stream of my consciousness, to see it for what it is, see the dualistic illusions behind it. Then take it out, throw it away and say: "I no longer need this in the stream of my consciousness."

Beloved Apollo, our vision we raise,
we see that the earth is in a new phase,
for nothing can stop the knowledge you bring,
exposing that there's no separate thing.

Beloved Apollo, thou Elohim Gold,
your radiant light our eyes now behold,
as pages of wisdom you gently unfold,
our planet is free from all that is old.

9. Maha Chohan, help me begin to lock in to the stillness behind the babbling of the mind, the eternal ongoing babbling of the ego. Help me see without seeing through the perception filter of the separate self. This is pure seeing, true seeing, naked awareness, pure awareness.

Beloved Apollo, in wisdom's great mirth,
we all are together uplifting the earth,
as you now the true Flame of Wisdom reveal,
all of earth's people can see what is real.

Beloved Apollo, thou Elohim Gold,
your radiant light our eyes now behold,
as pages of wisdom you gently unfold,
our planet is free from all that is old.

Part 2

1. Maha Chohan, help me see that creation is a two-fold process, whereby the One Creator creates individual self-aware extensions of itself, sends them into the latest sphere, and then they co-create the world of form from the inside, forming a figure-eight flow with the Creator.

Jophiel Archangel, in wisdom's great light,
all serpentine lies exposed to our sight.
So subtle the lies that creep through the mind,
yet you are the greatest teacher we find.

Jophiel Archangel, exposing all lies,
Jophiel Archangel, cutting all ties.
Jophiel Archangel, clearing the skies,
Jophiel Archangel, the mind truly flies.

2. Maha Chohan, help me see that I have been programmed to see the material universe as being separate from Spirit because God is a Spirit, but God supposedly created a world of form that is not Spirit, that is separated from Spirit.

Jophiel Archangel, your wisdom we hail,
your sword cutting through duality's veil.

As you show the way, we know what is real,
from serpentine doubt, we instantly heal.

Jophiel Archangel, exposing all lies,
Jophiel Archangel, cutting all ties.
Jophiel Archangel, clearing the skies,
Jophiel Archangel, the mind truly flies.

3. Maha Chohan, help me see that this image is non-constructive for my spiritual growth because Spirit cannot create something that is separate from Spirit. Spirit cannot create something that is not Spirit. Spirit creates by creating spirit.

Jophiel Archangel, your reality,
the best antidote to duality.
No lie can remain in your Presence so clear,
with you on our side, no serpent we fear.

Jophiel Archangel, exposing all lies,
Jophiel Archangel, cutting all ties.
Jophiel Archangel, clearing the skies,
Jophiel Archangel, the mind truly flies.

4. Maha Chohan, help me see that the Creator itself is beyond form, yet in order to create the world of form, the Creator does not create a form that is separate from itself. The Creator, which is Spirit, can create a form in only one way, namely by creating a spirit, a spirit that is created in two distinct phases.

Jophiel Archangel, God's mind is in me,
and through your clear light, its wisdom we see.
Divisions all vanish, as we see the One,
and truly, the wholeness of mind we have won.

Jophiel Archangel, exposing all lies,
Jophiel Archangel, cutting all ties.
Jophiel Archangel, clearing the skies,
Jophiel Archangel, the mind truly flies.

5. Maha Chohan, help me see that the Creator must envision a matrix, and then the Creator allows the stream of its own Being, consciousness and Spirit to flow through the matrix.

Jophiel Archangel, now show us the way,
that leads us beyond duality's fray,
we long to discern the truth and the lie,
so we the serpentine knots can untie.

Jophiel Archangel, exposing all lies,
Jophiel Archangel, cutting all ties.
Jophiel Archangel, clearing the skies,
Jophiel Archangel, the mind truly flies.

6. Maha Chohan, help me see that the matrix then becomes animated by the Creator's Spirit, and therefore becomes a spirit that has a distinct form. This spirit is now charged with the task of maintaining that form.

Jophiel Archangel, your Presence is here,
and therefore our minds are perfectly clear,
in wisdom's great fount we do take a bath,
and now we withstand the devil's own wrath.

Jophiel Archangel, exposing all lies,
Jophiel Archangel, cutting all ties.
Jophiel Archangel, clearing the skies,
Jophiel Archangel, the mind truly flies.

7. Maha Chohan, help me see that the Creator creates inanimate forms that are upheld by a spirit that has consciousness but does not have self-awareness.

Jophiel Archangel, it is your great task,
to raise all mankind, if only we ask,
so now on behalf of those who are blind,
we ask for your help in wisdom to find.

Jophiel Archangel, exposing all lies,
Jophiel Archangel, cutting all ties.
Jophiel Archangel, clearing the skies,
Jophiel Archangel, the mind truly flies.

8. Maha Chohan, help me see that the Creator creates co-creators, who also have a form and therefore also started out as a matrix in the Creator's mind, endowed by a portion of Spirit so concentrated that it makes them self-aware.

Jophiel Archangel, your Presence we hail,
your Light cutting through the serpentine veil,
the serpents can no longer people deceive,
for all now your Flame of Wisdom receive.

Jophiel Archangel, exposing all lies,
Jophiel Archangel, cutting all ties.
Jophiel Archangel, clearing the skies,
Jophiel Archangel, the mind truly flies.

9. Maha Chohan, help me see that the Creator creates spirits with awareness but no self-awareness, and Spirits with self-awareness.

Jophiel Archangel, where else can we go,
when we long the highest wisdom to know?
You share with us gladly all that you are,
and now our vision goes ever so far.

Jophiel Archangel, exposing all lies,
Jophiel Archangel, cutting all ties.
Jophiel Archangel, clearing the skies,
Jophiel Archangel, the mind truly flies.

Part 3

1. Maha Chohan, help me see that an "inanimate" spirit cannot transcend the basic matrix according to which it was created. It cannot consciously and deliberately transcend itself, recreate itself, redefine itself.

Master Lanto, golden wise,
expose in us the ego's lies.
Master Lanto, will to be,
we will to win our mastery.

Master Lanto, Wisdom's Fount,
with blessings we can hardly count,
you are for earth a shining light,
your Golden Wisdom oh so bright.

2. Maha Chohan, help me see that a spirit can evolve within the parameters set by its original matrix, which means that it can become more of that matrix. It can gather to itself energy, even consciousness, and therefore it can grow in power.

Master Lanto, balance all,
for wisdom's balance we do call.
Master Lanto, help us see,
that balance is the Golden Key.

**Master Lanto, Wisdom's Fount,
with blessings we can hardly count,
you are for earth a shining light,
your Golden Wisdom oh so bright.**

3. Maha Chohan, help me see that a self-aware "animate" Spirit, a co-creator, has the ability to step back, look at itself and decide that it wants to be something different than what it is right now. And therefore, it can remake itself, recreate itself, transcend itself.

Master Lanto, from Above,
we call forth discerning love.
Master Lanto, love's not blind,
through love, God vision we do find.

**Master Lanto, Wisdom's Fount,
with blessings we can hardly count,
you are for earth a shining light,
your Golden Wisdom oh so bright.**

4. Maha Chohan, help me see that a co-creative Spirit has the same ability as the Creator, which is to formulate a matrix in its mind and to direct the stream of its consciousness through the matrix. Thus, a co-creative Spirit can create form, a new form not seen before.

Master Lanto, we are sure
as Christic lamb intentions pure.
Master Lanto, we'll transcend,
acceleration is our truest friend.

Master Lanto, Wisdom's Fount,
with blessings we can hardly count,
you are for earth a shining light,
your Golden Wisdom oh so bright.

5. Maha Chohan, help me see that while a co-creative Spirit can envision a new matrix, there are limitations set by the matrix that defines the co-creative Spirit.

Master Lanto, we are whole,
no more division in the soul.
Master Lanto, healing flame,
all balance in your sacred name.

Master Lanto, Wisdom's Fount,
with blessings we can hardly count,
you are for earth a shining light,
your Golden Wisdom oh so bright.

6. Maha Chohan, help me see that there are two phases in the evolution of a co-creative Spirit. The first phase is that I am focused on creating forms, and the second phase is that I realize that in order to create forms that are completely new, I need to recreate myself.

Master Lanto, serve all life,
as we transcend all inner strife.

Master Lanto, peace you give,
to all who want to truly live.

Master Lanto, Wisdom's Fount,
with blessings we can hardly count,
you are for earth a shining light,
your Golden Wisdom oh so bright.

7. Maha Chohan, help me see that I start by exploring my co-creative abilities and expanding my self-awareness, but I am not doing this fully consciously.

Master Lanto, free to be,
in balanced creativity.
Master Lanto, we employ,
your balance as the key to joy.

Master Lanto, Wisdom's Fount,
with blessings we can hardly count,
you are for earth a shining light,
your Golden Wisdom oh so bright.

8. Maha Chohan, help me see that my self-awareness, my sense of self, is being expanded through the experiences I have of interacting with the material universe, by me co-creating within the matrix defined by my spiritual parents.

Master Lanto, balance all,
the seven rays upon our call.
Master Lanto, we take flight,
the threefold flame a blazing light.

Master Lanto, Wisdom's Fount,
with blessings we can hardly count,
you are for earth a shining light,
your Golden Wisdom oh so bright.

9. Maha Chohan, help me see that when I reach the 96th level, I need to step back, look at the matrix and realize that the next phase of my path is to consciously and deliberately expand my sense of self.

Lanto dear, your Presence here,
filling up the inner sphere.
Life is now a sacred flow,
God Wisdom we on all bestow.

Master Lanto, Wisdom's Fount,
with blessings we can hardly count,
you are for earth a shining light,
your Golden Wisdom oh so bright.

Part 4

1. Maha Chohan, help me see that anything I do is done with energy. Anything I do is done with consciousness.

Maha Chohan, I will to grow,
I feel the power of your flow.
Maha Chohan, the veil is rent,
creative will from heaven sent.

**O Holy Spirit, flow through me,
I am the open door for thee.
O mighty rushing stream of Light,
transcendence is my sacred right.**

2. Maha Chohan, help me see that the energy aspect is the Ma-ter light. I form a matrix in my mind, and then I allow my consciousness to flow through the matrix and thereby project that matrix upon the Ma-ter light, which then takes on the form.

Maha Chohan, your wisdom streams,
awaken all from matter's dreams.
Maha Chohan, your balance bring,
let bells of integration ring.

**O Holy Spirit, flow through me,
I am the open door for thee.
O mighty rushing stream of Light,
transcendence is my sacred right.**

3. Maha Chohan, help me see that anything that has consciousness flowing through it, becomes animated by consciousness. What I am actually doing is to create a spirit.

Maha Chohan, love's mighty call,
the prison walls are shattered all.
Maha Chohan, set all life free
through unconditionality.

**O Holy Spirit, flow through me,
I am the open door for thee.**

**O mighty rushing stream of Light,
transcendence is my sacred right.**

4. Maha Chohan, help me see that a new co-creator often takes on a pre-defined role in order to have a foundation for starting its creative efforts. Yet as I continue to co-create through that role, I gradually begin to create a spirit.

Maha Chohan, intentions pure,
all life is one, I know for sure.
Maha Chohan, I am awake,
surrender all for oneness' sake.

**O Holy Spirit, flow through me,
I am the open door for thee.
O mighty rushing stream of Light,
transcendence is my sacred right.**

5. Maha Chohan, help me see that this spirit does not have self-awareness, but it is a being that has a certain sense of awareness, a certain survival instinct, and therefore a built-in desire to grow.

Maha Chohan, help all men see,
through veils of unreality.
Maha Chohan, with single eye,
I know I am the greater "I."

**O Holy Spirit, flow through me,
I am the open door for thee.
O mighty rushing stream of Light,
transcendence is my sacred right.**

6. Maha Chohan, help me see that as I work my way up through the seven rays, I create an outer self that is a spirit. Yet the Conscious You, that has created this outer spirit, is not the spirit.

Maha Chohan, your peace I find,
Maitreya shows me to be kind.
Maha Chohan, all war will cease,
now flooding all with sacred peace.

**O Holy Spirit, flow through me,
I am the open door for thee.
O mighty rushing stream of Light,
transcendence is my sacred right.**

7. Maha Chohan, help me see that the Conscious You has not become the spirit and has not been changed by this spirit. The Conscious You is still what it always was created to be, an open door and nothing more—and nothing less.

Maha Chohan, you balance all,
the seven rays upon my call.
Maha Chohan, all life is free,
transcending for eternity.

**O Holy Spirit, flow through me,
I am the open door for thee.
O mighty rushing stream of Light,
transcendence is my sacred right.**

8. Maha Chohan, help me see that the test I face at this point is whether I will let the spirit I have created die, so that I can be reborn into a higher sense of self.

Maha Chohan, your sacred Flame,
what beauty in your blessed name.
Maha Chohan, what rushing flow,
the Spirit one with life below.

**O Holy Spirit, flow through me,
I am the open door for thee.
O mighty rushing stream of Light,
transcendence is my sacred right.**

9. Maha Chohan, help me see that the spirit I have created, often called the soul, cannot ascend. What can ascend are the positive experiences that I have had through that spirit and that become part of my causal body.

Maha Chohan, your Presence here,
filling up the inner sphere.
Life is now a sacred flow,
God Wisdom we on all bestow.

**O Holy Spirit, flow through me,
I am the open door for thee.
O mighty rushing stream of Light,
transcendence is my sacred right.**

Sealing:

In the name of the Divine Mother, I fully accept that the power of these calls is used to set free the Ma-ter light, so it can outpicture the perfect vision of Christ for my own life, for all people and for the planet. In the name I AM THAT I AM, it is done! Amen.

7 | LETTING OLD SPIRITS DIE

The Maha Chohan I AM. In this discourse we will again consider the question: "What is the Holy Spirit?" We are approaching the topic and answer gradually that you might have a greater understanding of this extremely important topic.

We go back to the concept of the 144 levels of consciousness and the fact that a new co-creator starts out at the 48th level. And then – if it chooses to raise its consciousness and engage in the Path of the Seven Veils, the Paths of the Seven Rays – it gradually works its way up through the seven rays towards the 96th level of consciousness.

Spirits and the seven rays

As I explained, anything you do is done with energy. Anything you do is done with consciousness. The energy aspect is what we have called the Ma-ter light. You form a matrix in your mind, and then you allow your consciousness to flow through the matrix and thereby project that matrix upon the Ma-ter light, which then takes on the form.

Anything that has consciousness flowing through it, becomes animated by consciousness. What you are actually doing is you are creating a spirit. We have given various teachings on this topic already. We have talked about how a new co-creator often takes on what we have called a pre-defined role in order to have a foundation for starting its creative efforts. Yet as you continue to co-create through that role, you gradually begin to create a spirit. This spirit, of course, does not have self-awareness as you do, but nevertheless it is a spirit. It is a being that has a certain sense of awareness, a certain survival instinct, and therefore a built-in desire to grow.

What happens is that as you work your way up through the first three rays, you are simply experimenting with your creative powers. There is the joy of experimenting with the First Ray. There is the desire to evaluate on the Second Ray, whether the results you produce are the results you want. Then there is the love of the Third Ray, which can be the pure love of creating, but eventually becomes the love for creating for some higher purpose.

This can lead you to the point where you accelerate yourself on the Fourth Ray and begin to evaluate your co-creation based on something outside yourself. For you are striving for some greater sense of purpose, something that has a positive effect on life beyond your own sphere of self. This continues through the Fifth, Sixth and Seventh Ray, until you end up at that 95-96th level consciousness where you then face the initiation of whether you will take a giant leap – a quantum leap – or whether you will continue to seek to reinforce what you have created up until this point.

You are not the spirit you create

And what is it that you have created? You have created the outer self that is a spirit. The extreme importance of the concept of the Conscious You is that it is the Conscious You that has created this outer spirit, but the Conscious You is not the spirit. The Conscious You has not become the spirit and has not been changed by this spirit. The Conscious You is still what it always was created to be, an open door and nothing more—and nothing less.

The test that you face at this point – when you have completed the initiations of the seven rays – is simply this: Will you now let that spirit that you have created die, so that you can be reborn into a higher sense of self? This is what Jesus alluded to in a mystical way, when he told Nicodemus that only the man who descended from heaven can ascend back to heaven. This refers to the Conscious You. Only the Conscious You can ascend back to the spiritual realm.

The spirit that you have created, what many people call the soul, cannot ascend. It cannot ascend, my beloved. What can ascend are the positive experiences that you have had through that spirit, and that becomes part of your causal body [See *The Power of Self*]. But the spirit itself cannot ascend; it must be allowed to die in order for the Conscious You to be allowed to rise to the next level, and go beyond the 96th level, moving towards the 144th level.

What needs to happen at the 96th level is that you actually allow the spirit you have created to die, so that you can – as Jesus put it – be born again, be born of water. When you are born of water, you take on a new self, which is, of course, not completely different from the old self. Yet it is a distinctly new self, and you consciously know that it is a new self.

Then you start growing towards the 144th level. As you do so, you are again creating a self, a spirit. When you come to the 144th level, you are – like Jesus demonstrated on the cross – you are paralyzed, you are crucified, and you realize you are crucified by your own creation. Therefore, you can, while hanging on the cross, realize that nobody is going to come and save you from your own creation and free you from the spirit you have created. You are the one who must give up the ghost and let that spirit die once more whereby you can then be born again, be reborn of fire in the ritual of the fire of the Ascension Flame that completely accelerates your being but does so by shattering the matrix of the spirit that took you to this point.

How the Holy Spirit is created

You now see, by illustrating the process that you go through as a co-creator on earth that this is the same process that has taken place over and over and over again in previous spheres. Self-aware beings started out as you do with a point-like sense of self-awareness. And then, they gradually expand that sense of self-awareness by creating a spirit. This spirit is by no means a dark or evil spirit; it can be a beautiful and bright spirit that is created from the positive momentum that these lifestreams build. Yet it is still a spirit that must be allowed to die, for the Conscious You to come up higher and come closer to its ultimate oneness with its creator, with its source, the I AM Presence in your case, being that you are in the material realm.

All previous beings in all previous spheres have gone through this process: first creating a spirit out of the seven rays, then allowing that spirit to die, being reborn, and starting to work on the higher rays – what we previously called the secret rays – until they build another spirit. Then allowing that spirit to die, being reborn in the fire of the Ascension Flame. Now finally being accelerated into being immortal lifestreams in the spiritual realm, in an ascended sphere, instead of in an unascended sphere. This entire process is part of what creates the Holy Spirit.

Even while you are creating this spirit before your ascension, you are contributing to the growth of your sphere. You are bringing light into the sphere, you are bringing the light of the seven rays at first, up until the 96th level, and then you bring the light of the higher rays beyond that. You are contributing to building and raising your sphere, building that ascending momentum of your sphere. What actually makes the spirit holy, what actually contributes to the Holy Spirit, is when you consciously see the spirit you have created and consciously choose to let it die, so that you are reborn.

That is when you contribute to the Holy Spirit, the One Spirit because now by letting the old spirit die, you move one step closer to oneness. And the final contribution to the Holy Spirit is when you let that last ghost die, and then you are accelerated into the Ascension Flame. Still, every time you withdraw the Conscious You from a particular spirit, see that spirit from the outside – see that it is not the real you – and allow it to die consciously, then you contribute to the upward momentum whereby the separate Spirit Sparks, the individualizations of the Creator, move one step closer to oneness with the Creator. And you begin to see that this is the Holy Spirit.

Your inherent drive to become More

The Creator decided to create individual extensions of its Self, to send them out with a point-like sense of self, so different from the omnipresent, non-linear, spherical sense of self of the Creator. And The Creator knew that these Spirit Sparks could become lost in their own creation. They could come to identify themselves with their creation and therefore stay in that creation indefinitely, unless there was some mechanism that pulled them to always grow, always seek to return to their source. The whole purpose for creation is that the Spirit Sparks go out and then return to their source. Not to return to go into oblivion, but to return as being More than when they went out. And that is how creation expands and how God is magnified.

Built into your life-stream is the desire to become More, the desire to expand. This is the very desire that drove the Creator to create in the first place, to create a world of form and to create individual sparks of its Self, so that all might become More in this process of going out and returning to source, but returning as More than what went out.

There is a drive inside of you to be More, and that is why you co-create. That is why you formulate an image and then imbue it with consciousness, imbue it with Spirit. This is also why any spirit that you create has that drive to become More, to expand, to grow and to intensify.

This becomes important, when you look again at the process of how free will outplays itself. Now you begin to realize that if you start at the 48th level of consciousness and choose to go up, then you will indeed build a spirit that has a desire to expand and to grow.

Yet take note of an important point. When you are following the process of initiation under the seven Chohans, what is the essential ability that you learn? It is the ability to draw the light of the seven rays from inside yourself – or rather from your I AM Presence – through the open door of the Conscious You into the outer self, the spirit you are creating. When you create the spirit between the 48th and the 96th level, you are creating a spirit that knows it can get light, it can get the driving force for its growth, from inside itself. This is a creative process because you do not need to take anything from other lifestreams, you do not have to take anything from the material world to drive your co-creative efforts. You know you can get it from within, through your momentum on using the seven rays.

Consciously letting a spirit die

As you grow toward the 96th level, this spirit you create becomes more and more powerful in using the seven rays. If you follow the instructions of the Chohans, you will actually become more and more detached from the spirit you are creating, knowing that this is just a vehicle, knowing that it is a servant that you have created, and that you – the Conscious You – is in charge.

You are not allowing this spirit to take on a self of its own and you actually – gradually – come to the point where, as you get closer to the 96th level, you become more and more aware that each time you step up one level in consciousness, you do so by letting the old spirit die and by being reborn into a new spirit that is more than the old because it has been reborn of water.

So as you come to the 96th level, you are familiar with the process of letting the old die without holding on to it because you know you will be reborn as More. Therefore, it is relatively easy for you to make that leap at the 96th level and completely let go of the momentum you have on the seven rays, realizing you now want something higher, which is the other rays, the secret rays. The higher rays are not meant to create material form, but are meant to create something beyond material form and thereby contribute to the raising of the collective awareness, rather than the physical manifestations that you see with the senses. Unfortunately, it is possible that a lifestream does not become more aware of this process of letting the old die, but is so focused on expanding the spirit, magnifying that spirit that it is creating more and more physical manifestations. It does not consciously see that it is letting the old die.

Therefore, when it comes to the 96th level and is now faced with the necessity to let the old die, then it can come as a shock to that lifestream, and it can actually decide that it is not willing to let the old die. It is not willing to give up that ghost; it wants to hold on to it. It wants to use its momentum to demonstrate some mastery of mind over matter that it may go out and create these phenomena that can impress those who are further down on the path. Thus, a lifestream can become attached to the spirit and decide that it will not let it go, and this causes the lifestream to fall.

What happens when beings fall

If you fall at the 96th level, you fall to the very lowest level, which does not mean you now have no momentum. It actually means that you have a great momentum on using the seven rays, but you have now perverted that momentum into using it for entirely selfish purposes where you are not using it to grow from within. You are seeking to hold on to what you have, and therefore you suddenly feel threatened. Now, you think you have to use your powers to control your environment, to control other lifestreams, to control Mother Nature herself. So you now become what Jesus talked about when he said that: "If the light that is in thee be darkness, how great is that darkness"

Suddenly, the light you had garnered on the Path of the Seven Rays has now turned into darkness where you are no longer on the path of self-transcendence. You are on the false path of seeking to produce outer phenomena and hold on to those phenomena. Thus, the light that you had garnered has been turned to darkness, and you have now become a black magician who is using your gifts, using your momentum, for an entirely self-centered purpose. You are therefore cut off from the flow of the Spirit, the flow of the spirit of self-transcendence, the Holy Spirit.

This means that you can no longer receive light through the seven rays. So what must you do? You must either become subject to the second law of thermodynamics and gradually return to that zero-point where there is no energy to do anything. Or you must go into the path of the black magicians, of stealing light from the material realm. Which means stealing it from other lifestreams, who are still receiving it from within.

It is, of course, possible for you to fall at any level between the 48th and the 96th level. And thus, there are different beings that have different momentums on this separate self. What you need to understand is that when you do go below the 48th level of awareness, no matter what point you go below, then the spirit that you had created up until that point now becomes a spirit that cannot see that it can get energy from inside itself.

It instantly reverts to a spirit, or is transformed into a spirit that now knows it must take light from outside itself. Yet it still has the basic drive that is the drive of all life, the drive that in a way is consciousness itself, namely the drive to multiply, the drive to become More.

Why spirits become aggressive

You now have a spirit that has a drive to become More, but cannot become More by getting the energy of the seven rays from inside itself. So what must this spirit do? It must seek to become More by taking energy from the level where it is at in the material realm. And that means it now becomes a spirit that by its very nature is an aggressive spirit that must and will take light from other spirits.

That is why you now have a spirit that cannot live and let live. It has no life in itself, the life of the Spirit. So it has in a sense become what Jesus talked about, when he talked about those who are dead in a spiritual sense, as when he said: "Let the dead bury their dead."

These are the ones who are no longer on that path of transcendence from within, but are on the false path of seeking to take from without. And they must, of course, take from without through either deceit or direct force. It is why we have, as we have talked about before, the two types of fallen beings:

1. Those who seek to use obvious force to take from others.

2. Those who use deceit, so that they can get others to voluntarily give them their energy.

Now you understand the basic teaching that the Holy Spirit is the Spirit of self-transcendence by taking energy from the spiritual realm and multiplying the talents, thereby needing to take nothing from the level where you are at, but only giving to that level. And you also have the dead spirit, the one that is not alive. The dead spirit seeks to take from its own level, for it cannot get from within; it cannot get from the higher level because it is no longer the open door.

So, there is the one Holy Spirit that always moves closer and closer to oneness. And then you have the multiplicity of the separate spirits, the dead spirits that are in fact moving further and further away from oneness the more power they gather to themselves. Each time they take from another, they move further away from oneness with that other. For how can you forcefully or deceitfully take from another and move closer to oneness with that other? It simply is not possible. Do you begin to see this?

This sets the foundation for what we will talk about in coming discourses. I will leave you to ponder this teaching, which will truly be mind-blowing for many people, who have been brought up in traditional religions or even in many spiritual or so-called New Age philosophies; even for many who have some familiarity with ascended master teachings. I leave you to ponder this, and I shall return with my next installment when the time is ready.

8 | INVOKING AWARENESS OF ENERGY

In the name I AM THAT I AM, Jesus Christ, I call to my I AM Presence to flow through the I Will Be Presence that I AM and give this invocation with full power. I call to beloved Elohim Heros and Amora, Archangel Chamuel and Charity, Paul the Venetian and the Maha Chohan to help me become aware of how I use both physical and non-physical energy. Help me see and surrender all patterns that block my oneness with the Maha Chohan and my oneness with my I AM Presence, including …

[Make personal calls]

Part 1

1. Maha Chohan, help me see that a spirit cannot ascend; it must be allowed to die in order for the

Conscious You to rise to the next level, and go beyond the 96th level.

> O Heros-Amora, in your love so pink,
> we care not what others about us may think,
> in oneness with you, we claim a new day,
> as innocent children, we frolic and play.
>
> **O Heros-Amora, we reap what we sow,**
> **yet this is Plan B for helping us grow,**
> **for truly, Plan A is that we join the flow,**
> **immersed in the Infinite Love you bestow.**

2. Maha Chohan, help me see that in order to rise to a higher level, I must allow the spirit I have created to die, so that I can be born again, be born of water.

> O Heros-Amora, a new life begun,
> we laugh at the devil, the serious one,
> the serpent is stuck in his duality,
> but we are set free by Love's reality.
>
> **O Heros-Amora, we reap what we sow,**
> **yet this is Plan B for helping us grow,**
> **for truly, Plan A is that we join the flow,**
> **immersed in the Infinite Love you bestow.**

3. Maha Chohan, help me see that when I am born of water, I take on a new self, which is not completely different from the old self. Yet it is a distinctly new self, and I consciously know that it is a new self.

> O Heros-Amora, awakened we see,
> in true love is no conditionality,
> we bathe in your glorious Ruby-Pink Sun,
> knowing our God allows life to be fun.

> **O Heros-Amora, we reap what we sow,**
> **yet this is Plan B for helping us grow,**
> **for truly, Plan A is that we join the flow,**
> **immersed in the Infinite Love you bestow.**

4. Maha Chohan, help me see that when I come to the 144th level, I am – like Jesus demonstrated on the cross – crucified by my own creation.

> O Heros-Amora, life is such a joy,
> we see that the world is like a great toy,
> whatever the mind into it projects,
> the mirror of life exactly reflects.

> **O Heros-Amora, we reap what we sow,**
> **yet this is Plan B for helping us grow,**
> **for truly, Plan A is that we join the flow,**
> **immersed in the Infinite Love you bestow.**

5. Maha Chohan, help me see that nobody is going to come and save me from my own creation and free me from the spirit I have created.

> O Heros-Amora, conditions you burn,
> we know we are free to take a new turn,
> Immersed in the stream of infinite Love,
> we know that the Spirit came from Above.

> **O Heros-Amora, we reap what we sow,**
> **yet this is Plan B for helping us grow,**
> **for truly, Plan A is that we join the flow,**
> **immersed in the Infinite Love you bestow.**

6. Maha Chohan, help me see that I am the one who must give up the ghost and let that spirit die once more, whereby I can be reborn of fire in the ritual of the Ascension Flame, that accelerates my being by shattering the matrix of the spirit that took me to this point.

> O Heros-Amora, we feel that at last,
> we've risen above the trap of the past,
> in true love we claim our freedom to grow,
> forever we're one with Love's Infinite Flow.

> **O Heros-Amora, we reap what we sow,**
> **yet this is Plan B for helping us grow,**
> **for truly, Plan A is that we join the flow,**
> **immersed in the Infinite Love you bestow.**

7. Maha Chohan, help me see that this is the same process that has taken place in previous spheres. Self-aware beings started out with a point-like sense of self-awareness and expanded it by creating a spirit.

> O Heros-Amora, conditions are ties,
> forming a net of serpentine lies,
> but you have the antidote setting us free,
> you take us beyond conditionality.

> **O Heros-Amora, we reap what we sow,**
> **yet this is Plan B for helping us grow,**

**for truly, Plan A is that we join the flow,
immersed in the Infinite Love you bestow.**

8. Maha Chohan, help me see that this spirit is not a dark or evil spirit; it can be a beautiful and bright spirit that is created from a positive momentum.

O Heros-Amora, your love is no bond,
for love only wants to take us beyond,
your love has no bounds, forever it flies,
raising all life into Ruby-Pink skies.

**O Heros-Amora, we reap what we sow,
yet this is Plan B for helping us grow,
for truly, Plan A is that we join the flow,
immersed in the Infinite Love you bestow.**

9. Maha Chohan, help me see that it is still a spirit that must be allowed to die for the Conscious You to come up higher, and come closer to its ultimate oneness with its creator, with its source, the I AM Presence.

O Heros-Amora, love bathing the earth,
filling all people with infinite mirth,
for fear and despair there is no more room,
as all are awakened by love's sonic boom.

**O Heros-Amora, we reap what we sow,
yet this is Plan B for helping us grow,
for truly, Plan A is that we join the flow,
immersed in the Infinite Love you bestow.**

Part 2

1. Maha Chohan, help me see that all previous beings in all previous spheres have gone through this process of first creating a spirit out of the seven rays, then allowing that spirit to die, then working on the higher rays, allowing that spirit to die, being reborn in the fire of the Ascension Flame. Finally, being accelerated into being immortal lifestreams. This process is part of what creates the Holy Spirit.

> Chamuel Archangel, in ruby ray power,
> we know we are taking a life-giving shower.
> Love burning away all perversions of will,
> we suddenly feel our desires falling still.

> **Chamuel Archangel, descend from Above,**
> **Chamuel Archangel, with ruby-pink love,**
> **Chamuel Archangel, so often thought-of,**
> **Chamuel Archangel, o come Holy Dove.**

2. Maha Chohan, help me see that even while I am creating this spirit before my ascension, I am contributing to the growth of my sphere. I am bringing the light of the seven rays at first and then I bring the light of the higher rays.

> Chamuel Archangel, a spiral of light,
> as ruby ray fire now pierces the night.
> All forces of darkness consumed by your fire,
> consuming all those who will not rise higher.

> **Chamuel Archangel, descend from Above,**
> **Chamuel Archangel, with ruby-pink love,**

**Chamuel Archangel, so often thought-of,
Chamuel Archangel, o come Holy Dove.**

3. Maha Chohan, help me see that I am contributing to building and raising my sphere, building that ascending momentum of my sphere.

Chamuel Archangel, your love so immense,
with clarified vision, our lives now make sense.
The purpose of life you so clearly reveal,
immersed in your love, God's oneness we feel.

**Chamuel Archangel, descend from Above,
Chamuel Archangel, with ruby-pink love,
Chamuel Archangel, so often thought-of,
Chamuel Archangel, o come Holy Dove.**

4. Maha Chohan, help me see that what makes the spirit holy, what contributes to the Holy Spirit, is when I consciously see the spirit I have created and choose to let it die, so that I am reborn.

Chamuel Archangel, what calmness you bring,
we see now that even death has no sting.
For truly, in love there can be no decay,
as love is transcendence into a new day.

**Chamuel Archangel, descend from Above,
Chamuel Archangel, with ruby-pink love,
Chamuel Archangel, so often thought-of,
Chamuel Archangel, o come Holy Dove.**

5. Maha Chohan, help me see that by letting the old spirit die, I move one step closer to oneness. The final contribution to the Holy Spirit is when I let that last ghost die, and then I am accelerated into the Ascension Flame.

> Chamuel Archangel, God's Love Flame bestow,
> on all those longing God's true love to know,
> conditions we know can never be real,
> and this is the love you always reveal.

> **Chamuel Archangel, descend from Above,**
> **Chamuel Archangel, with ruby-pink love,**
> **Chamuel Archangel, so often thought-of,**
> **Chamuel Archangel, o come Holy Dove.**

6. Maha Chohan, help me see that every time I withdraw the Conscious You from a particular spirit, see that spirit from the outside and allow it to die consciously, then I contribute to the upward momentum whereby the separate Spirit Sparks move one step closer to oneness with the Creator.

> Chamuel Archangel, love's seed you have sown,
> in hearts of all those who don't seek to own,
> for love that possesses is nothing but fear,
> that pierces the heart with duality's spear.

> **Chamuel Archangel, descend from Above,**
> **Chamuel Archangel, with ruby-pink love,**
> **Chamuel Archangel, so often thought-of,**
> **Chamuel Archangel, o come Holy Dove.**

7. Maha Chohan, help me see that the Creator decided to create individual extensions of its Self, to send them out with a

point-like sense of self, so different from the omnipresent, non-linear, spherical sense of self of the Creator.

Chamuel Archangel, we don't want control,
for this is the devil's hold on the soul,
your love will now break the serpentine chain,
so we are set free God's love to reclaim.

Chamuel Archangel, descend from Above,
Chamuel Archangel, with ruby-pink love,
Chamuel Archangel, so often thought-of,
Chamuel Archangel, o come Holy Dove.

8. Maha Chohan, help me see that the Creator knew that these Spirit Sparks could become lost in their own creation. They could come to identify themselves with their creation and therefore stay in that creation indefinitely, unless there was some mechanism that pulled them back to their source.

Chamuel Archangel, you are so adept,
at helping us God's true love to accept,
we know that the love for which we so yearn,
is not something we on earth have to earn.

Chamuel Archangel, descend from Above,
Chamuel Archangel, with ruby-pink love,
Chamuel Archangel, so often thought-of,
Chamuel Archangel, o come Holy Dove.

9. Maha Chohan, help me see that the purpose for creation is that the Spirit Sparks go out and then return to their source. Not to return to go into oblivion, but to return as being More

than when they went out. And that is how creation expands
and how God is magnified.

> Chamuel Archangel, for love to accept,
> we do not need to be so perfect,
> for love is not static but always a flow,
> demanding only we're willing to grow.

> **Chamuel Archangel, descend from Above,**
> **Chamuel Archangel, with ruby-pink love,**
> **Chamuel Archangel, so often thought-of,**
> **Chamuel Archangel, o come Holy Dove.**

Part 3

1. Maha Chohan, help me see that built into my life-stream is
the desire to become More, the desire to expand. This is the
very desire that drove the Creator to create in the first place.

> Master Paul, venetian dream,
> your love for beauty's flowing stream.
> Master Paul, in love's own womb,
> your power shatters ego's tomb.

> **Master Paul, your love so true,**
> **and therefore we apply to you,**
> **to set all free in the great love,**
> **that you are shining from Above.**

2. Maha Chohan, help me see that there is a drive inside of me
to be More, and that is why I co-create. That is why I formulate

an image and then imbue it with consciousness. This is also why any spirit that I create has that drive to become More, to expand, to grow and to intensify.

> Master Paul, your counsel wise,
> our minds are raised to lofty skies.
> Master Paul, in wisdom's love,
> such beauty flowing from Above.

> **Master Paul, your love so true,**
> **and therefore we apply to you,**
> **to set all free in the great love,**
> **that you are shining from Above.**

3. Maha Chohan, help me see that when I am following the process of initiation under the seven Chohans, I learn to draw the light of the seven rays from inside myself into the outer self, the spirit I am creating.

> Master Paul, love is an art,
> it opens up the secret heart.
> Master Paul, love's rushing flow,
> our hearts awash in sacred glow.

> **Master Paul, your love so true,**
> **and therefore we apply to you,**
> **to set all free in the great love,**
> **that you are shining from Above.**

4. Maha Chohan, help me see that this is a creative process, because I do not need to take anything from other lifestreams or the material world to drive my co-creative efforts.

> Master Paul, accelerate,
> upon pure love we meditate.
> Master Paul, intentions pure,
> our self-transcendence will ensure.

> **Master Paul, your love so true,**
> **and therefore we apply to you,**
> **to set all free in the great love,**
> **that you are shining from Above.**

5. Maha Chohan, help me become more and more detached from the spirit I am creating, knowing that this is just a vehicle, knowing that it is a servant that I have created, and that I am in charge.

> Master Paul, your love will heal,
> our inner light you do reveal.
> Master Paul, all life console,
> with you we're being truly whole.

> **Master Paul, your love so true,**
> **and therefore we apply to you,**
> **to set all free in the great love,**
> **that you are shining from Above.**

6. Maha Chohan, help me to not allow this spirit to take on a self of its own. Help me become aware that each time I step up one level in consciousness, I do so by letting the old spirit die and by being reborn into a new spirit that is more than the old.

> Master Paul, you serve the All,
> by helping us transcend the fall.

Master Paul, in peace we rise,
as ego meets its sure demise.

Master Paul, your love so true,
and therefore we apply to you,
to set all free in the great love,
that you are shining from Above.

7. Maha Chohan, help me become familiar with the process of letting the old die without holding on to it, because I know I will be reborn as More.

Master Paul, love all life free,
your love is for eternity.
Master Paul, you are the One,
to help us make the journey fun.

Master Paul, your love so true,
and therefore we apply to you,
to set all free in the great love,
that you are shining from Above.

8. Maha Chohan, help me so that when I come to the 96th level, I can let go of the momentum I have on the seven rays, realizing I now want something higher, which is the secret rays.

Master Paul, you balance all,
the seven rays upon our call.
Master Paul, you paint the sky,
with colors that delight the I.

Master Paul, your love so true,
and therefore we apply to you,

> **to set all free in the great love,**
> **that you are shining from Above.**

9. Maha Chohan, help me see that the higher rays are not meant to create material form, but are meant to create something beyond material form and thereby contribute to the raising of the collective awareness, rather than the physical manifestations that I see with the senses.

> Master Paul, your Presence here,
> filling up the inner sphere.
> Life is now a sacred flow,
> God Love we do on all bestow.

> **Master Paul, your love so true,**
> **and therefore we apply to you,**
> **to set all free in the great love,**
> **that you are shining from Above.**

Part 4

1. Maha Chohan, I am willing to let the old die, I am willing to give up the ghost. I hereby give up any desire to demonstrate some mastery of mind over matter and create phenomena that can impress other people.

> Maha Chohan, I will to grow,
> I feel the power of your flow.
> Maha Chohan, the veil is rent,
> creative will from heaven sent.

**O Holy Spirit, flow through me,
I am the open door for thee.
O mighty rushing stream of Light,
transcendence is my sacred right.**

2. Maha Chohan, help me see that if people are no longer on the path of self-transcendence, they become black magicians who are using their gifts for an entirely self-centered purpose. They are therefore cut off from the flow of the Spirit.

Maha Chohan, your wisdom streams,
awaken all from matter's dreams.
Maha Chohan, your balance bring,
let bells of integration ring.

**O Holy Spirit, flow through me,
I am the open door for thee.
O mighty rushing stream of Light,
transcendence is my sacred right.**

3. Maha Chohan, help me see that such people can no longer receive light through the seven rays. They must go into the path of the black magicians, of stealing light from those who are still receiving it from within.

Maha Chohan, love's mighty call,
the prison walls are shattered all.
Maha Chohan, set all life free
through unconditionality.

**O Holy Spirit, flow through me,
I am the open door for thee.**

**O mighty rushing stream of Light,
transcendence is my sacred right.**

4. Maha Chohan, help me see that when we go below the 48th level of awareness, then the spirit that we had created up until that point now becomes a spirit that cannot see that it can get energy from inside itself.

Maha Chohan, intentions pure,
all life is one, I know for sure.
Maha Chohan, I am awake,
surrender all for oneness' sake.

**O Holy Spirit, flow through me,
I am the open door for thee.
O mighty rushing stream of Light,
transcendence is my sacred right.**

5. Maha Chohan, help me see that such a spirit instantly reverts to a spirit that now knows it must take light from outside itself. Yet it still has the basic drive to multiply, the drive to become More.

Maha Chohan, help all men see,
through veils of unreality.
Maha Chohan, with single eye,
I know I am the greater "I."

**O Holy Spirit, flow through me,
I am the open door for thee.
O mighty rushing stream of Light,
transcendence is my sacred right.**

6. Maha Chohan, help me see that such a spirit must seek to become More by taking energy from the level where it is at in the material realm. It now becomes a spirit, that by its very nature is an aggressive spirit that must and will take light from other spirits.

> Maha Chohan, your peace I find,
> Maitreya shows me to be kind.
> Maha Chohan, all war will cease,
> now flooding all with sacred peace.

> **O Holy Spirit, flow through me,**
> **I am the open door for thee.**
> **O mighty rushing stream of Light,**
> **transcendence is my sacred right.**

7. Maha Chohan, help me see that this is why such a spirit cannot live and let live. It must take energy from without through either deceit or direct force. Some spirits seek to take by obvious force and some seek to take through deceit.

> Maha Chohan, you balance all,
> the seven rays upon my call.
> Maha Chohan, all life is free,
> transcending for eternity.

> **O Holy Spirit, flow through me,**
> **I am the open door for thee.**
> **O mighty rushing stream of Light,**
> **transcendence is my sacred right.**

8. Maha Chohan, help me see that the Holy Spirit is a living Spirit of self-transcendence that takes energy from the spiritual

realm and gives to the material. The one Holy Spirit always moves closer and closer to oneness.

> Maha Chohan, your sacred Flame,
> what beauty in your blessed name.
> Maha Chohan, what rushing flow,
> the Spirit one with life below.

> **O Holy Spirit, flow through me,**
> **I am the open door for thee.**
> **O mighty rushing stream of Light,**
> **transcendence is my sacred right.**

9. Maha Chohan, help me see that there is a multiplicity of the separate spirits that are moving further away from oneness the more power they gather to themselves. Each time they take from another, they move further away from oneness with that other. For how can one forcefully or deceitfully take from another and move closer to oneness with that other?

> Maha Chohan, your Presence here,
> filling up the inner sphere.
> Life is now a sacred flow,
> God Wisdom we on all bestow.

> **O Holy Spirit, flow through me,**
> **I am the open door for thee.**
> **O mighty rushing stream of Light,**
> **transcendence is my sacred right.**

Sealing:

In the name of the Divine Mother, I fully accept that the power of these calls is used to set free the Ma-ter light, so it can outpicture the perfect vision of Christ for my own life, for all people and for the planet. In the name I AM THAT I AM, it is done! Amen.

9 | THE SPIRITUAL SCENARIO ON EARTH

The Maha Chohan I AM. In this discourse we will look at the contrast between the ideal scenario for the growth of a new co-creator, and the scenario that is the current reality on planet earth.

As we have said, a new co-creator first descends at the 48th level of consciousness. At this level you have an intuitive, inner sense that you are connected to something greater than yourself. And this something greater is, of course, your I AM Presence. You also have the availability of a spiritual teacher—that is, of course, in the ideal scenario. You therefore have conscious contact with a spiritual teacher, who can guide you on the First Ray and then on the other rays as you move forward.

What happens in the ideal scenario is that you rise from the 48th through the 49th level of consciousness. And as you rise, you create a spirit. Then you allow that spirit to be reborn into a higher spirit, and this allows you to rise to the next level of consciousness. Take note that in this ideal scenario you are not actually dealing with the concept that you on earth today see as death. It is not truly necessary for you to let the old spirit die, in the sense you understand death on earth.

A spiritual view of death

You see, the way you have come to look at death is that this is something that definitively ends your life that breaks it off that stops it. You have come to see it as something that is forced upon you by some outside force.

Yet in the ideal scenario, you do not have to go through the process of letting the old spirit die, in the sense that it ceases to be that something is forced upon you, and that this is a loss or a cessation of consciousness. Instead, you realize that you can simply allow yourself to be reborn into a higher sense of self.

Therefore, one could say that what you do between the 48th and the 96th level of consciousness, is that you very smoothly allow one spirit to transcend itself into the next spirit—and the next, and the next, and the next. This is a process that does not entail any abrupt stoppages, as you associate with death today. You are simply flowing from one stage to the next, and therefore it is easy for a co-creator to get the sense that you have continuity between the spirit at one level of consciousness and the spirit at the next level of consciousness.

This can then give you, as I spoke about previously, the sense that you are building a continuous spirit instead of going from one spirit to the next. Yet at the same time, if you have contact with a spiritual teacher, then the teacher will prepare you for the fact that when you come to the 96th level, you do have to go through an abrupt change. Because at that point you actually have to "lay down your life for a friend," as Jesus expressed it.

You have to have that greater love of being willing to lay down the spirit that you have created at the first 48 levels of consciousness. For this spirit cannot take you beyond the 96th level, as it is a spirit that was focused on raising itself as an individual spirit. In order to transcend and go beyond the 96th level, you need to start creating a new spirit that is aimed at raising up more than your individual self that is aimed at raising up the whole.

In the ideal scenario, this is a more abrupt change than you have experienced before, but it is still not what you see as death today. Because truly, it is not a loss for the Conscious You. As you have become more and more conscious, as you grew towards the 96th level, you have also become conscious of the fact that you will not die if your spirit dies because you are more than the spirit. The spirit is not you. You have not created a "self;" you have not even recreated yourself as the spirit.

You are conscious of the fact that the spirit is just a vehicle that you are using to express yourself in the material world. Therefore, you will know that even if this spirit dies, you will not die. There will not even be a cessation of consciousness. There will not be an abrupt change or loss. This means that you can, when you are aware of this, smoothly let go of the old. You can lay down your life for a greater cause than raising up an individual self. You can therefore smoothly transition into that next phase.

Ideal versus current scenario

We will now look at the scenario that you face today, as you begin the path in a more conscious way than you have done before. What you have on planet earth today is not the ideal scenario by any means. It is very far from the ideal scenario.

Of course, my purpose for bringing out this book before I allow the seven Chohans to bring out books for each of the seven rays, is indeed to prepare you, so that you can more successfully navigate the seven rays and the initiations of the seven rays.

Truly, in the ideal scenario, you would not be confronted with what I, in the last discourse, talked about as the aggressive spirits. In the ideal scenario, you are creating a spirit, and a number of spirits, as you grow from the 48th to the 96th level. But these are spirits that have two interesting characteristics. One is that they know that you can draw enough energy from inside yourself to drive your creative efforts. Thus, you do not need to take anything from outside yourself, from other lifestreams, meaning there is nothing aggressive in this kind of spirit. Furthermore, the spirit you are creating has the over-all goal of growing towards a higher state of consciousness. You are not creating a static spirit; you are creating a spirit that wants to grow that wants to transition into a higher phase.

This is in stark contrast to what happens after you fall into the duality consciousness where you now begin to see yourself as a separate being. In order to go through this process, you have to be aware of a subtle psychological mechanism. Before you fall into a lower state of consciousness, you do have some inner sense that you are connected to something greater than yourself. This means that in order to enter into the conscious-ness of separation where you now see yourself as a separate being, you have to deny your connection to something greater than yourself.

Yet the Conscious You is created as an extension of the I AM Presence, as an extension of the ascended masters and ultimately as an extension of the Creator's Being. So you have to go through a deliberate denial of this connection to some-thing greater. And in order to do this, you have to justify the denial. You have to find a way, in your own mind, to justify that you are departing the path towards greater and greater oneness with something greater, and instead switching to the path that takes you deeper and deeper into separation. This is where you then seek to raise up your separate self – not as a connected being with greater and greater creative powers – but as a separate being with greater and greater powers to forcefully control your environment.

How you create an aggressive spirit

When you go into separation, and deny your connection to something greater, what is it exactly that happens? Well, if you deny that you are connected to something greater than yourself where are you going to get the energy to drive your creative efforts? You cannot get it from something greater than yourself, if you deny that you are connected to something greater than yourself. So in a sense you are shutting off that connection and the flow of energy through it, which now means that you have to get energy from some other source.

Of course, you still need energy in order to do anything, and this means you now need to get energy from the same level where you are focused, namely the material realm. Which essentially means you need to get it from other lifestreams, who are still connected to their source. So you need to find a way to either forcefully or deceitfully get other lifestreams to give their energy. This means you now create a new type of spirit that is not focused on getting energy from within and upon growing to another stage that is higher than its own stage.

Instead, you create a spirit that is focused on taking energy from the world around it, and it is focused on expanding itself as a powerful being in this world. In other words, instead of seeking to become more than you are; you now have a spirit who seeks to become more of what it already is—more powerful in terms of doing the things you can do in the material realm.

What you now see is that since the original fall, the beings that fell into the consciousness of separation have created innumerable spirits that are based on the illusion of separation. These are separate spirits that seek to aggressively influence other lifestreams. Their entire modus operandi, their entire design, is aimed at aggressively taking energy from others. Some of them seek to do this through obvious force, others seek to do this through fear, and others seek to do it through deception. Yet they are all aimed at this one goal: aggressively projecting their own matrix, the thought-matrix that created them, upon other lifestreams for the purpose of controlling them.

Overcoming false spirits

You now see that in the ideal scenario you have 48 levels, as you go through the Path of the Seven Rays. For each of them there is a certain spirit. In order to go from one level to the next, you have to leave that spirit behind and embrace the next spirit. Yet none of those spirits are aggressively seeking to control your mind, and thus it is not a hard process—in the ideal scenario.

But what you have on planet earth today is not the ideal scenario. It is a scenario where you now have false spirits that have been created at each of the 48 levels of consciousness between the 48th and the 96th level.

In other words, for each step that you take on the Path of the Seven Rays, there is a false spirit. And this false spirit will aggressively seek to prevent you from taking the next step on the path. It will seek to keep you on the level where you are at, and to keep you there indefinitely.

You also have the scenario that many beings have gone below the 48th level of consciousness, which is something you do not have to deal with in the ideal scenario. Yet what you have today on earth is that many beings have gone below the 48th level, and they have, of course, also created false spirits, or aggressive-spirits, for each of the levels between the 48th level and the 1st level, the lowest level of consciousness.

What you now have is an interesting interaction between the false spirits above the 48th level and the aggressive-spirits below. You now see that in order to pass from one level of consciousness to the next, you do not simply have to deal with the spirit that you yourself have created at your current level of consciousness. You also have to deal with the false spirit at that level, and then the aggressive spirit at the corresponding level beneath the 48th level of consciousness.

For example, if you are currently 10 levels above the 48th level of consciousness, then there is what we might call a true spirit at that level, which you use as a vehicle to get to the next level. But there is also a false spirit that justifies why you should not move from that level to the next level. And then, there is a corresponding aggressive spirit that is 10 levels below the 48th level, which is also aggressively seeking to draw you into its matrix.

False and aggressive spirits

Here is the difference. The false-spirit that is 10 levels above the 48th level is aimed at justifying why you do not go higher than that level of consciousness. But the aggressive spirit is aimed at drawing you into the dualistic struggle between you and some kind of opponent.

The false spirits that exist between the 48th and the 96th level are still focused on you as an individual lifestream because you are in the process of growing as an individual lifestream. So the false spirit will say to you: "You do not need to grow beyond this level, and here is why and here are all the justifications for why you should not grow. You should stay here and enjoy this level and expand your awareness at this level only." This is still not aimed at anything outside yourself; it is aimed at you.

Yet the corresponding aggressive spirit that is below the 48th level of consciousness, is trapped in the dualistic mindset. It sees itself as being opposed by an external enemy, and therefore it sees itself as being in a constant battle with this external enemy. The lower you go between the 48th level and the lowest level of consciousness, the more you find spirits who are completely trapped in what we have called the epic mindset. This is where you see the battle between the ultimate forces of good and evil, such as the traditional theistic view of God, and the equally theistic view of the devil as being in opposition to God. So you see the difference.

There is still a false spirit that is focused on you as an individual lifestream, but then there is the aggressive spirit where you are not even focused on yourself anymore; you are focused on dealing with some external opponent. At some level this will be other people, at other levels it will be a greater dark force, but at the very lowest level your external opponent is actually God. Because you now think – as the fallen ones fell into the original illusion – that God has made a mistake and created a faulty design for the universe. And it is your task to correct God's mistake and set things right, by forcing others to follow you in your vision of salvation.

The growth of the whole

You now see that, in a sense, there is a mirror image between the levels of consciousness from the 96th to the 144th level, and the levels below the 48th level. As you rise from the 96th to the 144th level, you must overcome and deal with these aggressive spirits. And you must not only overcome them in your own mind, but you must also make a contribution to slaying these spirits—to having them bound, judged and ultimately having the matrix shattered as you rise in consciousness.

Therefore, your personal growth from one level to the next, makes it easier for other lifestreams to grow beyond that particular aggressive spirit and the illusions behind it. This then is what facilitates the growth of the entire sphere of planet earth where you can eventually get to a point, as we have explained where the level of the 144 potential states of consciousness is raised, so that what is the lowest level right now, will no longer be allowed on earth. And the beings who are at that level, will have to go somewhere else whereby the earth is set free from the downward pull of these lifestreams. Yet, let us not get too far ahead of ourselves, for the focus on this series of discourses is to help you grow from the 48th to the 96th level.

Following a conscious path

Let me put it this way. You, of course, have had many previous lifetimes. You have in those lifetimes been engaged in the path in some way or another, whether you were consciously aware of this or not. Therefore, it is quite possible that in past lifetimes you have risen to a certain level of consciousness between the 48th and the 96th level. Nevertheless, if you have found this book and you are reading this, this means that you are now at a point on your personal path where you are ready to not walk this process in a largely unconscious way; but to walk it in a conscious, deliberate way.

This means that even if you are at, say the 72nd level of consciousness, you cannot jump in consciously to that level and start from there. Instead, the most constructive way to do this, is to have the humility and the realism to realize that you need to start at the basic level. You need to start with the very first initiation that a new lifestream would be given at the 48th level. Which is the point where you are initiated on the First Ray as both the Alpha and the Omega aspect of the initiation. When you pass this test, you can go to the 49th level where the First Ray is still the Alpha but the Second Ray is now the Omega. Then, of course, you move on to the First Ray being the Alpha and the Omega being the Third Ray, and this continues.

By being willing to go through this process of learning from each of the seven Chohans without worrying about where you are at, you will go through these steps in a conscious way. This will have a dual effect. It will first of all help yourself be more conscious of the initiation, which anchors it more firmly at all levels of your being. What you have attained in past lives is anchored in your three higher bodies – identity, mental and emotional – but not necessarily at the physical level, or you would obviously be conscious of it right now. You need to bring your past attainment to the conscious level, so you can use it consciously. And this is what you will do, by going through these levels.

The other important aspect of you starting at the 48th level with the First Ray, is that you then make it easier for other people to go through this process. Because you are adding to the momentum of going through the Path of the Seven Rays, and this is part of the momentum for the Holy Spirit for planet earth. Indeed, you will make it easier for others to tune in to the Holy Spirit, and therefore transcend their current level of consciousness, by tuning in to the momentum created by you and all other beings on earth, who have passed the initiations of the seven rays.

Two levels of motivation

This does not mean that the attainment and momentum you have built in past ages is of no use to you, until you reach the level of consciousness you reached in past ages. If you have a momentum, say on the 72nd level, you will make it much more easy for yourself to pass the initiations below that level. And thus, you can go through the process much more quickly, than someone who would start out at the 48th level or even start out below.

What we propose to do in this book, and in the coming releases from the seven Chohans, is to outline a path that anyone on earth can follow, regardless of their level of consciousness. In other words, someone even at the very lowest level of consciousness, could start with the initiations we describe, or will describe, for the First Ray and could then grow from there. Of course what we can do is only to outline the path; we can outline the steps that you must follow, taking one step and then the next.

But what we cannot do is supply the willingness to follow the path. That is your responsibility, your exclusive responsibility. Thus, we foresee, of course that there will be two levels of motivation. When you go below the 48th level you go into – or rather you create – a downward spiral. Of course, many other beings have already created a downward spiral on earth, and so when you go below the 48th level, you will be tied into these spirals. You will be sucked in by them, and this will accelerate your personal spiral. Nevertheless, you are still required to make a decision for each step you take down, so even though there is a magnetic force pulling you down, you have to decide to take that step down.

This, of course, also means that in order to reverse the process and start going back up, you have to make a decision to go back up. What will cause you to make that decision? Well, if you fall below the 48th level, it usually means that you have to come to a point that some people call "hitting bottom," or "hitting rock bottom." This is where things become so intense that you simply cannot do this anymore; you cannot live with yourself, you cannot live with the conditions you are facing in the material universe.

Beyond unpleasant situations

This is what we might call a negative motivation because you feel forced by external conditions into a situation where you simply cannot stand it anymore. So even though this is what we might call a negative motivation, it can still be a motivation—if you are willing to do one thing. If you are willing to look at yourself and say: "What is the self that cannot stand it anymore? What is the I that cannot stand it? Is there more than one self here?"

In other words, is there a difference between who I really am and the self that is experiencing my current situation as unbearable. If you will ask yourself this, you can then become open to the teaching I have given. Namely that at your current level of consciousness, whatever that is, you have created a spirit. That spirit is not you because you are still the Conscious You, which is pure awareness. You have not become this spirit. You are only seeing – you are perceiving – life through the perception filter of that spirit. Thus, it is not you who can't stand the situation; it is the spirit who can't stand the situation. For it has put itself into a blind alley – a catch-22 – where it seemingly cannot get out of it in any way that it can see. And it is perfectly true that if you look at your situation through the perception filter of that spirit, you cannot get out of it—there is no way out. But there is a way out, and that is to realize: "I am not that spirit, I am More than that spirit." And that means I have the potential to rise to the next level of consciousness, but how can I do this?

You can do this in only one way: by letting your current spirit die! Believe me because that spirit is an aggressive spirit, it will experience it as a death, as you currently see death on planet earth—where everything, every thought system, every philosophy, every religion – even most spiritual teachings – is influenced by the consciousness of death, the consciousness of separation and duality.

This is why you have to acknowledge a simple fact. In today's less than ideal scenario – whether you are below the 48th level or between the 48th and the 96th level – the only way to grow to the next level of your path, is that you must deal with the negative, aggressive spirit that corresponds to your current level. In order to free yourself from the downward pull of that spirit, you must look at the spirit of your self, and see it as a spirit that is different from the Conscious You, different from the real you. And you must consciously and deliberately say to that spirit: "I am not you, and I do not want to see life through the filter that you are. I acknowledge that you are unreal, and I am willing to let you die, so that I can be free to rise to a higher level."

This is the only way that you are going to be truly able to leave behind the lower level of consciousness and rise to the next level. Remember that this is not the way it was in the ideal scenario, but you are not in an ideal environment. You are in a very treacherous environment that is heavily infused by the death consciousness. And how you can deal with the death consciousness will be the topic of my next discourse, but for now I have given you plenty to contemplate.

10 | INVOKING A HIGHER AWARENESS OF EARTH

In the name I AM THAT I AM, Jesus Christ, I call to my I AM Presence to flow through the I Will Be Presence that I AM and give this invocation with full power. I call to beloved Elohim Astrea and Purity, Archangel Gabriel and Hope, Serapis Bey and the Maha Chohan to help me increase my awareness of what kind of planet I am on. Help me see and surrender all patterns that block my oneness with the Maha Chohan and my oneness with my I AM Presence, including …

[Make personal calls]

Part 1

1. Maha Chohan, help me see that as I rise to the next level of consciousness, I create a spirit. Then, I allow that spirit to be reborn into a higher spirit, and this allows me to rise to the next level of consciousness.

Beloved Astrea, your heart is so true,
your Circle and Sword of white and blue,
cut all life free from dramas unwise,
on wings of Purity our planet will rise.

**Beloved Astrea, in oneness with you,
your circle and sword of electric blue,
with Purity's Light cutting right through,
raising the earth into all that is true.**

2. Maha Chohan, help me see that in the ideal scenario, it is not necessary to let the old spirit die, in the sense we understand death on earth.

Beloved Astrea, in God Purity,
accelerate all of our life energy,
we're rising beyond every impurity,
as Purity's Light forever we see.

**Beloved Astrea, in oneness with you,
your circle and sword of electric blue,
with Purity's Light cutting right through,
raising the earth into all that is true.**

3. Maha Chohan, help me see that we tend to look at death as something that definitively ends a life, that breaks it off, that stops it. We have come to see it as something that is forced upon us by some outside force.

Beloved Astrea, from Purity's Ray,
send forth deliverance to all life today,
acceleration to Purity, we are now free
from all that is less than love's Purity.

**Beloved Astrea, in oneness with you,
your circle and sword of electric blue,
with Purity's Light cutting right through,
raising the earth into all that is true.**

4. Maha Chohan, help me see that in the ideal scenario, we do not have to go through the process of letting the old spirit die. Instead, we allow ourselves to be reborn into a higher sense of self.

Beloved Astrea, accelerate us all,
as for your deliverance we fervently call,
set all life free from vision impure
beyond fear and doubt, we're rising for sure.

**Beloved Astrea, in oneness with you,
your circle and sword of electric blue,
with Purity's Light cutting right through,
raising the earth into all that is true.**

5. Maha Chohan, help me see that between the 48th and the 96th level of consciousness, we allow one spirit to transcend itself into the next spirit.

Beloved Astrea, we're willing to see,
all of the lies that keep us unfree,
we surrender all lies causing the fall,
forever affirming the oneness of All.

**Beloved Astrea, in oneness with you,
your circle and sword of electric blue,
with Purity's Light cutting right through,
raising the earth into all that is true.**

6. Maha Chohan, help me see that this does not entail any abrupt stoppages, as we associate with death today. We are flowing from one stage to the next, and it is easy to get the sense that we have continuity between the spirit at one level and the spirit at the next level.

> Beloved Astrea, accelerate life
> beyond all duality's struggle and strife,
> consume all division between God and man,
> accelerate fulfillment of God's perfect plan.

> **Beloved Astrea, in oneness with you,**
> **your circle and sword of electric blue,**
> **with Purity's Light cutting right through,**
> **raising the earth into all that is true.**

7. Maha Chohan, help me see that this can give us the sense that we are building a continuous spirit instead of going from one spirit to the next.

> Beloved Astrea, we lovingly call,
> break down separation's invisible wall,
> raising our minds into true unity
> with the Masters of love in Infinity.

> **Beloved Astrea, in oneness with you,**
> **your circle and sword of electric blue,**
> **with Purity's Light cutting right through,**
> **raising the earth into all that is true.**

8. Maha Chohan, help me see that when we come to the 96th level, we do have to go through an abrupt change. At that

point we have to "lay down our lives for a friend," as Jesus expressed it.

Beloved Astrea, help all of us find,
the secret that we create with the mind,
and thus what in ignorance we decreate,
in knowledge we easily can recreate.

Beloved Astrea, in oneness with you,
your circle and sword of electric blue,
with Purity's Light cutting right through,
raising the earth into all that is true.

9. Maha Chohan, help me see that we must have the greater love of being willing to lay down the spirit that we have created at the first 48 levels of consciousness. For this spirit cannot take us beyond the 96th level, because it is a spirit that was focused on raising itself as an individual spirit.

Beloved Astrea, we all do aspire,
to learning to use your purity's fire,
to raise every form in infamy sown,
as Saint Germain makes this planet his own.

Beloved Astrea, in oneness with you,
your circle and sword of electric blue,
with Purity's Light cutting right through,
raising the earth into all that is true.

Part 2

1. Maha Chohan, help me see that in order to go beyond the 96th level, I need to start creating a new spirit that is aimed at raising up more than my individual self, that is aimed at raising up the whole.

> Gabriel Archangel, your light we revere,
> immersed in your Presence, nothing we fear.
> Disciples of Christ, we do leave behind,
> the ego's desire for responding in kind.

> **Gabriel Archangel, of this we are sure,**
> **Gabriel Archangel, Christ light is the cure.**
> **Gabriel Archangel, intentions so pure,**
> **Gabriel Archangel, in you we're secure.**

2. Maha Chohan, help me see that in the ideal scenario, this is a more abrupt change than I have experienced before, but it is still not what we see as death today. It is not a loss for the Conscious You.

> Gabriel Archangel, we fear not the light,
> in purifications' fire, we delight.
> With your hand in ours, each challenge we face,
> we follow the spiral to infinite grace.

> **Gabriel Archangel, of this we are sure,**
> **Gabriel Archangel, Christ light is the cure.**
> **Gabriel Archangel, intentions so pure,**
> **Gabriel Archangel, in you we're secure.**

3. Maha Chohan, help me become conscious of the fact that I will not die if my spirit dies, because I am more than the spirit. The spirit is not me. I have not created a "self;" I have not even recreated myself as the spirit.

> Gabriel Archangel, your fire burning white,
> ascending with you, out of the night.
> The ego has nowhere to run and to hide,
> in ascension's bright spiral, with you we abide.
>
> **Gabriel Archangel, of this we are sure,**
> **Gabriel Archangel, Christ light is the cure.**
> **Gabriel Archangel, intentions so pure,**
> **Gabriel Archangel, in you we're secure.**

4. Maha Chohan, help me see that the spirit is just a vehicle that I am using to express myself in the material world. If this spirit dies, I will not die. There will not even be a cessation of consciousness. There will not be an abrupt change or loss.

> Gabriel Archangel, your trumpet we hear,
> announcing the birth of Christ drawing near.
> In lightness of being, we now are reborn,
> rising with Christ on bright Easter morn.
>
> **Gabriel Archangel, of this we are sure,**
> **Gabriel Archangel, Christ light is the cure.**
> **Gabriel Archangel, intentions so pure,**
> **Gabriel Archangel, in you we're secure.**

5. Maha Chohan, help me see that I can smoothly let go of the old. I can lay down my life for a greater cause than raising

up an individual self. I can smoothly transition into the next
phase.

> Gabriel Archangel, the earth is now free,
> embracing a nondual reality,
> the judgment of Christ upon forces so dark,
> who deny that all have a spiritual spark.
>
> **Gabriel Archangel, of this we are sure,**
> **Gabriel Archangel, Christ light is the cure.**
> **Gabriel Archangel, intentions so pure,**
> **Gabriel Archangel, in you we're secure.**

6. Maha Chohan, help me see that on earth we do not have the
ideal scenario. In the ideal scenario, I would not be confronted
with aggressive spirits.

> Gabriel Archangel, with angels so white,
> raising our planet out of the dark night,
> as we now intone the Word of the Lord,
> the beings who fell are bound by your sword.
>
> **Gabriel Archangel, of this we are sure,**
> **Gabriel Archangel, Christ light is the cure.**
> **Gabriel Archangel, intentions so pure,**
> **Gabriel Archangel, in you we're secure.**

7. Maha Chohan, help me see that when I fall into the duality
consciousness, I begin to see myself as a separate being. In
order to see myself as a separate being, I have to deny my connection to something greater than myself.

Gabriel Archangel, we call now to you,
the astral plane your light burning through,
entities, demons, discarnates are bound,
as you and we intone Sacred Sound.

Gabriel Archangel, of this we are sure,
Gabriel Archangel, Christ light is the cure.
Gabriel Archangel, intentions so pure,
Gabriel Archangel, in you we're secure.

8. Maha Chohan, help me see that because the Conscious You is created as an extension of the I AM Presence, I have to go through a deliberate denial of this connection to something greater. In order to do this, I have to justify the denial.

Gabriel Archangel, what glorious day,
your radiant angels have come here to stay,
your purifications fire burning white,
intentions so pure, our hearts taking flight.

Gabriel Archangel, of this we are sure,
Gabriel Archangel, Christ light is the cure.
Gabriel Archangel, intentions so pure,
Gabriel Archangel, in you we're secure.

9. Maha Chohan, help me see that I had to find a way to justify that I was departing the path towards greater oneness, and instead switched to the path that takes me deeper into separation.

Gabriel Archangel, our planet so pure,
in our bright new future we do feel secure,

with your band of light encircling the earth,
Saint Germain's Golden Age is now given birth.

Gabriel Archangel, of this we are sure,
Gabriel Archangel, Christ light is the cure.
Gabriel Archangel, intentions so pure,
Gabriel Archangel, in you we're secure.

Part 3

1. Maha Chohan, help me see that I had to raise up my separate self, not as a connected being with creative powers, but as a separate being with greater powers to forcefully control my environment.

Serapis Bey, what power lies,
behind your purifying eyes.
Serapis Bey, it is a treat,
to enter your sublime retreat.

Serapis Bey, we call to you,
to help us dual lies see through,
come purify our inner sight,
we see the earth in your great light.

2. Maha Chohan, help me see that when I go into separation, and deny that I am connected to something greater than myself, the energy used to drive my creative efforts can no longer come from my I AM Presence, so it must come from some other source.

Serapis Bey, what wisdom found,
your words are always most profound.
Serapis Bey, we tell you true,
our minds have room for naught but you.

Serapis Bey, we call to you,
to help us dual lies see through,
come purify our inner sight,
we see the earth in your great light.

3. Maha Chohan, help me see that I still need energy in order to do anything, and this means I now need to get energy from the same level where I am focused, namely the material realm.

Serapis Bey, what love beyond,
our hearts do leap, as we respond.
Serapis Bey, your life a poem,
that calls us to our starry home.

Serapis Bey, we call to you,
to help us dual lies see through,
come purify our inner sight,
we see the earth in your great light.

4. Maha Chohan, help me see that this means I need to get it from other lifestreams, who are still connected to their source. So I need to find a way to either forcefully or deceitfully get other lifestreams to give me their energy.

Serapis Bey, your guidance sure,
our base is clear and white and pure.
Serapis Bey, no longer trapped,
by soul in which the self was wrapped.

**Serapis Bey, we call to you,
to help us dual lies see through,
come purify our inner sight,
we see the earth in your great light.**

5. Maha Chohan, help me see that this means I now create a new type of spirit that is not focused on taking energy from the world around it, and it is focused on expanding itself as a powerful being in this world.

Serapis Bey, what healing balm,
in mind that is forever calm.
Serapis Bey, our thoughts are pure,
your discipline we shall endure.

**Serapis Bey, we call to you,
to help us dual lies see through,
come purify our inner sight,
we see the earth in your great light.**

6. Maha Chohan, help me see that instead of seeking to become more than I am, I now have a spirit who seeks to become more of what it already is—more powerful in terms of doing the things I can do in the material realm.

Serapis Bey, what secret test,
for egos who want to be best.
Serapis Bey, expose the "me,"
that takes away our harmony.

**Serapis Bey, we call to you,
to help us dual lies see through,**

come purify our inner sight,
we see the earth in your great light.

7. Maha Chohan, help me see that the beings that fell into the consciousness of separation have created innumerable spirits that are based on the illusion of separation. These are separate spirits, that seek to aggressively influence other lifestreams.

Serapis Bey, what moving sight,
the self ascends to sacred height.
Serapis Bey, forever free,
in sacred synchronicity.

Serapis Bey, we call to you,
to help us dual lies see through,
come purify our inner sight,
we see the earth in your great light.

8. Maha Chohan, help me see that their entire design is aimed at aggressively taking energy from others. Some of them seek to do this through obvious force, some through fear and some through deception.

Serapis Bey, you balance all,
the seven rays upon our call.
Serapis Bey, in space and time,
the pyramid of self, we climb.

Serapis Bey, we call to you,
to help us dual lies see through,
come purify our inner sight,
we see the earth in your great light.

9. Maha Chohan, help me see that these spirits are all aimed at this one goal: aggressively projecting their own matrix, the thought-matrix that created them, upon other lifestreams for the purpose of controlling them.

> Serapis Bey, your Presence here,
> filling up the inner sphere.
> Life is now a sacred flow,
> God Purity we do bestow.

> **Serapis Bey, we call to you,**
> **to help us dual lies see through,**
> **come purify our inner sight,**
> **we see the earth in your great light.**

Part 4

1. Maha Chohan, help me see that on earth today we do not have the ideal scenario. We have a scenario where we have false spirits that have been created at each level of consciousness between the 48th and the 96th level.

> Maha Chohan, I will to grow,
> I feel the power of your flow.
> Maha Chohan, the veil is rent,
> creative will from heaven sent.

> **O Holy Spirit, flow through me,**
> **I am the open door for thee.**
> **O mighty rushing stream of Light,**
> **transcendence is my sacred right.**

2. Maha Chohan, help me see that for each step that I take on the Path of the Seven Rays, there is a false spirit. And this false spirit will aggressively seek to prevent me from taking the next step on the path. It will seek to keep me on the level where I am at, and to keep you there indefinitely.

Maha Chohan, your wisdom streams,
awaken all from matter's dreams.
Maha Chohan, your balance bring,
let bells of integration ring.

**O Holy Spirit, flow through me,
I am the open door for thee.
O mighty rushing stream of Light,
transcendence is my sacred right.**

3. Maha Chohan, help me see that many beings have gone below the 48th level of consciousness, and they have also created false spirits for each of the levels between the 48th level and the lowest level of consciousness.

Maha Chohan, love's mighty call,
the prison walls are shattered all.
Maha Chohan, set all life free
through unconditionality.

**O Holy Spirit, flow through me,
I am the open door for thee.
O mighty rushing stream of Light,
transcendence is my sacred right.**

4. Maha Chohan, help me see that there is an interaction between the false spirits above the 48th level and the aggressive spirits below.

> Maha Chohan, intentions pure,
> all life is one, I know for sure.
> Maha Chohan, I am awake,
> surrender all for oneness' sake.
>
> **O Holy Spirit, flow through me,**
> **I am the open door for thee.**
> **O mighty rushing stream of Light,**
> **transcendence is my sacred right.**

5. Maha Chohan, help me see that in order to pass from one level of consciousness to the next, I do not simply have to deal with the spirit that I created at my current level. I also have to deal with the false spirit at that level, and then the aggressive spirit at the corresponding level beneath the 48th level of consciousness.

> Maha Chohan, help all men see,
> through veils of unreality.
> Maha Chohan, with single eye,
> I know I am the greater "I."
>
> **O Holy Spirit, flow through me,**
> **I am the open door for thee.**
> **O mighty rushing stream of Light,**
> **transcendence is my sacred right.**

6. Maha Chohan, help me see that the false-spirit at my level above the 48th level is aimed at justifying why I do not go

higher than that level of consciousness. The aggressive spirit is aimed at drawing me into the dualistic struggle with some kind of opponent.

> Maha Chohan, your peace I find,
> Maitreya shows me to be kind.
> Maha Chohan, all war will cease,
> now flooding all with sacred peace.

> **O Holy Spirit, flow through me,**
> **I am the open door for thee.**
> **O mighty rushing stream of Light,**
> **transcendence is my sacred right.**

7. Maha Chohan, help me see that the false spirit will say to me: "You do not need to grow beyond this level, and here is why and here are all the justifications for why you should not grow. You should stay here and enjoy this level and expand your awareness at this level only."

> Maha Chohan, you balance all,
> the seven rays upon my call.
> Maha Chohan, all life is free,
> transcending for eternity.

> **O Holy Spirit, flow through me,**
> **I am the open door for thee.**
> **O mighty rushing stream of Light,**
> **transcendence is my sacred right.**

8. Maha Chohan, help me see that the corresponding aggressive spirit is trapped in the dualistic mindset. It sees itself as

being opposed by an external enemy, and therefore it sees itself as being in a constant battle with this enemy.

Maha Chohan, your sacred Flame,
what beauty in your blessed name.
Maha Chohan, what rushing flow,
the Spirit one with life below.

**O Holy Spirit, flow through me,
I am the open door for thee.
O mighty rushing stream of Light,
transcendence is my sacred right.**

9. Maha Chohan, help me see that at the lowest level of consciousness, we find spirits who are trapped in the epic mindset, the idea of a battle between the ultimate forces of good and evil.

Maha Chohan, your Presence here,
filling up the inner sphere.
Life is now a sacred flow,
God Wisdom we on all bestow.

**O Holy Spirit, flow through me,
I am the open door for thee.
O mighty rushing stream of Light,
transcendence is my sacred right.**

Part 5

1. Maha Chohan, help me see that there is still a false spirit, that is focused on me as an individual lifestream, and there is the aggressive spirit, where I am not focused on myself but on dealing with some external opponent.

Serapis Bey, what power lies,
behind your purifying eyes.
Serapis Bey, it is a treat,
to enter your sublime retreat.

Serapis Bey, we call to you,
to help us dual lies see through,
come purify our inner sight,
we see the earth in your great light.

2. Maha Chohan, help me see that my personal growth from one level to the next, makes it easier for other lifestreams to grow beyond that particular aggressive spirit and the illusions behind it.

Serapis Bey, what wisdom found,
your words are always most profound.
Serapis Bey, we tell you true,
our minds have room for naught but you.

Serapis Bey, we call to you,
to help us dual lies see through,
come purify our inner sight,
we see the earth in your great light.

3. Maha Chohan, help me see that I am now at a point on my personal path, where I am ready to no longer walk this process in a largely unconscious way; but to walk it in a conscious, deliberate way.

> Serapis Bey, what love beyond,
> our hearts do leap, as we respond.
> Serapis Bey, your life a poem,
> that calls us to our starry home.

> **Serapis Bey, we call to you,**
> **to help us dual lies see through,**
> **come purify our inner sight,**
> **we see the earth in your great light.**

4. Maha Chohan, I do have the humility and the realism to realize that I need to start at the basic level. I need to start with the very first initiation that a new lifestream would be given at the 48th level.

> Serapis Bey, your guidance sure,
> our base is clear and white and pure.
> Serapis Bey, no longer trapped,
> by soul in which the self was wrapped.

> **Serapis Bey, we call to you,**
> **to help us dual lies see through,**
> **come purify our inner sight,**
> **we see the earth in your great light.**

5. Maha Chohan, help me see that by being willing to go through the process of learning from each of the seven Chohans

without worrying about where I am at, I will go through these steps in a conscious way.

> Serapis Bey, what healing balm,
> in mind that is forever calm.
> Serapis Bey, our thoughts are pure,
> your discipline we shall endure.

> **Serapis Bey, we call to you,**
> **to help us dual lies see through,**
> **come purify our inner sight,**
> **we see the earth in your great light.**

6. Maha Chohan, help me see that this will help me be more conscious of the initiation, which anchors it more firmly in my being. What I have attained in past lives is anchored in my three higher bodies.

> Serapis Bey, what secret test,
> for egos who want to be best.
> Serapis Bey, expose the "me,"
> that takes away our harmony.

> **Serapis Bey, we call to you,**
> **to help us dual lies see through,**
> **come purify our inner sight,**
> **we see the earth in your great light.**

7. Maha Chohan, help me see that I need to bring my past attainment to the conscious level, so I can use it consciously. And this is what I will do, by going through these levels.

Serapis Bey, what moving sight,
the self ascends to sacred height.
Serapis Bey, forever free,
in sacred synchronicity.

Serapis Bey, we call to you,
to help us dual lies see through,
come purify our inner sight,
we see the earth in your great light.

8. Maha Chohan, help me see that by starting at the 48th level with the First Ray, I make it easier for other people to go through this process. I am adding to the momentum of going through the Path of the Seven Rays, and this is part of the momentum of the Holy Spirit for earth.

Serapis Bey, you balance all,
the seven rays upon our call.
Serapis Bey, in space and time,
the pyramid of self, we climb.

Serapis Bey, we call to you,
to help us dual lies see through,
come purify our inner sight,
we see the earth in your great light.

9. Maha Chohan, I am willing to make it easier for others to tune in to the Holy Spirit, and therefore transcend their current level of consciousness, by tuning in to the momentum created by me and all other beings on earth who have passed the initiations of the seven rays.

Serapis Bey, your Presence here,
filling up the inner sphere.
Life is now a sacred flow,
God Purity we do bestow.

Serapis Bey, we call to you,
to help us dual lies see through,
come purify our inner sight,
we see the earth in your great light.

Part 6

1. Maha Chohan, I am willing to look at myself and say: "What is the self that cannot stand my present situation anymore? What is the I that cannot stand it? Is there more than one self here?"

Maha Chohan, I will to grow,
I feel the power of your flow.
Maha Chohan, the veil is rent,
creative will from heaven sent.

O Holy Spirit, flow through me,
I am the open door for thee.
O mighty rushing stream of Light,
transcendence is my sacred right.

2. Maha Chohan, help me see that there is a difference between who I really am and the self that is experiencing my current situation as unbearable. At my current level of consciousness,

I have created a spirit. That spirit is not me because I am still
the Conscious You, which is pure awareness.

> Maha Chohan, your wisdom streams,
> awaken all from matter's dreams.
> Maha Chohan, your balance bring,
> let bells of integration ring.

> **O Holy Spirit, flow through me,**
> **I am the open door for thee.**
> **O mighty rushing stream of Light,**
> **transcendence is my sacred right.**

3. Maha Chohan, help me see that I have not become this
spirit. I am only perceiving life through the perception filter of
that spirit.

> Maha Chohan, love's mighty call,
> the prison walls are shattered all.
> Maha Chohan, set all life free
> through unconditionality.

> **O Holy Spirit, flow through me,**
> **I am the open door for thee.**
> **O mighty rushing stream of Light,**
> **transcendence is my sacred right.**

4. Maha Chohan, help me see that it is not me who can't stand
the situation; it is the spirit who can't stand the situation. For
it has put itself into a blind alley where it seemingly cannot get
out of it in any way that it can see.

Maha Chohan, intentions pure,
all life is one, I know for sure.
Maha Chohan, I am awake,
surrender all for oneness' sake.

**O Holy Spirit, flow through me,
I am the open door for thee.
O mighty rushing stream of Light,
transcendence is my sacred right.**

5. Maha Chohan, help me see that if I look at my situation through the perception filter of the spirit, I cannot get out of it—there is no way out. The only way out is to realize: "I am not that spirit, I am More than that spirit."

Maha Chohan, help all men see,
through veils of unreality.
Maha Chohan, with single eye,
I know I am the greater "I."

**O Holy Spirit, flow through me,
I am the open door for thee.
O mighty rushing stream of Light,
transcendence is my sacred right.**

6. Maha Chohan, help me see that I can rise to the next level of consciousness, but I can do this in only one way: by letting my current spirit die!

Maha Chohan, your peace I find,
Maitreya shows me to be kind.
Maha Chohan, all war will cease,
now flooding all with sacred peace.

**O Holy Spirit, flow through me,
I am the open door for thee.
O mighty rushing stream of Light,
transcendence is my sacred right.**

7. Maha Chohan, help me see that an aggressive spirit will experience it as a death, as we currently see death on planet earth, where every thought system is influenced by the consciousness of death, the consciousness of separation and duality.

Maha Chohan, you balance all,
the seven rays upon my call.
Maha Chohan, all life is free,
transcending for eternity.

**O Holy Spirit, flow through me,
I am the open door for thee.
O mighty rushing stream of Light,
transcendence is my sacred right.**

8. Maha Chohan, help me see that in today's less than ideal scenario, the only way to grow to the next level of my path, is that I must deal with the negative, aggressive spirit that corresponds to my current level.

Maha Chohan, your sacred Flame,
what beauty in your blessed name.
Maha Chohan, what rushing flow,
the Spirit one with life below.

**O Holy Spirit, flow through me,
I am the open door for thee.**

**O mighty rushing stream of Light,
transcendence is my sacred right.**

9. Maha Chohan, help me see that in order to free myself from the downward pull of that spirit, I must look at the spirit of my self, and see it as a spirit that is different from the Conscious You, different from the real me. I say to that spirit: "I am not you, and I do not want to see life through the filter that you are. I acknowledge that you are unreal, and I am willing to let you die, so that I can be free to rise to a higher level."

Maha Chohan, your Presence here,
filling up the inner sphere.
Life is now a sacred flow,
God Wisdom we on all bestow.

**O Holy Spirit, flow through me,
I am the open door for thee.
O mighty rushing stream of Light,
transcendence is my sacred right.**

Sealing:

In the name of the Divine Mother, I fully accept that the power of these calls is used to set free the Ma-ter light, so it can outpicture the perfect vision of Christ for my own life, for all people and for the planet. In the name I AM THAT I AM, it is done! Amen.

11 | THE DEATH CONSCIOUSNESS

The Maha Chohan I am, and I come to give you a discourse on the death consciousness, and how you might begin to build a better way to react to it, or rather, to stop reacting to it. For of course, what the death consciousness wants more than anything else is to get you to react, to engage, or even to fight or seek to destroy it.

This, of course, is in stark contrast to the Holy Spirit, to the Spirit of Life, which does not want you to fight, does not want you to oppose, does not want you to destroy anyone or anything or to put down any part of life. It wants you to flow with the Spirit, to flow with the Spirit that is life.

For truly, as I have said, in all previous spheres – and in the very long time span that has passed since your sphere has come into being – the combined effort of all self-aware beings, who have transcended themselves and become more, has formed the upward flow of the Holy Spirit. It truly is the River of Life that carries everything with it. And truly, even the earth is carried with the stream of the Holy Spirit.

The River of Life never stands still

As you might know, if you think about this more deeply, your planet is not simply revolving around the sun in an elliptical orbit, and therefore coming back to its starting point every time it has completed one revolution. For you must know, I am sure that the entire universe is expanding, with all of the galaxies moving away from each other. That means that your sun is not stationary in the universe. Your sun is moving along a line, which is not even a straight line.

This means that as the sun is moving and dragging the planets with it, then, when the earth is moving in an elliptical orbit around the sun, it is not stationary in that orbit, it is not a stable orbit. The sun is moving, and so the actual path formed by the earth through space is more like a spiral, a very complex spiral, which can nevertheless be described mathematically. And which will, at some point in the not-too-distant future, be described mathematically. This will open up important new scientific discoveries, but this is beside the point of this discourse.

What you need to realize is simply this: the River of Life is an ongoing, moving stream. There is nothing in the River of Life that stands still. But you also need to consider that the River of Life is not simply moving, as you consider movement in the macroscopic universe of your senses. For you have the concept that you can move from one place to the other and remain the same. But this is not the kind of movement you find in the River of Life. For in the River of Life, movement is always transcending itself.

It is not just a horizontal movement where you remain the same. You are transcending, you are growing, you are accelerating and you are multiplying the talents and becoming more. And this is the essence of the life consciousness, the consciousness of life, the River of Life.

What is the consciousness of death?

So, with this in mind, let me now give you a concentrated teaching about what is the consciousness of death:

[15 second pause]

So you have now received a taste of what is the consciousness of death. For the consciousness of death is what you experienced in this interval of silence. For of course, whether you were reading or listening to this, you were expecting that after my introduction, something more would follow, some teaching, some image, some description of the consciousness of death. And therefore, when your expectation was not met because there was an interval of silence, you had a reaction in your mind, did you not?

And this reaction, if you would care to look at it, to observe it, you would see that this is part of the death consciousness. For what did you expect? You were tuned in to the flow of my delivery, and I was giving you to understand that I would give you a description of the death consciousness. So in your mind there was an expectation. And so you see, the death consciousness has two aspects here that you can identify, if you think about this carefully.

One is that there is a knowing behind the death consciousness that life is an ongoing process. You know deep within your being that life is meant to be the River of Life that is constantly transcending itself. This is an inner knowing that comes from the fact that the Conscious You is an extension of your I AM Presence, and then an extension of ascended masters, reaching all the way back to the Creator.

The Creator extended itself as self-aware extensions of itself precisely to give them an opportunity to accelerate their sense of self awareness. So this is your entire purpose for being: to accelerate your self-awareness and flow with the River of Life. And therefore you cannot – even though you can dull your conscious faculties – you cannot escape this inner knowing that life is an ongoing process, life is meant to be an ongoing process.

And thus, the death consciousness cannot completely remove this inner knowing. It can cover it over. It can camouflage it. It can misdirect it. But it cannot completely silence your inner knowing that life is meant to be an ongoing process.

But now what is it that the death consciousness *can* do? It can cause you to build an expectation of what that process should be like where it should be going as the next step, and where it should be going as the ultimate goal. This is what the death consciousness can do, but how can it do this?

Side-tracked by death

It can do so only because the death consciousness itself is a resistance to the ongoingness, to the River of Life. And when you resist the ongoingness of the River of Life, you create a distance, a space, between where you are now and where you would have been if you had followed the River of Life. And in this distance, in this space, is where there is room to build the expectation of what life should be like and where it should be going. To give you an illustration of this from ordinary life on earth, let me consider the many people who every Saturday go to a sporting game, whether it be football or something else. Before you go to the game, you have an expectation, a hope, of what should happen and what should not happen. You want the home team to win. This is the ultimate goal that you look at. And in the time up to the game, you might be counting down, saying, "Now I need to do this to get ready, now I need to do that to get ready, now I need to go here and park my car and get into the stadium and so forth and so on."

So all of this time, there is an interval between you and the game, and you are trying to anticipate and you are building expectations about what should happen and what you hope will not happen. You might indeed sit there during the game, being so caught up in your own expectations that you cannot really enjoy the game until it is finally over and you know whether your home team won or not. You might be sitting there watching every move, hoping that the other team will not score, hoping that your home team will score.

But I want to point out to you that there are also times, at least for many people where they simply watch the game and become fully absorbed in the game, so that they are flowing with the game itself. And they have now forgotten their expectations of what should or should not happen. They have even forgotten to think about the ultimate goal of who wins, for they are enjoying the process of the game itself.

Well, it is in fact so that every Saturday many of the people, who otherwise cannot in any way tune in to the Holy Spirit, get at least some glimpse of it, when they get absorbed in a sporting game. This is, of course, not the highest way to be tuned in to the Holy Spirit. But being absorbed in an activity, rather than being detached from it and thinking about it – experiencing it through the mind and the filter of the mind and the activities and expectations and mental images of the mind – this is still being somewhat attuned to the Holy Spirit.

Because when you are flowing with the River of Life where is the space in your experience of life, the space where you can insert these expectations and fears and worries and concerns and judgments about what should and should not happen? There is no space, my beloved, for you are flowing with the River of Life.

Beyond the need to judge

Yes, I understand: sometimes you need to plan and think ahead. But that is not quite the same. There is a subtle difference between thinking ahead, making cool-headed, common-sense decisions, and then sitting there and evaluating everything based on a value-laden judgment of what should or should not happen, what is right or what is not right, what is good and what is bad—and all of these concerns that people have in their minds.

My beloved, one of the aspects of the death consciousness that I wish to bring to your attention at this point, is precisely this tendency to think that you have to judge, analyze and evaluate everything that is going on around you—what other people are doing, what other people are saying, what is happening in the world, what this or that person is doing, what the celebrities in the world are doing or not doing, who they marry or who they don't marry, and all of these things.

I am not saying you should not follow what is going on around you. But again, there is a subtle difference between being aware without judging, and constantly being in this state of judging, criticizing, evaluating whether this is good or bad. And then putting down that which is bad because the ego, after all, loves to feel that if it is not doing what the bad people are doing, it cannot be as bad as the bad people.

But you see, this is not the River of Life. For you are now in a space, and in that space there is room for all kinds of considerations, judgments, value judgments, expectations. This sets you apart from life. You are not fully engaged in the process of life. You are not truly enjoying life, enjoying watching it unfold. And this is not your highest potential.

For how can you be fully creative, unless you follow Jesus' call to become as little children, who can enter the kingdom of God because you enter the state of consciousness that is the kingdom of God where you are flowing with life? Do you see that what the death consciousness wants you to do, is to be constantly evaluating yourself and your own behavior, and the way you look or don't look, and the way you dress or don't dress, and all of these things?

The standard of death

What the death consciousness has done is that it has set up this earthly, worldly standard, about how you should be as a human being. From the moment you were even in your mother's womb, you have been subconsciously (and later consciously) programmed to follow whatever standard is defined in your culture. And you have come to think that in order to be a good human being, you have to live up to this standard.

Thus, when you find the spiritual path and the teachings of the ascended masters, you will – without even knowing it – transfer this to the teachings of the masters. You will think that the way to follow the teachings of the ascended masters, the way to come closer to your ascension, is to be a good spiritual person who lives up to some kind of standard. It may no longer be the standard, the exact standard, of your society or family, but yet it is still an outer standard that you have taken into your outer mind. And you are then using the outer mind to constantly evaluate everything you do: "Is this correct? Am I OK? Am I really spiritual if I do this? What if I say this; are people going to judge me as not being spiritual?"

Do you see that in your mind there is a space where there is supposedly always this judge, sitting there and judging your every action, your every word, or even your thoughts and feelings? My beloved, who is this judge that is sitting there, judging your innermost thoughts and feelings?

Ah, many religious people project that it is either the devil or it is God. And many ascended master students project that it is the ascended masters. But you see, the only being who knows your innermost thoughts and feelings is you.

I am the Maha Chohan. I am a God-free, ascended being. I am not sitting up here, looking at the innermost thoughts and feelings of each of the 7 billion people on planet earth. Neither is Master MORE or Saint Germain. They are focused on being who they are, unfolding their lifestreams as they flow with the River of Life. They are focused on goals for the golden age. But they are not goals that they have in the outer, critical mind that evaluates everything. They are not sitting up here, the Chohans, looking down on you, judging you according to some standard and criticizing you when you are wrong. This is not the way we work. This is not the way we think.

Can you not begin to see that this is an entirely human construct, and we have ascended because we have accelerated ourselves beyond that state of consciousness? And our only desire for you, is that you would see this state of consciousness for what it is, the death consciousness because it is separated from the River of Life. It exists in the space between the Consciousness You and the River of Life.

Beyond the death consciousness

When you see this, you can do what we have done: accelerate yourself beyond it. This is our joy, our desire, to have you come to that point where you see the need to accelerate yourself beyond the death consciousness, and therefore you say to us, the Chohans:

"Show me the way! I am willing to follow the path that you have followed and that you have proven. I am willing to follow the Path of the Seven Veils, the Path of the Seven Rays. Show me the way, and I will put one foot in front of the other and follow each direction I get, even if I do not see where it leads, even if it does not exactly correspond to my expectations. For I am beginning to realize that my expectations are indeed very limited."

"My culture, my view of life, is limited and truly influenced by the death consciousness in subtle ways. I do not see all of the ways in which my consciousness is influenced by the death consciousness, but I am beginning to see that it is influenced by the death consciousness—and that I want to be free of this influence. And I know that I am only able to be free by having a frame of reference from beings that have already accelerated themselves beyond it. That is why I am willing to follow you, the Chohans. So show me the next step, and I will take that next step."

This is when you are ready for the Chohans, for the ascended masters, and not some pretend-to-be master, not some pretend-to-be spiritual teacher or some angelic being from some star system or other galaxy or some spaceship that has come to earth to guide human beings.

Death consciousness and control

Do you not understand that there are beings in this universe who have embodied the death consciousness to the point where they in a sense realize at least some of the limitations of the death consciousness? And therefore, they have determined to use those limitations to enslave and control all other self-aware beings. Do you really not begin to see that these false hierarchy impostors, as we may call them, will use the death consciousness in all of its subtlety to keep you trapped?

When you are a spiritual person and begin to long for something beyond what the material world has to offer, they will come in and offer you a false path that gives you the expectation, the simple expectation that if you follow that path, then one day you will magically be transformed into a perfect being. You will reach enlightenment, cosmic consciousness, or you will ascend. Or you will shift into the 5th or 27th dimension.

You see, again, in the gap, the false teachers can build all kinds of false religions and false spiritual teachings. They are good at giving you the expectation that they will get you to the goal. But do you know why they can never get you to the goal? Do you begin to see why they can never get you to the goal? Because that which is created in the gap between you and the River of Life, cannot help you transcend the gap and come back into the River of Life.

What the false teachers have done is to create the impression that there is something wrong with the universe, and that is why you are separated from the River of Life. You see, they are creating the impression that something outside of you went wrong, and that is why you are separated from the River of Life.

Why do you fall for this trick? You have started to awaken and become more aware of your longing to come back into the

River of Life. You may not understand that it is the River of Life you want to come back to, but you are longing for something beyond your outer self. You know there must be something, and you are longing for it. And the false teachers can no longer keep you focused on the earth and this world, so they must misdirect your longing. But you are not yet at the point where you see exactly what it is you want to find. You do not understand or see that it is actually the feeling of flowing with the River of Life that you are longing for. For this is paradise, the lost paradise.

The false outer path

Because you do not see this, they make you believe that something went wrong outside of you. There is some problem in this world, in this universe, whether it be by God's design – who caused the vessels to be shattered or the angels to fall, or whatever it may have been, original sin or some of the many theories out there – there is some kind of problem that must be solved. And so, they either engage you in trying to solve this problem by changing other people, or they engage you in thinking that if you just follow a certain path and keep doing this exercise or keep following this outer guru, you will one day automatically arrive at the goal.

But do you see that what they are promising you is that one day you will close the gap by some kind of magic that happens outside of you? Look at the entire craze that has been going on up to this point in time with the year 2012. Oh, the earth is going to shift into the 5th dimension, and all people are going to be raised in consciousness and all problems are going to be solved. Yes, the earth might indeed shift into some other dimension at some point, but how is this shift going to happen? By some aliens in a spaceship coming in here and accelerating the planet?

Nay, it can happen only when the people on this planet accelerate their consciousness, and this has to be done individually. And it has to be done, not "out there" but "in here." The problem in the universe is that *you* have created a gap between where you are in consciousness and where you would be, if you were flowing with the River of Life.

The problem for you, individually, is to close that gap, and the gap exists in only one place: in your mind. For you are not separated from the River of Life, you only think you are. You have only separated yourself in your mind. And thus, the only place the gap can be closed is where the gap was created: in your mind.

There is no problem to solve here in this universe that you need to solve and all problems will disappear. The only problem, so to speak, to be solved is for you, individually, to close the gap, so that you are flowing with the River of Life. And that means that you must first of all see that this is your true goal. This is what your longing is all about. You are simply longing to flow with the River of Life, instead of standing apart from it and watching it flow by you. And then, you must begin the process of dismantling the mental images and expectations that are actually making up the gap and giving you the perception that you are separated from the River of Life.

Look inside your Self

And what is the very first step that you must take, in order to engage in that process of closing the gap and dismantling the veil that keeps you apart from the River? Well, the very first step you must take is: you must get your attention off seeking to change what is taking place outside yourself, and instead put your attention on what is going on inside yourself. You must, as Jesus said 2,000 years ago: "Why are you looking at the splinter in the eyes of your brother and not looking at the beam in your own eye?"

It may be that your brother has a gap between his consciousness and the River of Life. It may well be that he has all kinds of things that keep him apart from the River of Life. But you see, the vast majority of people on planet earth are not looking at their brothers that way. They are looking at them saying what is wrong with them according to an earthly standard.

And you see, even if you live up to your own earthly standard to absolute perfection, you would not be in the River of Life. You would still be apart from the River of Life because it is the standard that keeps you apart from the River of Life. So how can you help your brother by seeking to force him to live up to your standard, which is not his standard and does not have to be his standard?

For you all have free will. And as a result of free will, each of you, all 7 billion of you, have created your own individual standards. There are, of course, many common traits in the standards people have in a certain society or culture. Nevertheless, each of you have his or her own individual perception filter, through which you are looking at life and through which you are evaluating and judging everything including yourself. You have a right to create this because this is what gives you your unique Life experience.

Right now, you have created such a perception filter that it sets you apart from the River of Life. This is perfectly within the Law of Free Will. I have no objection. I am not here threatening you with hellfire and brimstone that if you do not follow my words, you will go to some fiery hell. All that will happen if you do not follow my words is that you stay in your current perception filter and stay separate from the River of Life. If this is what you desire to experience for another lifetime or another 10,000 lifetimes or another 2 million years, then I will still be here when you are ready to come back to the Path of Oneness.

Imposing a standard on the teacher

But if you are ready for that path right now, then *listen to what I am saying and stop judging what I am saying* based on the standard that is preventing you from following what I am saying. There is absolutely no point in you coming to a spiritual teacher, and then wanting to impose upon the teacher and the teaching your standard.

Because the entire purpose for a spiritual teacher, at least a true spiritual teacher, is to help you transcend your standard. How can a teacher do this, if you are imposing your standard upon the teacher or the teaching, so that you do not hear the teachings, but only hear a filtered version of it adapted to your standard? This makes no sense whatsoever, if you claim to be a true spiritual student who wants to get somewhere on the path.

If you want entertainment spirituality, then there is a myriad of false gurus who will give it to you, day and night, for as long as you want it. Again, I have no objections to this. But I am here to state clearly that we of the eight Chohans are not entertainment gurus. If you want feel-good spirituality, go somewhere else. We are not here to help you, until you are ready to transcend your consciousness, to transcend yourself, to close the gap and come back into the River of Life.

If this is what you want, I welcome you with open arms. If it is not, then I have no standard by which I judge you. I simply accept the fact that you desire another experience for a time, and I hold in my heart the readiness to welcome you back, whenever you decide you are ready and you want MORE and a deeper and richer life experience than what you can have through your current standard.

And thus, I shall assume that those who will move on from this point, and study the following discourses, will have made the decision that they want more than their standard that they want a guru, a teacher, who can take them beyond their standard. And who can help them close the gap and come closer and closer to the goal that they now see, which is to flow with the River of Life.

12 | INVOKING FREEDOM FROM THE DEATH CONSCIOUSNESS

In the name I AM THAT I AM, Jesus Christ, I call to my I AM Presence to flow through the I Will Be Presence that I AM and give this invocation with full power. I call to beloved Elohim Cyclopea and Virginia, Archangel Raphael and Mother Mary, Hilarion and the Maha Chohan to help me become aware of how I have been influenced by the death consciousness. Help me see and surrender all patterns that block my oneness with the Maha Chohan and my oneness with my I AM Presence, including …

[Make personal calls]

Part 1

1. Maha Chohan, help me see that the death consciousness
wants me to react to it, engage with it or even fight it.

> Cyclopea so dear, the truth you reveal,
> the truth that duality's ailments will heal,
> your Emerald Light is like a great balm,
> our emotional bodies are perfectly calm.
>
> **Cyclopea so dear, in Emerald Sphere,**
> **in raising perception we shall persevere,**
> **as deep in our hearts your truth we revere,**
> **to immaculate vision the earth does adhere.**

2. Maha Chohan, help me see that the Holy Spirit, the Spirit of
Life, does not want me to fight it, does not want me to oppose
it, does not want me to destroy anyone or anything or to put
down any part of life. It wants me to flow with the Spirit that
is life.

> Cyclopea so dear, with you we unwind,
> all negative spirals clouding the mind,
> we know pure awareness is truly our core,
> the key to becoming the wide-open door.
>
> **Cyclopea so dear, in Emerald Sphere,**
> **in raising perception we shall persevere,**
> **as deep in our hearts your truth we revere,**
> **to immaculate vision the earth does adhere.**

3. Maha Chohan, help me see that the combined effort of all self-aware beings, who have transcended themselves and become more, has formed the upward flow of the Holy Spirit. It is the River of Life that carries everything with it.

> Cyclopea so dear, clear our inner sight,
> empowered, we pierce the soul's fearful night,
> we now see our life through your single eye,
> beyond all disease we're ready to fly.

> **Cyclopea so dear, in Emerald Sphere,**
> **in raising perception we shall persevere,**
> **as deep in our hearts your truth we revere,**
> **to immaculate vision the earth does adhere.**

4. Maha Chohan, help me see that the River of Life is an ongoing, moving stream. There is nothing in the River of Life that stands still. For in the River of Life, movement is always transcending itself.

> Cyclopea so dear, life can only reflect,
> the images that the mind does project,
> the key to our healing is clearing the mind,
> from the images the ego is hiding behind.

> **Cyclopea so dear, in Emerald Sphere,**
> **in raising perception we shall persevere,**
> **as deep in our hearts your truth we revere,**
> **to immaculate vision the earth does adhere.**

5. Maha Chohan, help me see that in the River of Life I am transcending, I am growing, I am accelerating and I am multiplying the talents and becoming more. And this is the essence

of the life consciousness, the consciousness of life, the River of Life.

> Cyclopea so dear, we want to aim high,
> to your healing flame we ever draw nigh,
> through veils of duality we now take flight,
> bathed in your penetrating Emerald Light.

> **Cyclopea so dear, in Emerald Sphere,**
> **in raising perception we shall persevere,**
> **as deep in our hearts your truth we revere,**
> **to immaculate vision the earth does adhere.**

6. Maha Chohan, help me see that there is a knowing behind the death consciousness that life is an ongoing process. I know deep within my being, that life is meant to be the River of Life that is constantly transcending itself.

> Cyclopea so dear, your Emerald Flame,
> exposes every subtle, dualistic power game,
> including the game of wanting to say,
> that truth is defined in only one way.

> **Cyclopea so dear, in Emerald Sphere,**
> **in raising perception we shall persevere,**
> **as deep in our hearts your truth we revere,**
> **to immaculate vision the earth does adhere.**

7. Maha Chohan, help me see that this is an inner knowing that comes from the fact that the Conscious You is an extension of my I AM Presence, and then an extension of ascended masters, reaching all the way to the Creator.

Cyclopea so dear, we're feeling the flow,
as your Living Truth upon us you bestow,
from all dual vision we are now set free,
planet earth in immaculate matrix will be.

**Cyclopea so dear, in Emerald Sphere,
in raising perception we shall persevere,
as deep in our hearts your truth we revere,
to immaculate vision the earth does adhere.**

8. Maha Chohan, help me see that my entire purpose for being is to accelerate my self-awareness and flow with the River of Life. I cannot escape this inner knowing that life is meant to be an ongoing process.

Cyclopea so dear, the truth is now clear,
we see higher purpose for which we are here
we know truth transcends all systems below,
immersed in your light, we continue to grow.

**Cyclopea so dear, in Emerald Sphere,
in raising perception we shall persevere,
as deep in our hearts your truth we revere,
to immaculate vision the earth does adhere.**

9. Maha Chohan, help me see that the death consciousness cannot completely remove this inner knowing. It can cover it over, it can camouflage it, it can misdirect it. But it cannot completely silence my inner knowing that life is meant to be an ongoing process.

Cyclopea so dear, we're feeling your joy,
as creative vision we now do employ,

in lifting earth out of serpentine cage,
to manifest Saint Germain's Golden Age.

**Cyclopea so dear, in Emerald Sphere,
in raising perception we shall persevere,
as deep in our hearts your truth we revere,
to immaculate vision the earth does adhere.**

Part 2

1. Maha Chohan, help me see that the death consciousness *can* cause me to build an expectation of what that process should be like, where it should be going as the next step and as the ultimate goal.

Raphael Archangel, your light so intense,
raise us beyond all human pretense.
Mother Mary and you have a vision so bold,
to see that our highest potential unfold.

**Raphael Archangel, for vision we pray,
Raphael Archangel, show us the way,
Raphael Archangel, your emerald ray,
Raphael Archangel, our lives a new day.**

2. Maha Chohan, help me see that it can do so only because the death consciousness itself is a resistance to the ongoingness of the River of Life. When I resist the ongoingness, I create a space between where I am now and where I would have been if I had followed the River of Life.

Raphael Archangel, in emerald sphere,
to immaculate vision we always adhere.
Mother Mary enfolds us in her Sacred Heart,
from Mother's true love, we're never apart.

Raphael Archangel, for vision we pray,
Raphael Archangel, show us the way,
Raphael Archangel, your emerald ray,
Raphael Archangel, our lives a new day.

3. Maha Chohan, help me see that in this space, there is room to build the expectation of what life *should* be like and where it should be going.

Raphael Archangel, all ailments you heal,
each cell in our bodies in light now you seal.
Mother Mary's immaculate concept we see,
perfection of health our new reality.

Raphael Archangel, for vision we pray,
Raphael Archangel, show us the way,
Raphael Archangel, your emerald ray,
Raphael Archangel, our lives a new day.

4. Maha Chohan, help me see that the expectation causes me to be detached from life. I am thinking about it, experiencing it through the filter of the mind and the activities, expectations and mental images of the mind.

Raphael Archangel, your light is so real,
the vision of Christ in us you reveal.
Mother Mary now helps us to truly transcend,
in emerald light with you we ascend.

Raphael Archangel, for vision we pray,
Raphael Archangel, show us the way,
Raphael Archangel, your emerald ray,
Raphael Archangel, our lives a new day.

5. Maha Chohan, help me see that when I am flowing with the River of Life, there is no space in my experience where I can insert these expectations, fears, worries and judgments about what *should* and *should not* happen.

Raphael Archangel, diseases are done,
as you help us see that all life is One,
we no longer do your true love reject,
immaculate vision on all we project.

Raphael Archangel, for vision we pray,
Raphael Archangel, show us the way,
Raphael Archangel, your emerald ray,
Raphael Archangel, our lives a new day.

6. Maha Chohan, help me see that there is a subtle difference between thinking ahead, and then evaluating everything based on a value-laden judgment of what should or should not happen, what is right or what is not right, what is good and what is bad.

Raphael Archangel, we're healing the earth,
in immaculate vision we give her rebirth,
a new era has on this day begun,
your emerald light now shines like a sun.

Raphael Archangel, for vision we pray,
Raphael Archangel, show us the way,

Raphael Archangel, your emerald ray,
Raphael Archangel, our lives a new day.

7. Maha Chohan, help me see that one aspect of the death consciousness is the tendency to think that I have to judge, analyze and evaluate everything that is going on around me—what other people are doing or saying and what is happening in the world.

Raphael Archangel, the fall is behind,
as all of earth's people the Christ path do find,
we call now to you all people to heal,
as four lower bodies in love you do seal.

Raphael Archangel, for vision we pray,
Raphael Archangel, show us the way,
Raphael Archangel, your emerald ray,
Raphael Archangel, our lives a new day.

8. Maha Chohan, help me see that there is a subtle difference between being aware without judging, and constantly being in this state of judging, criticizing, evaluating whether this is good or bad.

Raphael Archangel, as you bring the light,
the forces of darkness swiftly take flight,
their day is now done as we claim the earth,
spreading to all an innocent mirth.

Raphael Archangel, for vision we pray,
Raphael Archangel, show us the way,
Raphael Archangel, your emerald ray,
Raphael Archangel, our lives a new day.

9. Maha Chohan, help me see that the ego loves to feel that if it is not doing what the bad people are doing, it cannot be as bad as the bad people. But this is not the River of Life, for I am now trapped in value judgments and expectations.

> Raphael Archangel, our vision set free,
> as we can now see God's reality,
> as Saint Germain's vision is manifest here,
> the earth is now sealed in immaculate sphere.
>
> **Raphael Archangel, for vision we pray,**
> **Raphael Archangel, show us the way,**
> **Raphael Archangel, your emerald ray,**
> **Raphael Archangel, our lives a new day.**

Part 3

1. Maha Chohan, help me see that the death consciousness wants me to be constantly evaluating myself and my own behavior, and the way I look or don't look, and the way I dress or don't dress.

> Hilarion, on emerald shore,
> we're free from all that's gone before.
> Hilarion, we let all go,
> that keeps us out of sacred flow.
>
> **Hilarion, with light so green,**
> **we see behind the matter screen,**
> **immaculate our inner sight,**
> **we see the earth is taking flight.**

2. Maha Chohan, help me see that the death consciousness has set up this worldly standard, about how I should be as a human being. I have been programmed to follow whatever standard is defined in my culture.

> Hilarion, the secret key,
> is wisdom's own reality.
> Hilarion, all life is healed,
> the ego's face no more concealed.

> **Hilarion, with light so green,**
> **we see behind the matter screen,**
> **immaculate our inner sight,**
> **we see the earth is taking flight.**

3. Maha Chohan, help me see that I have come to think that in order to be a good human being, I have to live up to this standard.

> Hilarion, your love for life,
> helps us surrender inner strife.
> Hilarion, your loving words,
> thrill our hearts like song of birds.

> **Hilarion, with light so green,**
> **we see behind the matter screen,**
> **immaculate our inner sight,**
> **we see the earth is taking flight.**

4. Maha Chohan, help me see that when I find the spiritual path, I will transfer this to the teachings of the masters. I will think that the way to follow the teachings is to be a good spiritual person who lives up to some kind of standard.

> Hilarion, invoke the light,
> your sacred formulas recite.
> Hilarion, your secret tone,
> philosopher's most sacred stone.
>
> **Hilarion, with light so green,**
> **we see behind the matter screen,**
> **immaculate our inner sight,**
> **we see the earth is taking flight.**

5. Maha Chohan, help me see that I have a standard that I have taken into my mind, and I am using the outer mind to constantly evaluate everything I do: "Is this correct? Am I OK? Am I really spiritual if I do this? What if I say this; are people going to judge me as not being spiritual?"

> Hilarion, with love you greet,
> us in your temple over Crete.
> Hilarion, your emerald light,
> the third eye sees with Christic sight.
>
> **Hilarion, with light so green,**
> **we see behind the matter screen,**
> **immaculate our inner sight,**
> **we see the earth is taking flight.**

6. Maha Chohan, help me see that in my mind there is a space where there is this judge who is judging my actions, words or even my thoughts and feelings.

> Hilarion, you give us fruit,
> of truth that is so absolute.

Hilarion, all stress decrease,
as our ambitions we release.

**Hilarion, with light so green,
we see behind the matter screen,
immaculate our inner sight,
we see the earth is taking flight.**

7. Maha Chohan, help me see that the judge that is judging my innermost thoughts and feelings is neither the devil, God or the ascended masters. It is something in my own psyche.

Hilarion, our chakras clear,
as we let go of subtlest fear.
Hilarion, we are sincere,
as freedom's truth we do revere.

**Hilarion, with light so green,
we see behind the matter screen,
immaculate our inner sight,
we see the earth is taking flight.**

8. Maha Chohan, help me see the need to accelerate myself beyond the death consciousness. I say to you, the Chohans: "Show me the way! I am willing to follow the path that you have followed and that you have proven. I am willing to follow the Path of the Seven Veils, the Path of the Seven Rays."

Hilarion, you balance all,
the seven rays upon our call.
Hilarion, you keep us true,
as we remain all one with you.

**Hilarion, with light so green,
we see behind the matter screen,
immaculate our inner sight,
we see the earth is taking flight.**

9. Maha Chohan, I say: "Show me the way, and I will put one foot in front of the other and follow each direction I get, even if I do not see where it leads, even if it does not exactly correspond to my expectations. For I am beginning to realize that my expectations are very limited."

Hilarion, your Presence here,
filling up the inner sphere.
Life is now a sacred flow,
God Vision we on all bestow.

**Hilarion, with light so green,
we see behind the matter screen,
immaculate our inner sight,
we see the earth is taking flight.**

Part 4

1. Maha Chohan, help me see that my culture, my view of life, is limited and influenced by the death consciousness in subtle ways. I am beginning to see that my consciousness is influenced by the death consciousness—and I want to be free of this influence.

Maha Chohan, I will to grow,
I feel the power of your flow.

Maha Chohan, the veil is rent,
creative will from heaven sent.

**O Holy Spirit, flow through me,
I am the open door for thee.
O mighty rushing stream of Light,
transcendence is my sacred right.**

2. Maha Chohan, help me see that I am only able to be free by having a frame of reference from beings that have already accelerated themselves beyond it. That is why I am willing to follow you, the Chohans. So show me the next step, and I will take that next step.

Maha Chohan, your wisdom streams,
awaken all from matter's dreams.
Maha Chohan, your balance bring,
let bells of integration ring.

**O Holy Spirit, flow through me,
I am the open door for thee.
O mighty rushing stream of Light,
transcendence is my sacred right.**

3. Maha Chohan, help me see that there are beings in this universe who have decided to use the limitations of the death consciousness to enslave and control all other self-aware beings. These false hierarchy impostors will use the death consciousness in all of its subtlety to keep me trapped.

Maha Chohan, love's mighty call,
the prison walls are shattered all.

Maha Chohan, set all life free
through unconditionality.

O Holy Spirit, flow through me,
I am the open door for thee.
O mighty rushing stream of Light,
transcendence is my sacred right.

4. Maha Chohan, help me see that the false teachers will offer
me a false path that gives me the expectation that if I follow
that path, then one day I will magically be transformed into a
perfect being.

Maha Chohan, intentions pure,
all life is one, I know for sure.
Maha Chohan, I am awake,
surrender all for oneness' sake.

O Holy Spirit, flow through me,
I am the open door for thee.
O mighty rushing stream of Light,
transcendence is my sacred right.

5. Maha Chohan, help me see that in this gap, the false teachers
can build all kinds of false religions and false spiritual teachings. They are good at producing the expectation that they will
get me to the goal.

Maha Chohan, help all men see,
through veils of unreality.
Maha Chohan, with single eye,
I know I am the greater "I."

**O Holy Spirit, flow through me,
I am the open door for thee.
O mighty rushing stream of Light,
transcendence is my sacred right.**

6. Maha Chohan, help me see that the false teachers can never get me to the goal. Because that which is created in the gap between me and the River of Life, cannot help me transcend the gap and come back to the River of Life.

Maha Chohan, your peace I find,
Maitreya shows me to be kind.
Maha Chohan, all war will cease,
now flooding all with sacred peace.

**O Holy Spirit, flow through me,
I am the open door for thee.
O mighty rushing stream of Light,
transcendence is my sacred right.**

7. Maha Chohan, help me see that the false teachers have created the impression that there is something wrong with the universe, and that is why I am separated from the River of Life. They are creating the impression that something outside of me went wrong, and that is why I am separated from the River of Life.

Maha Chohan, you balance all,
the seven rays upon my call.
Maha Chohan, all life is free,
transcending for eternity.

**O Holy Spirit, flow through me,
I am the open door for thee.
O mighty rushing stream of Light,
transcendence is my sacred right.**

8. Maha Chohan, help me see that the false teachers seek to misdirect my longing. They make me believe that something went wrong outside of me. There is some problem in this world that must be solved.

Maha Chohan, your sacred Flame,
what beauty in your blessed name.
Maha Chohan, what rushing flow,
the Spirit one with life below.

**O Holy Spirit, flow through me,
I am the open door for thee.
O mighty rushing stream of Light,
transcendence is my sacred right.**

9. Maha Chohan, help me see that the false teachers seek to get me to engage in trying to solve this problem by changing other people, or they engage me in thinking that if I just follow a certain path and keep doing this exercise or keep following this outer guru, I will one day automatically arrive at the goal.

Maha Chohan, your Presence here,
filling up the inner sphere.
Life is now a sacred flow,
God Wisdom we on all bestow.

**O Holy Spirit, flow through me,
I am the open door for thee.**

**O mighty rushing stream of Light,
transcendence is my sacred right.**

Part 5

1. Maha Chohan, help me see that they are promising me that one day I will close the gap by some kind of magic that happens outside of me. The problem in the universe is that *I* have created a gap between where I am in consciousness and where I would be, if I were flowing with the River of Life.

> Hilarion, on emerald shore,
> we're free from all that's gone before.
> Hilarion, we let all go,
> that keeps us out of sacred flow.

> **Hilarion, with light so green,
> we see behind the matter screen,
> immaculate our inner sight,
> we see the earth is taking flight.**

2. Maha Chohan, help me see that the problem for me individually, is to close that gap, and the gap exists only in my mind. For I am not separated from the River of Life, I only think I am.

> Hilarion, the secret key,
> is wisdom's own reality.
> Hilarion, all life is healed,
> the ego's face no more concealed.

Hilarion, with light so green,
we see behind the matter screen,
immaculate our inner sight,
we see the earth is taking flight.

3. Maha Chohan, help me see that I have only separated myself in my mind. And thus, the only place the gap can be closed is where the gap was created: in my mind.

Hilarion, your love for life,
helps us surrender inner strife.
Hilarion, your loving words,
thrill our hearts like song of birds.

Hilarion, with light so green,
we see behind the matter screen,
immaculate our inner sight,
we see the earth is taking flight.

4. Maha Chohan, help me see that there is no riddle that I need to solve and then all problems will disappear. The only problem to be solved for me, individually, is to close the gap so that I am flowing with the River of Life.

Hilarion, invoke the light,
your sacred formulas recite.
Hilarion, your secret tone,
philosopher's most sacred stone.

Hilarion, with light so green,
we see behind the matter screen,
immaculate our inner sight,
we see the earth is taking flight.

5. Maha Chohan, help me see that this is my true goal, this is what my longing is all about. I am longing to flow with the River of Life, instead of standing apart from it and watching it flow by me.

Hilarion, with love you greet,
us in your temple over Crete.
Hilarion, your emerald light,
the third eye sees with Christic sight.

**Hilarion, with light so green,
we see behind the matter screen,
immaculate our inner sight,
we see the earth is taking flight.**

6. Maha Chohan, help me begin the process of dismantling the mental images and expectations that are making up the gap, and giving me the perception that I am separated from the River of Life.

Hilarion, you give us fruit,
of truth that is so absolute.
Hilarion, all stress decrease,
as our ambitions we release.

**Hilarion, with light so green,
we see behind the matter screen,
immaculate our inner sight,
we see the earth is taking flight.**

7. Maha Chohan, help me see that the first step I must take is to get my attention off seeking to change what is taking place

outside myself, and instead put my attention on what is going
on inside myself.

> Hilarion, our chakras clear,
> as we let go of subtlest fear.
> Hilarion, we are sincere,
> as freedom's truth we do revere.

> **Hilarion, with light so green,**
> **we see behind the matter screen,**
> **immaculate our inner sight,**
> **we see the earth is taking flight.**

8. Maha Chohan, help me see that even if I live up to my earthly
standard to absolute perfection, I would not be in the River of
Life. I would still be apart from the River of Life because it is
the standard that keeps me apart.

> Hilarion, you balance all,
> the seven rays upon our call.
> Hilarion, you keep us true,
> as we remain all one with you.

> **Hilarion, with light so green,**
> **we see behind the matter screen,**
> **immaculate our inner sight,**
> **we see the earth is taking flight.**

9. Maha Chohan, help me see that I have my individual perception filter, through which I am looking at life and through
which I am evaluating and judging everything, including myself.

Hilarion, your Presence here,
filling up the inner sphere.
Life is now a sacred flow,
God Vision we on all bestow.

Hilarion, with light so green,
we see behind the matter screen,
immaculate our inner sight,
we see the earth is taking flight.

Part 6

1. Maha Chohan, help me see that I have a right to create this filter, because this is what gives me a unique Life experience. Yet my perception filter sets me apart from the River of Life and I have had enough of this experience. I am willing to come back to the Path of Oneness.

Maha Chohan, I will to grow,
I feel the power of your flow.
Maha Chohan, the veil is rent,
creative will from heaven sent.

O Holy Spirit, flow through me,
I am the open door for thee.
O mighty rushing stream of Light,
transcendence is my sacred right.

2. Maha Chohan, help me listen to what you are saying and stop judging what you are saying based on the standard that is preventing me from following what you are saying.

> Maha Chohan, your wisdom streams,
> awaken all from matter's dreams.
> Maha Chohan, your balance bring,
> let bells of integration ring.

> **O Holy Spirit, flow through me,**
> **I am the open door for thee.**
> **O mighty rushing stream of Light,**
> **transcendence is my sacred right.**

3. Maha Chohan, help me see that there is no point in me coming to a spiritual teacher, and then wanting to impose my standard upon the teacher and the teaching.

> Maha Chohan, love's mighty call,
> the prison walls are shattered all.
> Maha Chohan, set all life free
> through unconditionality.

> **O Holy Spirit, flow through me,**
> **I am the open door for thee.**
> **O mighty rushing stream of Light,**
> **transcendence is my sacred right.**

4. Maha Chohan, help me see that the purpose for a true spiritual teacher is to help me transcend my standard. How can a teacher do this, if I am imposing my standard upon the teacher, so that I do not hear the teachings, but only hear a filtered version adapted to my standard?

> Maha Chohan, intentions pure,
> all life is one, I know for sure.

Maha Chohan, I am awake,
surrender all for oneness' sake.

**O Holy Spirit, flow through me,
I am the open door for thee.
O mighty rushing stream of Light,
transcendence is my sacred right.**

5. Maha Chohan, I see that this·makes no sense whatsoever, since I am a true spiritual student who wants to get somewhere on the path.

Maha Chohan, help all men see,
through veils of unreality.
Maha Chohan, with single eye,
I know I am the greater "I."

**O Holy Spirit, flow through me,
I am the open door for thee.
O mighty rushing stream of Light,
transcendence is my sacred right.**

6. Maha Chohan, I do not want entertainment spirituality, I do not want feel-good spirituality.

Maha Chohan, your peace I find,
Maitreya shows me to be kind.
Maha Chohan, all war will cease,
now flooding all with sacred peace.

**O Holy Spirit, flow through me,
I am the open door for thee.**

**O mighty rushing stream of Light,
transcendence is my sacred right.**

7. Maha Chohan, I am ready to transcend my consciousness, to transcend myself, to close the gap and come back into the River of Life.

Maha Chohan, you balance all,
the seven rays upon my call.
Maha Chohan, all life is free,
transcending for eternity.

**O Holy Spirit, flow through me,
I am the open door for thee.
O mighty rushing stream of Light,
transcendence is my sacred right.**

8. Maha Chohan, help me see that you do not have a standard by which you judge me, for you allow me to have the experience I want.

Maha Chohan, your sacred Flame,
what beauty in your blessed name.
Maha Chohan, what rushing flow,
the Spirit one with life below.

**O Holy Spirit, flow through me,
I am the open door for thee.
O mighty rushing stream of Light,
transcendence is my sacred right.**

9. Maha Chohan, I desire you to welcome me back, for I decide that I am ready and I want MORE, I want a deeper and

richer life experience than what I can have through my current standard.

Maha Chohan, your Presence here,
filling up the inner sphere.
Life is now a sacred flow,
God Wisdom we on all bestow.

**O Holy Spirit, flow through me,
I am the open door for thee.
O mighty rushing stream of Light,
transcendence is my sacred right.**

Sealing:

In the name of the Divine Mother, I fully accept that the power of these calls is used to set free the Ma-ter light, so it can outpicture the perfect vision of Christ for my own life, for all people and for the planet. In the name I AM THAT I AM, it is done! Amen.

13 | AFFECTED BY DEATH

I am the Maha Chohan. Let us now take another look at the death consciousness. I need you to start looking back at your life. I need you to start recognizing, how you have been affected by the death consciousness in many ways, some obvious, some not so obvious. You may think – and this is in fact a common occurrence among people on earth, even the spiritual people – that death is a passive thing. You may have come to believe that after death there is nothing. It is just like an eternal sleep, as indeed some scientific materialists say.

Yet I can assure you that the death consciousness is not a passive force. It is an extremely aggressive force, although it is in fact capable of camouflaging itself, so that most people do not even see the attacks to which they are being exposed 24 hours a day, 7 days a week, 365 days a year for an entire lifetime. And even throughout all of their embodiments on this planet where everything is so influenced by the death con-sciousness that it can be extremely difficult for people to see something that is not influenced by the death consciousness.

And thus, of course, the most profound and subtle effect of the death consciousness is that when people have been enveloped in it for so long, they have no longer any frame of reference that there is something outside of the death consciousness. And they hardly ever see it, they hardly ever experience it in their daily lives.

Inner experience of the Holy Spirit

This, of course, is one of the primary functions of religion, or rather, spirituality. It is indeed to take people to the point where they have a direct inner experience of the Holy Spirit, the consciousness of life, the River of Life. So that they not only know intellectually that there is something outside the death consciousness, but they have experienced it. Until you have experienced that there is something outside the death consciousness, you do not actually have a frame of reference. Intellectual knowledge will not shift your consciousness; only that direct inner experience of something beyond the death consciousness.

And thus, what is truly meant to happen is that all true religions are meant to take people on a path where they raise their consciousness gradually through many levels. Where they shed certain illusions of the death consciousness, until they finally come to that point where they can go through some kind of ritual or ceremony, and then they have that experience of snapping out of their normal state of consciousness, so influenced by the death consciousness, and experiencing something more.

Even that something more that you can hear in my voice that you can "hear" between the lines in the words, if you are reading them. And you can know, from what I am saying that there is more that I AM MORE. That I am more than the death consciousness, and that because I am not in the death consciousness, I feel no obligation to conform to it. I have no intention whatsoever of conforming to it, and I will not conform to it.

So if you have projections that you project upon me as a spiritual teacher, or that you project upon the seven Chohans, then we cannot help you—unless you are willing to reconsider those expectations. And unless you are willing to, as our first order of business, allow us to shatter your expectations, by not living up to them, by challenging them, by deliberately going beyond them. Do you see that this is an essential, an absolutely essential, point on the spiritual path?

You cannot escape the death consciousness on your own, once you are enveloped in it. Your mind has become a closed system. For the overall effect of the death consciousness is that it is a closed system that is shut off from the life-giving power of the River of Life, from the Holy Spirit.

From separateness to oneness

The death consciousness is made up of innumerable false spirits, innumerable separate spirits, and they cannot see the Holy Spirit. If they were to see and acknowledge the Holy Spirit, they would instantly cease to exist as separate spirits. Do you see this, my beloved? Do you begin to at least glimpse this? You cannot be separate and in oneness at the same time. You cannot have your cake and eat it too.

This is one of the essential turning points on the spiritual path where you realize that if you want something more than what you have right now, you cannot stay in the state of consciousness you are in right now. You cannot remain comfortable, if you want spiritual growth. For the death consciousness can indeed make people so comfortable that they are absolutely convinced that if they keep doing that which they are doing right now – and keep believing what they are believing right now, and keep going to church every Sunday – then God simply has to save them and take them into heaven.

Yet the death consciousness can, of course, also make people extremely uncomfortable. And this will happen because of the second law of thermodynamics, which is actually the reinforcing spiral where everything is reinforced, whether it is separate or out of Oneness. And thus, the death consciousness must become more and more extreme, until it makes you more and more uncomfortable.

But nevertheless, they are the two aspects of it, the Alpha and Omega where some people become extremely comfortable and other people become extremely uncomfortable. And of course, those who are comfortable are not likely to change, are they? For why should they, when they are comfortable thinking that one day Jesus will arrive in the sky and save them? Or some other external savior will come and do the work for them.

The alternative to the struggle

Therefore, after people have been comfortable for a while, it is inevitable that they will start going into a downward spiral, which will intensify until you come to that breaking point where you realize, "I cannot do this anymore, something must change!" And then you start looking at it realistically, and you say, "Well, I can either try to control the world around me, but isn't that what I have been doing, and isn't that what hasn't worked for me and that has brought me into my current bind where I feel like I have nowhere to go and my life is a continuous struggle because I am always struggling against something inside myself?"

And then there comes that point of clarity where you say, "Is there an alternative to this struggle? Is there an alternative to trying to change someone or something outside of myself? Ah, indeed there is. What if I decided to look in the mirror and decided to pull the beam in my own eye and change my own consciousness?"

When you come to that point, you can then realize that you cannot change your own consciousness by remaining comfortable and believing what you are believing right now. Whatever beliefs and expectations you have about life, about spirituality, spiritual growth and ascended masters, you cannot maintain it and at the same time make progress on the path. Do you understand what I am saying?

There are many people who have known about the ascended masters for decades, who have been studying teachings and practicing rituals. But many of them have not moved any closer to stepping on to the real path because they still consider the path offered by the ascended masters an external path where they can do outer things and study outer teachings, but they do not have to look at themselves. They do not really have to change their own state of consciousness. And so, this is still the death consciousness. You may know about ascended masters, you may have studied our teachings and practiced our rituals, but you can still be in the death consciousness.

The Pearl of Great Price

After decades of thinking that you are on the path, you can *still* be in the death consciousness. And you will be in the death consciousness until you do what I have talked about in the previous discourses, and realize that you are looking at everything through a perception filter. And that perception filter is influenced by the death consciousness, and the only way to grow beyond your present level of consciousness is to be willing to have that perception filter challenged by a spiritual teacher, who is not inside your mental box or inside the death consciousness.

This is what we can offer you as the Chohans of the seven rays. We can offer you a frame of reference. We can offer you that we will systematically challenge your expectations. We will challenge your comfortability. We will challenge the death consciousness. And if you are willing to endure this, then we can help you. If you are not willing to endure it, then we cannot help you. And then you must go elsewhere. Or you must remain where you are, being absolutely convinced that you are on the right path and that one day – poof – you will make your ascension.

But I can tell you that there are people who for lifetimes have been waiting for the "poof," and they have not yet ascended. And so, those of us who have ascended, ascended because we stopped waiting for the "poof," we stopped looking for the magic, and instead we started looking at ourselves. And that is when you are ready, and that is when the true teachers of the ascended masters will appear in your life in one form or another – be it an outer book, an outer teaching to begin with – but then eventually also directly in your heart. Where you will begin to hear us, sense us, sense our presence, sense our vibration.

And when you sense the vibration of an ascended master that is when you attain a frame of reference that is beyond words and beyond anything that can be put into a book. It is truly the priceless opportunity, the Pearl of Great Price, to come up higher, to attune your consciousness to our vibration.

And therefore allow us to raise you up, so that you can rise beyond the death consciousness.

Death is an aggressive force

If you look back at your life, you will see that you have been exposed to the death consciousness in many ways. Consider the obvious outer, physical action. As a child were you not sometimes teased by other children? Where you not mobbed, as the saying goes these days, in some ways? Were you not exposed to children who tried to physically intimidate you or beat you up? This is an example of the aggressiveness of the death consciousness.

Of course, you can see this even more clearly on a greater scale. Crime, anybody who tries to steal your property or kill you, all of these things are expressions of the death consciousness. And then, on an even larger scale, governments that suppress their own people, governments that try to conquer other nations. Even the entire warring culture that has been around this planet for so long.

Why should you have to grow up being afraid that nuclear missiles could be sent at the push of a button and obliterate you and your entire country? This is an expression of the death consciousness. The fear of war, the fear of some calamity, is an expression of the death consciousness.

So you will, of course, know that you have been exposed to this in various forms throughout your life. And if you have grown up in the West, in a more modern, civilized, economically well-to-do part of the world, you may not have been exposed to some of the lower manifestations, but surely you are aware of them. And you know that this is the death consciousness because it is obvious that this is an aggressive force.

And what I am telling you, indeed, is that the death consciousness is an aggressive force.

Feeling superior to others

And so, what you will see here is something very simple. I have talked about the 144 levels of consciousness. I have said that between the 48th and the 96th level, you are walking the Path of the Seven Rays, the Path of the Seven Veils. I have said that you can go below it, to the 47th level and below, and that you do so by perverting the seven rays.

If you look at people who have gone into these perversions, you can see that at their highest level, on the 47th level and down, you have people who have perverted the First Ray. On the next level down, you have people who have perverted the First and the Second. And of course, at the very lowest level you have people who have perverted all seven rays. These are the ones who become more and more aggressive, more and more sure that they are right, more and more willing to try to suppress other people and control other people in various ways.

Common for all people who are below the 48th level of consciousness is that they tend to separate themselves from other people. They love setting themselves apart in a category where they are special and somehow superior. You will see this in many ways. You will see it in certain political movements where, for example, those in the Soviet Union were brought up to think they were superior to those who were not in a communist country. You see the same with Nazism. You also see it with many religions.

How many of you know people who think they are superior because they belong to this or that religion? Or even this or that spiritual movement, or even an ascended master teaching that nobody else has, and therefore they are more advanced than those who are not in that movement or teaching?

This, however, is the death consciousness. It is the lower levels of it. It is where you think that you are better than others because of some characteristic here on earth. In the River of Life you do not even have time to consider, whether some people are better than others because it is completely irrelevant. You are constantly focused on transcending yourself and helping all of life transcend itself.

You pay a price for superiority

What is the point in even comparing? There is no comparison. There is not even a thought of better or worse, or higher or lower. How can there be, when you know that everyone is one, and all are expressions of the One. And so you see, indeed, when you come into this consciousness of thinking that you are better than others, you will automatically pay a price, as you do in all elements of the death consciousness. Because when you enter the death consciousness, you pay a price; you have to pay the piper, as they say. And the price you pay is that there is always something for which you must compensate.

For you see the subtle reality: the Conscious You is out of the very being of the Creator. It knows that it is out of Oneness, and so in order to go into separation, it has to justify and explain. This is the price you pay. You constantly have to maintain that justification, and when you go into this consciousness of wanting to be better than others, you are obviously instantly threatened by those who are different from you, and by those who appear to be superior according to whatever measure you set up.

There was a time, when there were many people in the United States, who thought that people with black skin where inferior to whites in all ways. Then, when black people started entering different kinds of sports and did better than white people, the white people felt greatly threatened by this. But of course, the death consciousness always has a way out. It can create other criteria where you can still feel superior.

Nevertheless, you see my point: you are always threatened. And what must you do to avoid this threat? You must lock in to the aggressive force – that has been around this earth since the first fallen beings came here – of always seeking to project out, seeking to control others and hold them back in some way.

The lowest way to do this is of course physical force, physical control, such as you have seen in various dictatorships from the Roman Empire and forward—and even further back in time where a government is seeking to suppress the people with violent means. Yet, I trust that most of the spiritual people, most of the people who might be open to these discourses, have transcended this need and this desire to suppress other people with physical violence.

You may still have some remnants of it. For example, there are those who still believe it is necessary to have an army, such as many Americans who are spiritual people and yet believe that America should maintain a superior army and go out anywhere in the world and fight for whatever ideas have been raised up. But you see, my beloved, these are things that also need to go, as you move closer to Oneness. Indeed, there is no army in heaven, regardless of what might have been said in the Book of Revelation and elsewhere that there is an aggressive force. There is only, as Archangel Michael has said, the immovability of those who stand upon the Rock of Christ and cannot be moved by the consciousness of anti-christ.

Submitting to death

My point is this. Those of you who are open to these discourses, will not be willing to suppress and control others through physical violence. You will have raised yourselves beyond the need for physical violence in the sense that this is justified, at least on a personal scale. Yet, you may still have a very characteristic remnant of the lower aspects of the death consciousness, and that is this desire to prove other people wrong, to see ideas be proven wrong, to see other people be somehow humiliated or exposed or put down or judged.

This is a very, very aggressive force, and I would like you to look back at your life and see that beyond the direct, obvious, physical force, you have, from the moment you entered your mother's womb, been exposed to a more subtle aggressive force, which plays on your emotions and your thoughts. It is a constant projection upon your emotional body, to try to stir and agitate you into lower emotions, emotions that are based on fear and not on love.

And beyond that is a constant projection on your mental body, to get you to engage in certain thoughts, certain patterns of thoughts that end up forming closed loops. So that your mind goes round and round and round because you are always projecting out that the change needs to happen out there that other people are the ones who need to change, in order for your superior goal, however you define it, to be fulfilled.

This then, is what I need you to start recognizing, so you can see that you have been exposed to this force for many, many lifetimes on this planet. It has come at you relentlessly, my beloved. Throughout all of your embodiments, it has pounded on you, pounded on your chakras, pounded on your subconscious mind. Until in many cases, as has been the case with all of us who have taken embodiment on this planet, you have been pounded into submission, you have given in, you have somehow said, "Okay, I will surrender to this, to get some kind of peace for the rest of this lifetime."

Do you think that we who are ascended masters have not been subjected to this force and have not submitted to it at one point or another? You will notice that there are some masters who have had embodiments as famous people from history where they have stood out as being beyond the average. But you might notice that even those of us who have exposed a number of such embodiments have also – if you look at it from a linear, logical timeline – have had times where we have not given any famous embodiments.

But that did not mean we were not in embodiment. We have indeed, all of us, had many embodiments as so-called ordinary people, who did not stand out. And I can assure you that all of us have in those embodiments, from time to time, submitted to the death consciousness and this aggressive force.

I am telling you this because I want you to understand that we have all gone through what you have gone through. We all understand exactly how aggressive this force is, and we all understand how difficult it is to not submit to it. This I want you to understand because I want you to realize that we do not in any way judge or condemn you.

Awakening without guilt

We understand that there is always a danger here, there is always a danger for a spiritual teacher. So far, you may have lived your entire life without being aware of the problem I am bringing to your attention. And so, what happens when I bring to your attention that there is an element of the death consciousness? Well, you might look in the mirror and you might see, "Oh, but I have been under this consciousness, I have been influenced by this consciousness." You might even see that you have allowed yourself to become an expression of this consciousness, doing some of the things to others that others have done to you.

And so, what always happens is this: there are some spiritual students who will see this but who will immediately go into denial about it. And this will block their progress. There are others who are willing to see their own faults, but who are so willing to see them that they now go into condemnation and feeling guilty about it. This will also block their progress.

Do you see what I am saying? The death consciousness attempts to create this catch-22 where it becomes impossible for us, who are the true spiritual teachers, to actually raise you up. When we make you aware of the death consciousness, the death consciousness will use that to hold you back on the path, to put you down, or to get you to go into denial, so that you cannot actually transcend the death consciousness.

And this, of course, is not what I or the other Chohans desire to see happen. We desire you to openly and freely and consciously acknowledge the death consciousness on this planet. But we do not desire you to go into denial or into feeling guilty, for that will block your progress. And indeed, both denial and guilt are expressions of the death consciousness. You cannot overcome the death consciousness by using the death consciousness. This I trust should be obvious to those who are open to these teachings.

So, do not go into denial. Do not go into guilt and self-condemnation. You are no worse than anyone else who has ever embodied on this planet. This planet is a dark planet where the death consciousness is very strong. And there simply is no way to embody on this planet without in some ways submitting to or compromising with the death consciousness.

There never has been anyone who embodied here and was not affected by it. You may think, if you come from a certain religious tradition that Jesus or Buddha or Krishna did not submit to the death consciousness. But I tell you, they all had previous embodiments on this planet, and they did submit to the death consciousness.

Beyond the death consciousness

Do you understand that you simply cannot take embodiment here without submitting to the death consciousness in some way because otherwise your lifestream, the Conscious You, cannot even enter into a physical body on a planet like earth? It simply is not possible.

So what I am saying here is this: forget about the fact that you have entered into the death consciousness. Forget about feeling guilty. Forget about denying it. It is irrelevant. It is a fact. You cannot jump into the ocean without getting wet. Don't feel guilty about it. Don't swim around in the ocean and say, "I'm not wet, I'm not wet!" Just accept the fact that you have submitted to the death consciousness that everybody has done this, but that now it is time to turn around and say:

"Okay, I see this, I accept it, how do I now go beyond it? Maha Chohan, seven Chohans, show me the way. I am willing to rise beyond the death consciousness. I realize I cannot see right now how I have been influenced by the death consciousness. I want you to teach me. I want you to show me. I want to come up higher. And I am willing to look at myself and look at my expectations and my mental images and my perception filter. And I am willing to have you challenge it. I may not be able to have you challenge it all at once, but I am willing to have it challenged in bits and pieces, so that I can gradually come up higher while maintaining some sense of continuity of who I am."

Do you see, my beloved, you are looking at my release here. You are experiencing my release, whether you listen to it or whether you read it. You are experiencing it through the perception filter that you have right now. I know this. I see this. I am not in your perception filter. I do not have a perception filter based on the death consciousness. That is why I am an ascended master.

Thus, I see very clearly the challenges that you face. I do not expect you to awaken and shatter your perception filter in one moment. For we all, when we are in embodiment, have built a sense of self that gives us not only identity but a sense of continuity. And so, if you were to shed that sense of self instantly, you would go into a very severe identity crises and most likely end up in a mental institution because you would not be able to function. And we, of course, have no desire to have our students end up in mental institutions, or end up having to withdraw from the world, so they cannot function in the world.

Spirituality in the Age of Aquarius

You see, the ascended masters do not encourage their students to withdraw from the world, to withdraw from an active life. We encourage you to walk the spiritual path while participating in life on this planet. That is what we want you to demonstrate because this is the spirituality of the Golden Age of Saint Germain. In the Age of Pisces, it was a viable model that at least some people would withdraw from the world, retreat into the wilderness like Jesus did, or in a cave in the Himalayas, and therefore focus on going within and meditating on God because they could then hold the spiritual balance for many. But this is not the model for the Age of Aquarius. The Age of Aquarius is the age of the Holy Spirit, but the Holy Spirit flows through many people. It is also the age of community where you are participating in life.

And when you see or hear that the Golden Age is the age of community, do not misunderstand this. We are not talking about creating a new religion that will be *the* dominant religion for the Golden Age. This is not the ascended master's vision, for we know that in the Age of Pisces, you saw these religions that claimed exclusivity. "We are the only true religion. We are the only religion that can get you into heaven." And thus, they were trying to get everyone else to come into their religion, and they were trying to portray all other religions as false. Can you see that this is simply an expression of the death consciousness that I spoke about, of wanting you to feel superior to others? This is not the model for the Age of Aquarius.

Community means "come ye into unity." How can you come into unity, if you set yourself apart? You may come into unity with a few people—or rather, you may think so. But you are doing it at the price of setting yourself sharply apart from all other people. And I can tell you with absolute certainty that those religions and spiritual movements that have had this consciousness – that we have the only true religion and therefore we are superior to all others – even the members of all such religions cannot come into unity. How can they, when the basic culture of their movement is based on division? How can you?

You can even, if you are honest, look at ascended master movements and ascended master students and see that the students have not been able to come into unity precisely because the organization or culture, as with so many religions and so many spiritual movements, is based upon setting yourself apart. So what we are looking for in the Aquarian Age, is those who will come into unity with the greater community of all of mankind by taking active part in life, yet demonstrating their spirituality.

Coming apart from death

So then, do you see that this is, again, a very delicate challenge posed by the death consciousness? I need you to recognize that you have been exposed to the death consciousness. I need to you decide that you are willing to come apart from the death consciousness. In going through this process, you will go through a phase where you have to set yourself apart from all of the people who are in the mass consciousness. It is, as the Bible says: "Come apart and be a separate and chosen people, elect onto God." Because you have elected to reach for a higher ideal than what the people in the mass consciousness can see.

And so, you *do* need to come apart in order to come up higher. But I want you to know from the very beginning that the ultimate goal is not that you continue to set yourself apart. But that there actually comes a point where now you have separated yourself enough from the death consciousness that you are no longer blinded and pulled down by it. This is when you do not stay in your cave, but you go out in society, and you take an active part and you demonstrate the consciousness of life. And you may already have come to that point where you are able to live an active life and still express your spiritually. What I then propose is to simply help you free yourself even more from the death consciousness and be able to express your spiritually even more clearly. For those of you who have not yet come to this point, I propose to take you apart, take you aside;

not to pick you apart—although in a sense your ego will feel that it is being taken apart, it is being picked into pieces. For what can we do as spiritual teachers, when you have an ego that believes it knows everything and has everything under control based on this or that belief system? Well, we must pick it apart, we must take it apart in bits and pieces, for you cannot overcome it all at once.

So you must be able to see: "Ahh, here is this piece. This I can see today. This I can overcome today. I do not need to worry about the rest right now, for I know that I have made contact with a true spiritual teacher, who can see the whole and who will take me up step by step, up this spiral staircase of my personal path."

So then, my point for this discourse is this: start contemplating how you have been exposed to the death consciousness as an aggressive force that preys on your feelings and your thoughts, creating these merry-go-rounds, or rather these downward spirals where your thoughts and feelings, your psychic energies, keep being engaged in these patterns that you seemingly cannot break out of. I need you to begin to identity some of these patterns that you can see, and then, as both I and the other Chohans take you up the staircase of the seven veils, the seven rays, we will help you see more and more of them.

But for now, I need you to look at one. Do you recognize in yourself the desire to be set apart from others and the desire to somehow feel superior by seeing other people proven wrong, or their beliefs proven wrong? Do you see this? Do you see that you have been exposed to it? Do you see that you might have engaged in it yourself in some way? And if you do, then acknowledge this. Seek to become more conscious of it, and I will address it further in my next discourse.

14 | INVOKING THE EXPOSURE OF THE DEATH CONSCIOUSNESS

In the name I AM THAT I AM, Jesus Christ, I call to my I AM Presence to flow through the I Will Be Presence that I AM and give this invocation with full power. I call to beloved Elohim Peace and Aloha, Archangel Uriel and Aurora, Nada and the Maha Chohan to help me see the aspects of the death consciousness that are holding me back on the path. Help me see and surrender all patterns that block my oneness with the Maha Chohan and my oneness with my I AM Presence, including …

[Make personal calls]

Part 1

1. Maha Chohan, help me recognize how I have been affected by the death consciousness in many ways, some obvious, some not so obvious.

> O Elohim Peace, in Unity's Flame,
> there is no more room for duality's game,
> we know that all form is from the same source,
> empowering us to plot a new course.
>
> **O Elohim Peace, through your tranquility,**
> **we are free from the chaos of duality,**
> **in oneness with God a new identity,**
> **we are raising the earth into Infinity.**

2. Maha Chohan, help me see that the death consciousness is not a passive force. It is an aggressive force, although it is capable of camouflaging itself, so that most people do not see the attacks to which they are being exposed.

> O Elohim Peace, the bell now you ring,
> causing all atoms to vibrate and sing,
> we give up the sense of a separate "me,"
> we're crossing Samsara's turbulent sea.
>
> **O Elohim Peace, through your tranquility,**
> **we are free from the chaos of duality,**
> **in oneness with God a new identity,**
> **we are raising the earth into Infinity.**

3. Maha Chohan, help me see that on this planet everything is so influenced by the death consciousness, that it can be difficult to see something that is not influenced by the death consciousness.

O Elohim Peace, you help us to know,
that Jesus has come your Flame to bestow,
upon all who are ready to give up the strife,
by following Christ into infinite life.

O Elohim Peace, through your tranquility,
we are free from the chaos of duality,
in oneness with God a new identity,
we are raising the earth into Infinity.

4. Maha Chohan, help me see that the most profound and subtle effect of the death consciousness is that we no longer have any frame of reference that there is something outside of the death consciousness.

O Elohim Peace, through your eyes we see,
that only in oneness will we ever be free,
we now see that there is no separate thing,
to the ego-based self we no longer cling.

O Elohim Peace, through your tranquility,
we are free from the chaos of duality,
in oneness with God a new identity,
we are raising the earth into Infinity.

5. Maha Chohan, help me see that one of the primary functions of spirituality is to give us a direct inner experience of the Holy Spirit, the consciousness of life.

O Elohim Peace, you show us the way,
for clearing the mind from duality's fray,
you pierce the illusions of both time and space,
separation consumed by your Infinite Grace.

**O Elohim Peace, through your tranquility,
we are free from the chaos of duality,
in oneness with God a new identity,
we are raising the earth into Infinity.**

6. Maha Chohan, help me experience that there is something outside the death consciousness, so I have a frame of reference to shift my consciousness.

O Elohim Peace, what beauty your name,
consuming within us duality's shame,
the earth is set free from burden of fear,
accepting your peace is now manifest here.

**O Elohim Peace, through your tranquility,
we are free from the chaos of duality,
in oneness with God a new identity,
we are raising the earth into Infinity.**

7. Maha Chohan, help me raise my consciousness and shed certain illusions of the death consciousness, until I have the experience of snapping out of my normal state of consciousness and experiencing something more.

O Elohim Peace, with Christ at our side,
no force of duality can evermore hide,
It was through the vibration of your Golden

Flame,
that Christ the illusion of death overcame.

O Elohim Peace, through your tranquility,
we are free from the chaos of duality,
in oneness with God a new identity,
we are raising the earth into Infinity.

8. Maha Chohan, help me experience that you are more than the death consciousness, and that because you are not in the death consciousness, you feel no obligation to conform to it.

O Elohim Peace, you bring now to earth,
the unstoppable flame of Cosmic Rebirth,
we give up the sense that something is "mine,"
allowing your Light through our beings to shine.

O Elohim Peace, through your tranquility,
we are free from the chaos of duality,
in oneness with God a new identity,
we are raising the earth into Infinity.

9. Maha Chohan, help me see if I have expectations that I project upon you or the seven Chohans. Help me shatter my expectations, by not living up to them, by challenging them, by deliberately going beyond them.

O Elohim Peace, as peace now we feel,
all records of war you totally heal,
the earth is now free from forces of war,
restoring her purity known from before.

**O Elohim Peace, through your tranquility,
we are free from the chaos of duality,
in oneness with God a new identity,
we are raising the earth into Infinity.**

Part 2

1. Maha Chohan, help me see that I cannot escape the death consciousness on my own, once I am enveloped in it. My mind has become a closed system, for the overall effect of the death consciousness is that it is a closed system. It is shut off from the life-giving power of the River of Life, from the Holy Spirit.

Uriel Archangel, immense is the power,
of angels of peace, all war to devour.
The demons of war, no match for your light,
consuming them all, with radiance so bright.

**Uriel Archangel, use your great sword,
Uriel Archangel, consume all discord,
Uriel Archangel, we're of one accord,
Uriel Archangel, we walk with the Lord.**

2. Maha Chohan, help me see that the death consciousness is made up of innumerable false spirits, innumerable separate spirits, and they cannot see the Holy Spirit.

Uriel Archangel, intense is the sound,
when millions of angels, their voices compound.
They build a crescendo, piercing the night,
life's glorious oneness revealed to our sight.

Uriel Archangel, use your great sword,
Uriel Archangel, consume all discord,
Uriel Archangel, we're of one accord,
Uriel Archangel, we walk with the Lord.

3. Maha Chohan, help me see that if they were to see and acknowledge the Holy Spirit, they would instantly cease to exist as separate spirits. One cannot be separate and in oneness at the same time.

Uriel Archangel, from out the Great Throne,
your millions of trumpets, sound the One Tone.
Consuming all discord with your harmony,
the sound of all sounds will set all life free.

Uriel Archangel, use your great sword,
Uriel Archangel, consume all discord,
Uriel Archangel, we're of one accord,
Uriel Archangel, we walk with the Lord.

4. Maha Chohan, help me realize that if I want something more than what I have right now, I cannot stay in the state of consciousness I am in right now. I cannot remain comfortable, if I want spiritual growth.

Uriel Archangel, all war is now done,
for you bring a message, from heart of the One.
The hearts of all men, now singing in peace,
the spirals of love, forever increase.

Uriel Archangel, use your great sword,
Uriel Archangel, consume all discord,

**Uriel Archangel, we're of one accord,
Uriel Archangel, we walk with the Lord.**

5. Maha Chohan, help me see that the death consciousness can make people so comfortable that they are convinced, that if they keep doing what they are doing right now, then God has to take them into heaven.

Uriel Archangel, your infinite peace,
from all warring beings our planet release,
war is a prison from which we are free,
embracing the peace of true unity.

**Uriel Archangel, use your great sword,
Uriel Archangel, consume all discord,
Uriel Archangel, we're of one accord,
Uriel Archangel, we walk with the Lord.**

6. Maha Chohan, help me see that the death consciousness can also make people extremely uncomfortable. The death consciousness must become more and more extreme, until it makes people more and more uncomfortable.

Uriel Archangel, we send forth the call,
reveal now the oneness that unifies all,
help us the vision of peace now to see,
so we from all conflicts and struggles are free.

**Uriel Archangel, use your great sword,
Uriel Archangel, consume all discord,
Uriel Archangel, we're of one accord,
Uriel Archangel, we walk with the Lord.**

7. Maha Chohan, help me see that if I want to change, I can potentially try to control the world around me, but that is what I have been doing, and it has brought me into my current bind, where I feel like I have nowhere to go and my life is a continuous struggle.

Uriel Archangel, in service to life,
you give us release from struggle and strife,
forgetting the self is truly the key,
to living a life in true harmony.

Uriel Archangel, use your great sword,
Uriel Archangel, consume all discord,
Uriel Archangel, we're of one accord,
Uriel Archangel, we walk with the Lord.

8. Maha Chohan, help me see that there is an alternative to the struggle. Instead of trying to change someone or something outside of myself, I can look in the mirror and pull the beam in my own eye and change my own consciousness.

Uriel Archangel, the earth now you raise,
out of duality's death-bringing haze,
we call now upon your great Flame of Peace,
commanding that all petty squabbles do cease.

Uriel Archangel, use your great sword,
Uriel Archangel, consume all discord,
Uriel Archangel, we're of one accord,
Uriel Archangel, we walk with the Lord.

9. Maha Chohan, help me realize, that I cannot change my own consciousness by remaining comfortable and believing what I am believing right now.

Uriel Archangel, as peace is the norm,
to your higher vision the earth does conform,
as people have found your peace from within,
a Golden Age is the prize that we win.

Uriel Archangel, use your great sword,
Uriel Archangel, consume all discord,
Uriel Archangel, we're of one accord,
Uriel Archangel, we walk with the Lord.

Part 3

1. Maha Chohan, help me see that the false path is an external path where I can do outer things and study outer teachings, but I do not have to look at myself. This is still the death consciousness.

Master Nada, beauty's power,
unfolding like a sacred flower.
Master Nada, so sublime,
a will that conquers even time.

Master Nada, peace you give,
forevermore in peace we live,
our planet has a peaceful morn,
the Golden Age is hereby born.

2. Maha Chohan, help me realize that I am looking at every-thing through a perception filter, and that perception filter is influenced by the death consciousness.

Master Nada, you bestow,
upon us wisdom's rushing flow.
Master Nada, mind so strong
rising on your wings of song.

**Master Nada, peace you give,
forevermore in peace we live,
our planet has a peaceful morn,
the Golden Age is hereby born.**

3. Maha Chohan, help me see that the only way to grow beyond my present level of consciousness is to be willing to have that perception filter challenged by a spiritual teacher, who is not inside my mental box or inside the death consciousness.

Master Nada, precious scent,
your love is truly heaven-sent.
Master Nada, kind and soft
on wings of love we rise aloft.

**Master Nada, peace you give,
forevermore in peace we live,
our planet has a peaceful morn,
the Golden Age is hereby born.**

4. Maha Chohan, I want to have you as my frame of reference, so I can systematically challenge my expectations, my com-fortability, the death consciousness. I am willing to endure this.

> Master Nada, mother light,
> our hearts are rising like a kite.
> Master Nada, from your view,
> all life is pure as morning dew.
>
> **Master Nada, peace you give,**
> **forevermore in peace we live,**
> **our planet has a peaceful morn,**
> **the Golden Age is hereby born.**

5. Maha Chohan, I will stop looking for the magic wand and start looking at myself. I am ready for the true teachers of the ascended masters to appear in my life. I want to hear you, sense you, sense your presence, sense your vibration.

> Master Nada, truth you bring,
> as morning birds in love do sing.
> Master Nada, we now feel,
> your love that all four bodies heal.
>
> **Master Nada, peace you give,**
> **forevermore in peace we live,**
> **our planet has a peaceful morn,**
> **the Golden Age is hereby born.**

6. Maha Chohan, help me sense the vibration of an ascended master, so I attain a frame of reference that is the Pearl of Great Price, the opportunity to come up higher, to attune my consciousness to your vibration. I want to rise beyond the death consciousness.

> Master Nada, serve in peace,
> as all emotions we release.

Master Nada, life is fun,
the solar plexus is a sun.

Master Nada, peace you give,
forevermore in peace we live,
our planet has a peaceful morn,
the Golden Age is hereby born.

7. Maha Chohan, help me see that I have been exposed to the death consciousness because it is a very aggressive force on this planet.

Master Nada, love is free,
conditions we no longer see.
Master Nada, rise above,
all human forms of lesser love.

Master Nada, peace you give,
forevermore in peace we live,
our planet has a peaceful morn,
the Golden Age is hereby born.

8. Maha Chohan, help me see that people who are below the 48th level of consciousness tend to separate themselves from other people. They set themselves apart in a category where they are special and somehow superior.

Master Nada, balance all,
the seven rays upon our call.
Master Nada, rise and shine,
your radiant beauty most divine.

> **Master Nada, peace you give,**
> **forevermore in peace we live,**
> **our planet has a peaceful morn,**
> **the Golden Age is hereby born.**

9. Maha Chohan, help me see that the lower levels of the death consciousness make people think they are better than others because of some characteristic here on earth.

> Nada Dear, your Presence here,
> filling up the inner sphere.
> Life is now a sacred flow,
> God Peace we do on all bestow.

> **Master Nada, peace you give,**
> **forevermore in peace we live,**
> **our planet has a peaceful morn,**
> **the Golden Age is hereby born.**

Part 4

1. Maha Chohan, help me see that in the River of Life we do not even have time to consider whether some people are better than others because it is completely irrelevant. We are constantly focused on transcending ourselves and helping all of life transcend itself.

> Maha Chohan, I will to grow,
> I feel the power of your flow.
> Maha Chohan, the veil is rent,
> creative will from heaven sent.

**O Holy Spirit, flow through me,
I am the open door for thee.
O mighty rushing stream of Light,
transcendence is my sacred right.**

2. Maha Chohan, help me see that here is no comparison. How can there be when we know that everyone is one, and all are expressions of the One.

Maha Chohan, your wisdom streams,
awaken all from matter's dreams.
Maha Chohan, your balance bring,
let bells of integration ring.

**O Holy Spirit, flow through me,
I am the open door for thee.
O mighty rushing stream of Light,
transcendence is my sacred right.**

3. Maha Chohan, help me see that when we go into this consciousness of thinking that we are better than others, we will automatically pay a price, as we do in all elements of the death consciousness.

Maha Chohan, love's mighty call,
the prison walls are shattered all.
Maha Chohan, set all life free
through unconditionality.

**O Holy Spirit, flow through me,
I am the open door for thee.
O mighty rushing stream of Light,
transcendence is my sacred right.**

4. Maha Chohan, help me see that when we enter the death consciousness, we pay a price. The price we pay is that there is always something for which we must compensate.

> Maha Chohan, intentions pure,
> all life is one, I know for sure.
> Maha Chohan, I am awake,
> surrender all for oneness' sake.

> **O Holy Spirit, flow through me,**
> **I am the open door for thee.**
> **O mighty rushing stream of Light,**
> **transcendence is my sacred right.**

5. Maha Chohan, help me see that the Conscious You is out of the being of the Creator. It knows that it is out of Oneness, and so in order to go into separation, it has to justify and explain everything. This is the price I pay.

> Maha Chohan, help all men see,
> through veils of unreality.
> Maha Chohan, with single eye,
> I know I am the greater "I."

> **O Holy Spirit, flow through me,**
> **I am the open door for thee.**
> **O mighty rushing stream of Light,**
> **transcendence is my sacred right.**

6. Maha Chohan, help me see that I constantly have to maintain that justification. When I go into the consciousness of wanting to be better than others, I am instantly threatened by

those who are different from me, and by those who appear to be superior according to whatever measure I set up.

Maha Chohan, your peace I find,
Maitreya shows me to be kind.
Maha Chohan, all war will cease,
now flooding all with sacred peace.

O Holy Spirit, flow through me,
I am the open door for thee.
O mighty rushing stream of Light,
transcendence is my sacred right.

7. Maha Chohan, help me see that in the death consciousness we are always threatened, and in order to avoid this threat, we must lock in to the aggressive force of always seeking to project out, seeking to control others and hold them back.

Maha Chohan, you balance all,
the seven rays upon my call.
Maha Chohan, all life is free,
transcending for eternity.

O Holy Spirit, flow through me,
I am the open door for thee.
O mighty rushing stream of Light,
transcendence is my sacred right.

8. Maha Chohan, help me see if I still have a remnant of the lower aspects of the death consciousness, namely a desire to prove other people wrong, to see ideas be proven wrong, to see other people be humiliated, exposed, put down or judged.

Maha Chohan, your sacred Flame,
what beauty in your blessed name.
Maha Chohan, what rushing flow,
the Spirit one with life below.

**O Holy Spirit, flow through me,
I am the open door for thee.
O mighty rushing stream of Light,
transcendence is my sacred right.**

9. Maha Chohan, help me look back at my life and see that beyond the direct physical force, I have been exposed to a more subtle aggressive force, which is projecting upon my emotional body. It tries to stir and agitate me into lower emotions that are based on fear and not on love.

Maha Chohan, your Presence here,
filling up the inner sphere.
Life is now a sacred flow,
God Wisdom we on all bestow.

**O Holy Spirit, flow through me,
I am the open door for thee.
O mighty rushing stream of Light,
transcendence is my sacred right.**

Part 5

1. Maha Chohan, help me see that there is a constant projection on my mental body, to get me to engage in certain

thoughts that end up forming closed loops, so that my mind goes round and round.

> Master Nada, beauty's power,
> unfolding like a sacred flower.
> Master Nada, so sublime,
> a will that conquers even time.

> **Master Nada, peace you give,**
> **forevermore in peace we live,**
> **our planet has a peaceful morn,**
> **the Golden Age is hereby born.**

2. Maha Chohan, help me see the spirit that is projecting out that the change needs to happen out there, that other people are the ones who need to change, in order for my superior goal to be fulfilled.

> Master Nada, you bestow,
> upon us wisdom's rushing flow.
> Master Nada, mind so strong
> rising on your wings of song.

> **Master Nada, peace you give,**
> **forevermore in peace we live,**
> **our planet has a peaceful morn,**
> **the Golden Age is hereby born.**

3. Maha Chohan, help me recognize that I have been exposed to this force for lifetimes. It has pounded on my chakras, pounded on my subconscious mind, until I have been pounded into submission and said, "Okay, I will surrender to this, to get some kind of peace for the rest of this lifetime."

Master Nada, precious scent,
your love is truly heaven-sent.
Master Nada, kind and soft
on wings of love we rise aloft.

**Master Nada, peace you give,
forevermore in peace we live,
our planet has a peaceful morn,
the Golden Age is hereby born.**

4. Maha Chohan, help me see that even those who have
ascended, have submitted to this force. Help me see that you
understand how aggressive this force is, and you do not judge
or condemn me.

Master Nada, mother light,
our hearts are rising like a kite.
Master Nada, from your view,
all life is pure as morning dew.

**Master Nada, peace you give,
forevermore in peace we live,
our planet has a peaceful morn,
the Golden Age is hereby born.**

5. Maha Chohan, help me recognize that when you help me see
that I have been influenced by the death consciousness, there
is a danger that I might go into denial about it. And this will
block my progress.

Master Nada, truth you bring,
as morning birds in love do sing.

Master Nada, we now feel,
your love that all four bodies heal.

**Master Nada, peace you give,
forevermore in peace we live,
our planet has a peaceful morn,
the Golden Age is hereby born.**

6. Maha Chohan, help me see if I am so willing to see my own faults that I go into condemnation and feeling guilty about it. This will also block my progress.

Master Nada, serve in peace,
as all emotions we release.
Master Nada, life is fun,
the solar plexus is a sun.

**Master Nada, peace you give,
forevermore in peace we live,
our planet has a peaceful morn,
the Golden Age is hereby born.**

7. Maha Chohan, help me see that the death consciousness attempts to create a catch-22, where it becomes impossible for you as my teacher to raise me up.

Master Nada, love is free,
conditions we no longer see.
Master Nada, rise above,
all human forms of lesser love.

**Master Nada, peace you give,
forevermore in peace we live,**

**our planet has a peaceful morn,
the Golden Age is hereby born.**

8. Maha Chohan, help me see that when you make me aware of the death consciousness, the death consciousness will use that to hold me back on the path, to put me down, or to get me to go into denial, so that I cannot actually transcend the death consciousness.

Master Nada, balance all,
the seven rays upon our call.
Master Nada, rise and shine,
your radiant beauty most divine.

**Master Nada, peace you give,
forevermore in peace we live,
our planet has a peaceful morn,
the Golden Age is hereby born.**

9. Maha Chohan, I will openly and consciously acknowledge the death consciousness. I will not go into denial or into feeling guilty, for that will block my progress.

Nada Dear, your Presence here,
filling up the inner sphere.
Life is now a sacred flow,
God Peace we do on all bestow.

**Master Nada, peace you give,
forevermore in peace we live,
our planet has a peaceful morn,
the Golden Age is hereby born.**

Part 6

1. Maha Chohan, help me see that both denial and guilt are expressions of the death consciousness. I cannot overcome the death consciousness by using the death consciousness.

Maha Chohan, I will to grow,
I feel the power of your flow.
Maha Chohan, the veil is rent,
creative will from heaven sent.

**O Holy Spirit, flow through me,
I am the open door for thee.
O mighty rushing stream of Light,
transcendence is my sacred right.**

2. Maha Chohan, help me see that I am no worse than anyone else who has ever embodied on this planet. There is no way to embody on this planet without in some ways submitting to or compromising with the death consciousness.

Maha Chohan, your wisdom streams,
awaken all from matter's dreams.
Maha Chohan, your balance bring,
let bells of integration ring.

**O Holy Spirit, flow through me,
I am the open door for thee.
O mighty rushing stream of Light,
transcendence is my sacred right.**

3. Maha Chohan, help me see that there never has been anyone who embodied here and was not affected by it. Even Jesus, Buddha or Krishna had previous embodiments, and they did submit to the death consciousness.

Maha Chohan, love's mighty call,
the prison walls are shattered all.
Maha Chohan, set all life free
through unconditionality.

**O Holy Spirit, flow through me,
I am the open door for thee.
O mighty rushing stream of Light,
transcendence is my sacred right.**

4. Maha Chohan, help me see that I cannot take embodiment here without submitting to the death consciousness in some way, because otherwise my lifestream, the Conscious You, cannot even enter a physical body on a planet like earth.

Maha Chohan, intentions pure,
all life is one, I know for sure.
Maha Chohan, I am awake,
surrender all for oneness' sake.

**O Holy Spirit, flow through me,
I am the open door for thee.
O mighty rushing stream of Light,
transcendence is my sacred right.**

5. Maha Chohan, help me see that I have entered into the death consciousness. I accept the fact that I have submitted to

the death consciousness, that everybody has done this, but that now it is time to turn around.

> Maha Chohan, help all men see,
> through veils of unreality.
> Maha Chohan, with single eye,
> I know I am the greater "I."

> **O Holy Spirit, flow through me,**
> **I am the open door for thee.**
> **O mighty rushing stream of Light,**
> **transcendence is my sacred right.**

6. Maha Chohan, seven Chohans, show me the way. I am willing to rise beyond the death consciousness. I realize I cannot see right now how I have been influenced by the death consciousness. I want you to teach me. I want you to show me. I want to come up higher.

> Maha Chohan, your peace I find,
> Maitreya shows me to be kind.
> Maha Chohan, all war will cease,
> now flooding all with sacred peace.

> **O Holy Spirit, flow through me,**
> **I am the open door for thee.**
> **O mighty rushing stream of Light,**
> **transcendence is my sacred right.**

7. Maha Chohan, I am willing to look at myself and look at my expectations and my mental images and my perception filter. I am willing to have you challenge it. I may not be able to have you challenge it all at once, but I am willing to have it

challenged, so that I can gradually come up higher while maintaining some sense of continuity of who I am.

Maha Chohan, you balance all,
the seven rays upon my call.
Maha Chohan, all life is free,
transcending for eternity.

O Holy Spirit, flow through me,
I am the open door for thee.
O mighty rushing stream of Light,
transcendence is my sacred right.

8. Maha Chohan, help me see that I am experiencing your release through the perception filter that I have right now. Help me see the challenges that I face.

Maha Chohan, your sacred Flame,
what beauty in your blessed name.
Maha Chohan, what rushing flow,
the Spirit one with life below.

O Holy Spirit, flow through me,
I am the open door for thee.
O mighty rushing stream of Light,
transcendence is my sacred right.

9. Maha Chohan, help me walk the spiritual path while participating in life on this planet, so I can demonstrate the spirituality of the Golden Age of Saint Germain.

Maha Chohan, your Presence here,
filling up the inner sphere.

Life is now a sacred flow,
God Wisdom we on all bestow.

**O Holy Spirit, flow through me,
I am the open door for thee.
O mighty rushing stream of Light,
transcendence is my sacred right.**

Part 7

1. Maha Chohan, I am willing to come apart from the death consciousness. I will go through a phase where I have to set myself
apart from the people who are in the mass consciousness.

Maha Chohan, I will to grow,
I feel the power of your flow.
Maha Chohan, the veil is rent,
creative will from heaven sent.

**O Holy Spirit, flow through me,
I am the open door for thee.
O mighty rushing stream of Light,
transcendence is my sacred right.**

2. Maha Chohan, help me see that I *do* need to come apart in
order to come up higher. Yet the ultimate goal is not that I
continue to set myself apart.

Maha Chohan, your wisdom streams,
awaken all from matter's dreams.

Maha Chohan, your balance bring,
let bells of integration ring.

O Holy Spirit, flow through me,
I am the open door for thee.
O mighty rushing stream of Light,
transcendence is my sacred right.

3. Maha Chohan, help me see that there comes a point where I have separated myself enough from the death consciousness, that I am no longer blinded and pulled down by it.

Maha Chohan, love's mighty call,
the prison walls are shattered all.
Maha Chohan, set all life free
through unconditionality.

O Holy Spirit, flow through me,
I am the open door for thee.
O mighty rushing stream of Light,
transcendence is my sacred right.

4. Maha Chohan, help me see that this is when I need to go out in society, and I take an active part and I demonstrate the consciousness of life.

Maha Chohan, intentions pure,
all life is one, I know for sure.
Maha Chohan, I am awake,
surrender all for oneness' sake.

O Holy Spirit, flow through me,
I am the open door for thee.

**O mighty rushing stream of Light,
transcendence is my sacred right.**

5. Maha Chohan, help me live an active life and still express my spiritually. Help me free myself even more from the death consciousness and be able to express my spiritually even more clearly

Maha Chohan, help all men see,
through veils of unreality.
Maha Chohan, with single eye,
I know I am the greater "I."

**O Holy Spirit, flow through me,
I am the open door for thee.
O mighty rushing stream of Light,
transcendence is my sacred right.**

6. Maha Chohan, help me see that my ego will feel that it is being taken apart, it is being picked into pieces. For the ego believes it knows everything and has everything under control based on this or that belief system. So you must pick it apart in bits and pieces, for I cannot overcome it all at once.

Maha Chohan, your peace I find,
Maitreya shows me to be kind.
Maha Chohan, all war will cease,
now flooding all with sacred peace.

**O Holy Spirit, flow through me,
I am the open door for thee.
O mighty rushing stream of Light,
transcendence is my sacred right.**

7. Maha Chohan, help me focus on what I can overcome today and not worry about the rest. For you will take me up step by step, up this spiral staircase of my personal path.

Maha Chohan, you balance all,
the seven rays upon my call.
Maha Chohan, all life is free,
transcending for eternity.

**O Holy Spirit, flow through me,
I am the open door for thee.
O mighty rushing stream of Light,
transcendence is my sacred right.**

8. Maha Chohan, help me start contemplating how I have been exposed to the death consciousness as an aggressive force that preys on my feelings and thoughts, creating these downward spirals where my psychic energies are engaged in patterns that I seemingly cannot break out of.

Maha Chohan, your sacred Flame,
what beauty in your blessed name.
Maha Chohan, what rushing flow,
the Spirit one with life below.

**O Holy Spirit, flow through me,
I am the open door for thee.
O mighty rushing stream of Light,
transcendence is my sacred right.**

9. Maha Chohan, help me begin to identity some of these patterns. Help me especially see the desire to be set apart from others and the desire to feel superior by seeing other people

proven wrong. Help me become more conscious of this aspect of the death consciousness.

> Maha Chohan, your Presence here,
> filling up the inner sphere.
> Life is now a sacred flow,
> God Wisdom we on all bestow.

> **O Holy Spirit, flow through me,**
> **I am the open door for thee.**
> **O mighty rushing stream of Light,**
> **transcendence is my sacred right.**

Sealing:

In the name of the Divine Mother, I fully accept that the power of these calls is used to set free the Ma-ter light, so it can outpicture the perfect vision of Christ for my own life, for all people and for the planet. In the name I AM THAT I AM, it is done! Amen.

15 | GOING BEYOND AGGRESSIVE INTENT

The Maha Chohan I am. And I come to carry on, by building on the foundation I have set in the previous discourses. I have said that there is a tendency to form an aggressive intent of seeking to change other people. This is a tendency that started with the original fallen beings but has been perpetuated both in previous spheres and in this sphere by them, and by people who have been ensnared by them into taking part in this downward spiral.

What is the plan of these fallen beings? It is simply to drag as many people and lifestreams as possible into their downward spiral. If they can, they will drag every self-aware being into the downward spiral, which of course cannot be done, as there are already so many beings in this sphere who have entered the upward spiral, the ascension spiral that is the Holy Spirit.

Nevertheless, there are relatively few planets where fallen beings are allowed to embody, as an act of mercy towards them and as an act of testing towards the lifestreams who need this kind of test. They can maintain the illusion that one day they will be successful and prove God wrong by causing all self-aware beings to fall. And thus, God will be forced to change his design for the plan of raising awareness, self-awareness. So you need to see, when you are a spiritual student on the path, what is the modus operandi of the fallen beings.

The tendency to ignore dark forces

As I have said before, in the ideal scenario you would be able to walk the Path of the Seven Veils between the 48th and 96th level of consciousness without dealing with the fallen consciousness, without dealing with anyone aggressively seeking to influence you. It would be all between you and the spiritual teacher. But because planet earth is not an ideal scenario or environment, you will have to recognize – and you need to recognize as a spiritual student – that you will have to deal with the fallen consciousness on each level, up until the 96th level, and even beyond, but you deal with it in a different way after the 96th level.

I would like you now to take a look at the many spiritual movements that are out there on this planet, and you will indeed see that many of them have no teachings about fallen beings and dark forces. You will see that many spiritual people prefer to ignore these topics and indeed become kind of squeamish, when they are confronted with the potential that there could be dark forces.

There are some who say that you should focus only on the positive, for if you focus on the negative, you give it power. Well, my beloved, you do not necessarily give the dark forces power by being aware of them. You do give them power if you engage them with fear or seek to battle them. But I can tell you with absolute surety that you also give power to dark forces by ignoring and denying them.

For you see, ignorance, ignoring something and denying its existence, these are not passive measures. They are active measures for one very simple reason: the dark forces are aggressive. They seek to influence anyone on this planet. Therefore, you cannot be in existence on this planet without having an aggressive force directed against you.

And how can you ignore or deny this force? Only by directing a force back that blinds you to what is being directed at you. This should be known by simple wave dynamics where you need to have a certain basic understanding that everything is energy and energy moves in waves. And when two waves meet, they create an interference pattern. This means that one wave can cancel out or change the vibration of another wave.

What is coming at you from the fallen beings of the mass consciousness is a wave of energy. If you are neutral and attentive, you will notice this energy. So the only way you can go into a state where you ignore it or deny it, is that you are sending out energy, which will not neutralize the negative energy, it will only neutralize it at the level of your conscious awareness, so that you are not consciously aware of it. And therefore, you can ignore or deny the dark forces.

Yet they will still influence your subconscious mind. And I can tell you with all honesty that I can look at the millions of sincere spiritual seekers on this planet, and I can assure you that if they are not consciously aware of the dark forces, then they are indeed influenced by those dark forces.

Earth is one of the lower planets

This, of course, does not mean that they feel this influence because many of them don't. And the reason is partly what I just said that they have created an outgoing energy that prevents their conscious minds from noticing the attack from dark forces. But it is also due to the fact that once the dark forces have directed you onto a false path, a path that cannot lead you to the Christ consciousness and the ascension, then they will tend to not necessarily leave you alone, but they will allow you to stay in the illusion that you are doing exactly the right thing.

That is why you can see in the Western world many Christians, who are absolutely convinced that Jesus will come and save them because they are the chosen ones by being members of a particular church or by declaring Jesus as their Lord and Savior. Likewise, you will see many spiritual people who have similar beliefs that if they are only kind and loving towards everybody and don't put their attention on anything negative, then they are guaranteed to one day become enlightened.

This is all a lie created by the fallen beings specifically to trap those who are beginning to awaken, but have not yet awakened to the absolute reality that the spiritual path, the path towards enlightenment or the ascension, is a conscious path. You cannot walk it by being unconscious. You cannot walk it by ignoring or denying. You can walk it only by looking at anything and everything.

And you cannot, my beloved, walk the spiritual path on planet earth without recognizing and acknowledging what kind of planet you have landed upon. This is not an ideal planet. This is a treacherous planet. This is one of the lower planets in the material universe; not the lowest, but one of the lower ones. And you need to recognize this, and you need to be aware of it. I am not saying you need to be afraid of dark forces. I am not saying you need to battle them. But you need to be aware because only by being aware can you follow the call of Jesus: "Be ye wise as serpents and harmless as doves."

There are many spiritual people who think they are harmless as doves, but you cannot be harmless as a dove unless you are wise as a serpent, wise to the serpents and their attempts to direct you into a blind alley that does not lead to true self-transcendence. It leads to the automatic path where you think that because you follow certain outer requirements, you no longer need to look at the beam in your own eye, and that you can be saved automatically by belonging to this or that church, following this or that guru or doing this or that technique. It simply does not work that way.

Why dark forces attack you

Back to the scheme of the fallen beings, which is two things. Their first order of business is to attack any lifestream on earth with an aggressive force. Physical if possible, but in today's world it is not as easy for them to attack people physically, at least not in certain parts of the world. And thus, they also attack you through psychic means in your mental body, emotional body and, of course, the identity body.

So what is the purpose of this attack? It is not to destroy you. It is to draw you into reacting to the attack. This is their first order of business. They want nothing more than to draw you into an action-reaction game where you are exposed to an action from them and then you react, and then there is another action and another reaction. And pretty soon you are so far into this downward spiral that you have forgotten your spiritual goals for coming here in the first place. This then is their primary way whereby they seek to take you below the 48th level of consciousness into this aggressive state of mind that I have spoken about where you are constantly feeling under attack and feeling in need to defend yourself.

Now, if they cannot draw you into this or keep you into it because you start refusing to engage in these aggressive games, then their second plan is to get you to a certain level where you feel comfortable where you feel you are spiritual or religious where you feel you are saved and doing the right thing. And then they want to keep you there indefinitely.

For you see, what have I said is the Holy Spirit? What have I said is the true path? It is the River of Life, which is constantly, perpetually transcending itself. So if you are standing still at a certain level, you may feel ever so saved and spiritual. But you are not growing if you are not transcending yourself, and therefore you are not moving closer to the ascension point—and therefore you are stuck in the material world. If they cannot get you to go down, they will at least want you to be stuck. And then they feel they have you under control, and they do have you under control.

Let us return to the very fact that when you do allow yourself to get pulled into the action-reaction game of reacting to the aggressive intent of the fallen beings that is when you go below the 48th level of consciousness. My purpose for this discourse is to reach out to those who have gone below, but also to those who have actually started climbing between the 48th and 96th level.

When spirits react to other spirits

Now, when you take what I have said earlier, you should be able to see a simple fact. What is it that the fallen beings do to attack you with this aggressive force? What is that force? It is what I have talked about earlier: a spirit. The fallen beings have created a spirit that goes out and attacks you. But what do you create, when you react to this attack—whether you seek to escape it or whether you seek to fight back? Well, you also create a spirit. You create your own personal spirit. And for each step you go down below the 48th level, you are creating a new spirit.

What is it that happens, when a person reaches what they call rock bottom and says, "No, I can no longer do this?" This is when you decide that you will no longer create another spirit, and that you will attempt to stop feeding the spirits that you have created. You may not be consciously aware of this, but this is actually what happens.

So what is it that is required, for you to climb back up the spiral staircase towards the 96th level of consciousness? It is that you must go through the journey of confronting the spirits you have created and slaying them, as Saint George slew the dragon.

Some of you may be aware that the Maha Chohan was in a previous time embodied as the poet Homer, who wrote the Greek plays of the Iliad and the Odyssey. What is the Odyssey? It is a coded message, a symbol for the journey that all souls must complete. Odysseus was simply a symbol for each lifestream, and how you must travel around away from your home until you have met, confronted and overcome each of the spirits that you have personally created. And only then can you return home to the direct inner contact with your I AM Presence, with your Christ self, with your ascended teachers. Only then will your journey have come to one of those turning points where you know you have transcended the consciousness of seeing yourself as a separate, disconnected being opposed by other separate, disconnected beings.

For you see, which part of you is it that can feel it is being opposed by the dark spirits created by the fallen beings? Well, it is only the spirits that you have created. For only a separate spirit can feel opposed by other separate spirits. The One Spirit, the undivided Spirit, the indivisible Spirit, the Holy Spirit, does not feel opposed by separate spirits because it knows it is beyond them, beyond their reach. Because as soon as it feels their attack, what does it do? It does not go into denial. It does not go into fighting. It simply transcends itself, so that it becomes transparent to the force that is directed towards it.

Starting the true path

Now then, my aim for this book is to prepare you for the initiations of the seven Chohans, so that you can start the Path of the Seven Veils of climbing from the 48th to the 96th level of consciousness. What then, will it take to even start this path? Well, you live in the physical octave on planet earth. We of the ascended masters have given various teachings that are available in books or on the internet. It is possible for you to find such a teaching. It is not likely you will find it until you have hit that bottom experience and decided to turn around and that you want more than the struggle. Nevertheless, it is possible for you to find it before you are at the 48th level of consciousness, for of course, how could you ever climb back up to the 48th level of consciousness, if you did not have some frame of reference?

So what I am attempting to explain here is this: before you can rise beyond the 48th level, you must slay the spirits you have created beneath that level. But beyond the individual spirits, there is one spirit you need to slay, and that is the spirit of feeling what I have described earlier as being threatened, as having a need to project into the minds of other people because you seek to change them instead of changing yourself.

Listen to what I am saying—not just the words, but what I am saying between the lines, between the words. There are three stages among the 144 levels of consciousness, but there are two main ones: below the 48th level and beyond the 96th level. The absolute difference is that before you reach the 96th level, you are climbing the path as an individual being. That means one thing, very simply: you need to be completely focused on changing yourself and not seeking to change anyone else.

You need to be focused on the ideal that Jesus set up 2,000 years ago where you are not even concerned about the splinter in the eyes of your brother, for you are focusing all of your attention on the beam in your own eye. After you pass the 96th level, you go into a different phase where you no longer need to raise up the individual self. In fact, you need to be able and willing to lay down your life, to lay down that individual self, the individual attainment, in order to raise all life. But this is a shift you can only make at the 96th level and above.

Justifying your lower spirits

So what is it that happens below the 48th level? It is that you go into a perversion of the upper levels of consciousness, the levels beyond the 96th level where you now start directing an aggressive spirit. You start creating aggressive spirits that are aimed at controlling the minds of other people. But not only do you do this, you justify this by some greater cause—that you are doing this to help God's cause and not out of selfish reasons. This is the one spirit you must slay before you can rise above the 48th level. That is why I say to you, with as much clarity as can be put into words: "If you want to make it to the 96th level of consciousness, if you want to follow the true spiritual path, if you want to qualify for initiation under the seven Chohans, you must fulfill this one requirement: stop focusing on changing other people or the world! Withdraw all attention from seeking to change anything outside yourself. Instead, focus all attention on changing your own state of consciousness, slaying the spirits you have created and embodying the positive lessons of the seven rays, so that you build the individual self."

You will not make it to the 96th level by changing the world or other people. You will make it there only as an individual being. Then, at the 96th level, there is a shift. But that should not be your concern right now, for the simple reason that if you are reading or listening to these words, the next step on your personal path is to lock in to the initiations under the seven Chohans. Do not delude yourself into thinking you are beyond being initiated by the seven Chohans.

I have said that you may be above the 48th level of consciousness, and therefore you can more quickly catch up. But you still need to be humble, realistic and honest enough to start at the beginning, to start with the Chohan of the First Ray and work your way up, so that you do not skip steps and leave any spirits lingering in the subconscious, who will later come out and seek to devour you, for they will actually grow when they can stay hidden.

You see, the consequence of my teaching earlier – that even if you manage to ignore or deny the existence of dark spirits or the spirits you have created – is simply this: there will still be energy directed into your subconscious mind, and that means that whatever the spirits that are lurching there, they will grow in the hiding places that are maintained by your unwillingness to look at yourself.

Being unwilling to look at your own consciousness, to look into your subconscious mind, is the surest way to feed the spirits that are there. And they will keep growing, until you decide to abandon your willful ignorance and instead shine the light of your I AM Presence, the light of the seven rays, into the caves of the subconscious mind, flushing out those spirits into the open, so that you can see them. And then, with the expert guidance of the seven Chohans, you slay them one by one.

You are not alone

You do not need to fear this, for you will not have to confront them all at once, and you will not have to confront any spirit until you are ready to slay it. Neither will you have to confront it alone. You are walking the path of the seven Chohans. This is what we offer you in this book and the coming books, and we have already set you on this path by our first book in this series.

So you see, you are not walking alone. You will not have to face your spirits all alone. You will have one of the Chohans with you. You will have a corresponding Archangel and the Elohim. Thus, you will, if you are willing, have all the guidance, and all the tools, and all the knowledge needed to see through those spirits and slay them one by one.

Yet you cannot even begin this path until you at least acknowledge the one spirit that causes you to direct your attention outside yourself. This is the one requirement. For you see, my beloved, a simple reality here. We of the seven Chohans, and the eighth of myself, we are the true spiritual teachers of humankind. We have been given a task by cosmic hierarchies, and this task is to raise up the lifestreams of earth. But what are we seeking to raise up? We are seeking to raise up what

Jesus referred to, when he told Nicodemus that no man can ascend back to heaven except he that descended from heaven. And what descended from heaven was the Conscious You that state of pure awareness. What you have created since then is a separate self, a separate sense of identity that is made up of many individual spirits.

We, of the Chohans, are not charged with raising those spirits. This is not our job, and we will not compromise our calling. We will not help you to raise up the separate self. So unless you come to the point where you realize that the true goal of the path is to raise up the true self, we cannot even begin to help you. And the one requirement for your realizing this, is that you acknowledge the fact that you are here to raise up yourself to the 96th level. And that requires you to stop focusing on changing anyone or anything outside yourself. Is this not beginning to be clear?

I trust that it is clear for those who are ready. And for those who are not ready, well then, the teacher has really not appeared to you, has it? For you are not seeing me. You are not hearing me. You are not truly acknowledging the message that is streaming forth here.

You are still so identified with one of the separate spirits you have created that you have come to the spiritual path thinking that you would get help to raise and perfect that spirit, until it becomes acceptable to God and will be allowed entry into heaven. But as Jesus said, you will not enter the wedding feast without a wedding garment. And a wedding garment is what you weave up until the 96th level of consciousness and beyond. And that, I can assure you, is a process where there is no cheating.

Validating a spirit

I understand very well that when you look at the world and yourself through the filter of a separate spirit, you think you can get the world to conform. What is it that you are seeking to do, when you are seeking to change the world or change other people? You are seeking to get the world and other people to validate your separate self, your separate spirit. Because you think – or rather, the separate self and the ego thinks – that if the entire world acknowledges the perfection of your spirit, then God must allow it into Heaven. But you see, this is the essential illusion on the path.

When you are so identified with and blinded by this separate spirit, you think this spirit can fool God. You think you can get God and the ascended masters, including the Chohans, to look at life through the perception filter of that spirit, but it will never happen, my beloved. We will never acknowledge your perception filter as reality. Nor will we ever allow this separate spirit entry into the higher realms of our mystery schools and our etheric retreats.

We are not here to raise up the separate spirit. We are not here to raise up the unreal you. We are here to raise up the real you. This is our task. This is our love. We have infinite and unconditional love for the real you.

We also have an infinite and unconditional love for the unreal you, which is why we can see through all of its illusions. And therefore, we will not allow the separate spirits to bring their conditions into the spiritual realm, the realm of unconditionally and infinity.

You see, do you not that this is realty; the reality that I AM? For I AM the Maha Chohan.

16 | INVOKING FREEDOM FROM AGGRESSIVE INTENT

In the name I AM THAT I AM, Jesus Christ, I call to my I AM Presence to flow through the I Will Be Presence that I AM and give this invocation with full power. I call to beloved Elohim Arcturus and Victoria, Archangel Zadkiel and Amethyst, Saint Germain and the Maha Chohan to help me free myself from aggressive intent from within and without. Help me see and surrender all patterns that block my oneness with the Maha Chohan and my oneness with my I AM Presence, including …

[Make personal calls]

Part 1

1. Maha Chohan, help me see that the fallen beings plan to drag as many people as possible into their downward spiral of blaming others.

> Beloved Arcturus, release now the flow,
> of Violet Flame to help all life grow,
> in ever-expanding circles of light,
> it pulses within every atom so bright.

> **Beloved Arcturus, your Violet Flame pure,**
> **is for every ailment the ultimate cure,**
> **against it no darkness could ever endure,**
> **earth's freedom it will forever ensure.**

2. Maha Chohan, help me recognize that I will have to deal with the fallen consciousness on each level, up until the 96th level, and even beyond.

> Beloved Arcturus, thou Elohim Free,
> we open our hearts to your reality,
> we have no attachments to life here on earth,
> we claim a new life in your Flame of Rebirth.

> **Beloved Arcturus, your Violet Flame pure,**
> **is for every ailment the ultimate cure,**
> **against it no darkness could ever endure,**
> **earth's freedom it will forever ensure.**

3. Maha Chohan, help me see that I do not necessarily give the dark forces power by being aware of them. I do give them power if I engage them with fear or seek to battle them, but I also give power to dark forces by ignoring and denying them.

> Beloved Arcturus, be with us alway,
> reborn, we are ready to face a new day,
> expanding our hearts into Infinity,
> your flame is the key to our God-victory.

Beloved Arcturus, your Violet Flame pure,
is for every ailment the ultimate cure,
against it no darkness could ever endure,
earth's freedom it will forever ensure.

4. Maha Chohan, help me see that ignoring something and denying its existence is not a passive measure. It is an active measure because the dark forces are aggressive. They seek to influence anyone on this planet.

Beloved Arcturus, your bright violet fire,
now fills every atom, raising them higher,
the space in each atom all filled with your light,
as matter itself is shining so bright.

Beloved Arcturus, your Violet Flame pure,
is for every ailment the ultimate cure,
against it no darkness could ever endure,
earth's freedom it will forever ensure.

5. Maha Chohan, help me see that I cannot be in existence on this planet without having an aggressive force directed against me. I can ignore or deny this force only by directing a force back that blinds me to what is being directed at me.

Beloved Arcturus, your transforming Grace,
empowers us now every challenge to face,
with your Freedom's Song filling the ear,
we know that to God we're ever so dear.

Beloved Arcturus, your Violet Flame pure,
is for every ailment the ultimate cure,

**against it no darkness could ever endure,
earth's freedom it will forever ensure.**

6. Maha Chohan, help me see that what is coming at me from the fallen beings and the mass consciousness is a wave of energy. The only way to ignore or deny it, is that I am sending energy back.

Beloved Arcturus, we surrender all fear,
we're feeling your Presence so tangibly near,
as your violet light floods our inner space,
towards the ascension we willingly race.

**Beloved Arcturus, your Violet Flame pure,
is for every ailment the ultimate cure,
against it no darkness could ever endure,
earth's freedom it will forever ensure.**

7. Maha Chohan, help me see that my energy will not neutralize the negative energy, it will only neutralize it at the level of my conscious awareness so that I am not aware of it. And therefore, I can ignore or deny the dark forces.

Beloved Arcturus, bring in a new age,
help earth and humanity turn a new page,
your transforming light gives us certainty,
Saint Germain's Golden Age is a reality.

**Beloved Arcturus, your Violet Flame pure,
is for every ailment the ultimate cure,
against it no darkness could ever endure,
earth's freedom it will forever ensure.**

8. Maha Chohan, help me see that they will still influence my subconscious mind. If we are not consciously aware of the dark forces, then we are being influenced by those dark forces.

Beloved Arcturus, illusions you pierce,
no serpent can stand against angels so fierce,
no forces of darkness can stop Violet Flame,
all discord on earth it will instantly tame.

**Beloved Arcturus, your Violet Flame pure,
is for every ailment the ultimate cure,
against it no darkness could ever endure,
earth's freedom it will forever ensure.**

9. Maha Chohan, help me see that once the dark forces have directed me onto a false path, they will either leave me alone or allow me to stay in the illusion that I am doing the right thing.

Beloved Arcturus, we love Saint Germain,
and therefore we call forth again and again,
your Violet Flame to flood all the earth,
so Saint Germain's eyes are filling with mirth.

**Beloved Arcturus, your Violet Flame pure,
is for every ailment the ultimate cure,
against it no darkness could ever endure,
earth's freedom it will forever ensure.**

Part 2

1. Maha Chohan, help me see that many spiritual people think that if they are only kind and loving towards everybody and don't put their attention on anything negative, then they are guaranteed to one day become enlightened.

> Zadkiel Archangel, your flow is so swift,
> in your violet light, we instantly shift,
> into a vibration in which we are free,
> from all limitations of the lesser me.

> **Zadkiel Archangel, encircle the earth,**
> **Zadkiel Archangel, with your violet girth,**
> **Zadkiel Archangel, unstoppable mirth,**
> **Zadkiel Archangel, our planet's rebirth.**

2. Maha Chohan, help me see that this is a lie created by the fallen beings specifically to trap those who are beginning to awaken, but have not yet awakened to the absolute reality that the spiritual path is a conscious path.

> Zadkiel Archangel, we truly aspire,
> to being the master of your violet fire,
> wielding the power, of your alchemy,
> we use Sacred Word, to set all life free.

> **Zadkiel Archangel, encircle the earth,**
> **Zadkiel Archangel, with your violet girth,**
> **Zadkiel Archangel, unstoppable mirth,**
> **Zadkiel Archangel, our planet's rebirth.**

3. Maha Chohan, help me see that I cannot walk the path by being unconscious. I cannot walk it by ignoring or denying anything. I can walk it only by looking at anything and everything.

Zadkiel Archangel, your violet light,
transforming the earth, with unstoppable might,
so swiftly our planet, beginning to spin,
with legions of angels, our victory we win.

Zadkiel Archangel, encircle the earth,
Zadkiel Archangel, with your violet girth,
Zadkiel Archangel, unstoppable mirth,
Zadkiel Archangel, our planet's rebirth.

4. Maha Chohan, help me see that I cannot walk the path without recognizing and acknowledging what kind of planet I am on. This is not an ideal planet. This is one of the lower planets in the material universe.

Zadkiel Archangel, the earth is now free,
from burdens put on her by humanity,
all people are free from their inner strife,
embracing the freedom to start a new life.

Zadkiel Archangel, encircle the earth,
Zadkiel Archangel, with your violet girth,
Zadkiel Archangel, unstoppable mirth,
Zadkiel Archangel, our planet's rebirth.

5. Maha Chohan, help me see that I do not need to be afraid of dark forces or battle them. I need to be aware because only by being aware can I follow the call of Jesus to be wise as serpents and harmless as doves.

Zadkiel Archangel, the earth will now spin,
much faster as we Christ victory win,
for in Christ the captives are truly set free,
bathed in Christ Light the earth now will be.

Zadkiel Archangel, encircle the earth,
Zadkiel Archangel, with your violet girth,
Zadkiel Archangel, unstoppable mirth,
Zadkiel Archangel, our planet's rebirth.

6. Maha Chohan, help me see that I cannot be harmless as a dove unless I am wise as a serpent, wise to the serpents and their attempts to direct me into a blind alley that does not lead to self-transcendence.

Zadkiel Archangel, the forces of night,
are bound by your penetrating Freedom Light,
the earth is now cleared from forces so dark,
as your Violet Light provides a new spark.

Zadkiel Archangel, encircle the earth,
Zadkiel Archangel, with your violet girth,
Zadkiel Archangel, unstoppable mirth,
Zadkiel Archangel, our planet's rebirth.

7. Maha Chohan, help me see that the fallen beings attack any lifestream on earth with an aggressive force. Physical force if possible, but also through psychic means in my emotional, mental and identity body.

Zadkiel Archangel, we truly love you,
and to Saint Germain we will always be true,

help us now see our plans so Divine,
so we on this planet our full light can shine.

**Zadkiel Archangel, encircle the earth,
Zadkiel Archangel, with your violet girth,
Zadkiel Archangel, unstoppable mirth,
Zadkiel Archangel, our planet's rebirth.**

8. Maha Chohan, help me see that the purpose of this attack is not to destroy me. It is to draw me into reacting to the attack. They want to draw me into an action-reaction game, where I am exposed to an action from them and then I react.

Zadkiel Archangel, there is no more night,
a new day is born from your great Violet Light,
transforming all manifestations of fear,
we know that the Golden Age is now here.

**Zadkiel Archangel, encircle the earth,
Zadkiel Archangel, with your violet girth,
Zadkiel Archangel, unstoppable mirth,
Zadkiel Archangel, our planet's rebirth.**

9. Maha Chohan, help me see that pretty soon I am so far into this downward spiral that I have forgotten my spiritual goals and have gone below the 48th level of consciousness into this aggressive state of mind, constantly feeling under attack and feeling in need to defend myself.

Zadkiel Archangel, your violet flame,
the earth and humanity, never the same,
Saint Germain's Golden Age, is a reality,
what glorious wonder, we joyously see.

Zadkiel Archangel, encircle the earth,
Zadkiel Archangel, with your violet girth,
Zadkiel Archangel, unstoppable mirth,
Zadkiel Archangel, our planet's rebirth.

Part 3

1. Maha Chohan, help me see that their second plan is to make me feel comfortable, feeling that I am spiritual or religious, and then they want to keep me there indefinitely.

Saint Germain, your alchemy,
with violet fire now sets us free.
Saint Germain, we ever grow,
in freedom's overpowering flow.

O Saint Germain, your Golden Age,
sets people free from psychic cage,
the earth is raised to starry height,
as we project with Freedom's Sight.

2. Maha Chohan, help me see that the Holy Spirit, the true path, is the River of Life, which is constantly, perpetually transcending itself.

Saint Germain, your mastery,
of violet flame geometry.
Saint Germain, in you we see,
the formulas that set us free.

**O Saint Germain, your Golden Age,
sets people free from psychic cage,
the earth is raised to starry height,
as we project with Freedom's Sight.**

3. Maha Chohan, help me see that if I am standing still at a certain level, I may feel saved and spiritual, but I am not growing, I am stuck in the material world. If they cannot get me to go down, they will at least want me to be stuck.

Saint Germain, in Liberty,
you give the love that sets all free.
Saint Germain, we do adore,
the violet flame that makes all more.

**O Saint Germain, your Golden Age,
sets people free from psychic cage,
the earth is raised to starry height,
as we project with Freedom's Sight.**

4. Maha Chohan, help me see that the fallen beings attack me with an aggressive force, and that force is a spirit. The fallen beings have created a spirit that attacks me.

Saint Germain, in unity,
we will transcend duality.
Saint Germain, the self so pure,
your violet chemistry so sure.

**O Saint Germain, your Golden Age,
sets people free from psychic cage,
the earth is raised to starry height,
as we project with Freedom's Sight.**

5. Maha Chohan, help me see that when I react to this attack, I also create a spirit. I create my own personal spirit, and for each step I go below the 48th level, I am creating a new spirit.

> Saint Germain, reality,
> in violet light we are carefree.
> Saint Germain, our auras seal,
> your violet flame our chakras heal.

> **O Saint Germain, your Golden Age,**
> **sets people free from psychic cage,**
> **the earth is raised to starry height,**
> **as we project with Freedom's Sight.**

6. Maha Chohan, help me see that in order to climb back to higher levels, I must go through the journey of confronting the spirits I have created and slaying them.

> Saint Germain, your chemistry,
> with violet fire set atoms free.
> Saint Germain, from lead to gold,
> transforming vision we behold.

> **O Saint Germain, your Golden Age,**
> **sets people free from psychic cage,**
> **the earth is raised to starry height,**
> **as we project with Freedom's Sight.**

7. Maha Chohan, help me see that the journey home to contact with my I AM Presence requires me to meet, confront and overcome each of the spirits I have personally created.

Saint Germain, transcendency,
as we are always one with thee.
Saint Germain, from soul we're free,
we so delight in knowing thee.

O Saint Germain, your Golden Age,
sets people free from psychic cage,
the earth is raised to starry height,
as we project with Freedom's Sight.

8. Maha Chohan, help me see that when I feel I am being opposed by the dark spirits created by the fallen beings, this is only the spirits that I have created. For only a separate spirit can feel opposed by other separate spirits.

Saint Germain, nobility,
the key to sacred alchemy.
Saint Germain, you balance all,
the seven rays upon our call.

O Saint Germain, your Golden Age,
sets people free from psychic cage,
the earth is raised to starry height,
as we project with Freedom's Sight.

9. Maha Chohan, help me see that the One Spirit, the undivided Spirit, the indivisible Spirit, the Holy Spirit, does not feel opposed by separate spirits. It knows it is beyond their reach because it simply transcends itself, so that it becomes transparent to the force that is directed towards it.

Saint Germain, your Presence here,
filling up the inner sphere.

Life is now a sacred flow,
God Freedom we on all bestow.

O Saint Germain, your Golden Age,
sets people free from psychic cage,
the earth is raised to starry height,
as we project with Freedom's Sight.

Part 4

1. Maha Chohan, help me see that before I can rise beyond the 48th level, I must slay the spirits I have created beneath that level.

Maha Chohan, I will to grow,
I feel the power of your flow.
Maha Chohan, the veil is rent,
creative will from heaven sent.

O Holy Spirit, flow through me,
I am the open door for thee.
O mighty rushing stream of Light,
transcendence is my sacred right.

2. Maha Chohan, help me see that beyond the individual spirits, there is one spirit I need to slay, and that is the spirit of feeling threatened, therefore having a need to project into the minds of other people and change them instead of changing myself.

Maha Chohan, your wisdom streams,
awaken all from matter's dreams.
Maha Chohan, your balance bring,
let bells of integration ring.

O Holy Spirit, flow through me,
I am the open door for thee.
O mighty rushing stream of Light,
transcendence is my sacred right.

3. Maha Chohan, help me see that before I reach the 96th level, I am climbing the path as an individual being. I need to be completely focused on changing myself and not seeking to change anyone else.

Maha Chohan, love's mighty call,
the prison walls are shattered all.
Maha Chohan, set all life free
through unconditionality.

O Holy Spirit, flow through me,
I am the open door for thee.
O mighty rushing stream of Light,
transcendence is my sacred right.

4. Maha Chohan, help me go beyond being concerned about the splinter in the eye of my brother, for I am focusing all of my attention on the beam in my own eye.

Maha Chohan, intentions pure,
all life is one, I know for sure.
Maha Chohan, I am awake,
surrender all for oneness' sake.

**O Holy Spirit, flow through me,
I am the open door for thee.
O mighty rushing stream of Light,
transcendence is my sacred right.**

5. Maha Chohan, help me see that below the 48th level we start creating aggressive spirits that are aimed at controlling the minds of other people. We justify this by some greater cause and not out of selfish reasons.

Maha Chohan, help all men see,
through veils of unreality.
Maha Chohan, with single eye,
I know I am the greater "I."

**O Holy Spirit, flow through me,
I am the open door for thee.
O mighty rushing stream of Light,
transcendence is my sacred right.**

6. Maha Chohan, I want to make it to the 96th level of consciousness, I want to follow the true spiritual path, I want to qualify for initiation under the seven Chohans, and I will stop focusing on changing other people or the world!

Maha Chohan, your peace I find,
Maitreya shows me to be kind.
Maha Chohan, all war will cease,
now flooding all with sacred peace.

**O Holy Spirit, flow through me,
I am the open door for thee.**

**O mighty rushing stream of Light,
transcendence is my sacred right.**

7. Maha Chohan, I will withdraw all attention from seeking to change anything outside myself. I will focus all attention on changing my own state of consciousness, slaying the spirits I have created and embodying the positive lessons of the seven rays, so that I build the individual self.

Maha Chohan, you balance all,
the seven rays upon my call.
Maha Chohan, all life is free,
transcending for eternity.

**O Holy Spirit, flow through me,
I am the open door for thee.
O mighty rushing stream of Light,
transcendence is my sacred right.**

8. Maha Chohan, help me see that the next step on my personal path is to lock in to the initiations under the seven Chohans. I will not delude myself into thinking I am beyond being initiated by the seven Chohans.

Maha Chohan, your sacred Flame,
what beauty in your blessed name.
Maha Chohan, what rushing flow,
the Spirit one with life below.

**O Holy Spirit, flow through me,
I am the open door for thee.
O mighty rushing stream of Light,
transcendence is my sacred right.**

9. Maha Chohan, I will be humble, realistic and honest enough to start at the beginning, to start with the Chohan of the First Ray, and work my way up, so that I do not skip steps and leave any spirits lingering in the subconscious.

Maha Chohan, your Presence here,
filling up the inner sphere.
Life is now a sacred flow,
God Wisdom we on all bestow.

O Holy Spirit, flow through me,
I am the open door for thee.
O mighty rushing stream of Light,
transcendence is my sacred right.

Part 5

1. Maha Chohan, help me see that if I ignore or deny the existence of dark spirits, there will still be energy directed into my subconscious mind. Whatever the spirits are there, they will grow in the hiding places that are maintained by my unwillingness to look at myself.

Saint Germain, your alchemy,
with violet fire now sets us free.
Saint Germain, we ever grow,
in freedom's overpowering flow.

O Saint Germain, your Golden Age,
sets people free from psychic cage,

**the earth is raised to starry height,
as we project with Freedom's Sight.**

2. Maha Chohan, help me see that being unwilling to look at my own consciousness, to look into my subconscious mind, is the surest way to feed the spirits that are there.

Saint Germain, your mastery,
of violet flame geometry.
Saint Germain, in you we see,
the formulas that set us free.

**O Saint Germain, your Golden Age,
sets people free from psychic cage,
the earth is raised to starry height,
as we project with Freedom's Sight.**

3. Maha Chohan, I hereby decide to abandon my willful ignorance and shine the light of my I AM Presence, the light of the seven rays, into the caves of the subconscious mind, flushing out those spirits into the open so that I can see them. And then, with the guidance of the seven Chohans, I will slay them one by one.

Saint Germain, in Liberty,
you give the love that sets all free.
Saint Germain, we do adore,
the violet flame that makes all more.

**O Saint Germain, your Golden Age,
sets people free from psychic cage,
the earth is raised to starry height,
as we project with Freedom's Sight.**

4. Maha Chohan, help me see that I do not need to fear this, for I will not have to confront them all at once, and I will not have to confront any spirit until I am ready to slay it. Neither will I have to confront it alone.

> Saint Germain, in unity,
> we will transcend duality.
> Saint Germain, the self so pure,
> your violet chemistry so sure.

> **O Saint Germain, your Golden Age,**
> **sets people free from psychic cage,**
> **the earth is raised to starry height,**
> **as we project with Freedom's Sight.**

5. Maha Chohan, help me see that I will not have to face my spirits all alone. I will have one of the Chohans with me. I will have the corresponding Archangel and the Elohim. I will have all the guidance, all the tools and all the knowledge needed to see through those spirits and slay them one by one.

> Saint Germain, reality,
> in violet light we are carefree.
> Saint Germain, our auras seal,
> your violet flame our chakras heal.

> **O Saint Germain, your Golden Age,**
> **sets people free from psychic cage,**
> **the earth is raised to starry height,**
> **as we project with Freedom's Sight.**

6. Maha Chohan, I acknowledge the one spirit that causes me to direct my attention outside myself.

Saint Germain, your chemistry,
with violet fire set atoms free.
Saint Germain, from lead to gold,
transforming vision we behold.

**O Saint Germain, your Golden Age,
sets people free from psychic cage,
the earth is raised to starry height,
as we project with Freedom's Sight.**

7. Maha Chohan, help me see that what descended from heaven was the Conscious You, the state of pure awareness. What I have created since then is a separate self, a separate sense of identity, that is made up of many individual spirits.

Saint Germain, transcendency,
as we are always one with thee.
Saint Germain, from soul we're free,
we so delight in knowing thee.

**O Saint Germain, your Golden Age,
sets people free from psychic cage,
the earth is raised to starry height,
as we project with Freedom's Sight.**

8. Maha Chohan, help me see that the Chohans are not charged with raising those spirits. You will not help me raise up the separate self. I realize that the true goal of the path is to raise up the true self.

Saint Germain, nobility,
the key to sacred alchemy.

> Saint Germain, you balance all,
> the seven rays upon our call.

> **O Saint Germain, your Golden Age,**
> **sets people free from psychic cage,**
> **the earth is raised to starry height,**
> **as we project with Freedom's Sight.**

9. Maha Chohan, I acknowledge the fact, that I am here to raise up myself to the 96th level. I therefore stop focusing on changing anyone or anything outside myself.

> Saint Germain, your Presence here,
> filling up the inner sphere.
> Life is now a sacred flow,
> God Freedom we on all bestow.

> **O Saint Germain, your Golden Age,**
> **sets people free from psychic cage,**
> **the earth is raised to starry height,**
> **as we project with Freedom's Sight.**

Part 6

1. Maha Chohan, help me see that when I look at the world and myself through the filter of a separate spirit, I think I can get the world to conform.

> Maha Chohan, I will to grow,
> I feel the power of your flow.

Maha Chohan, the veil is rent,
creative will from heaven sent.

**O Holy Spirit, flow through me,
I am the open door for thee.
O mighty rushing stream of Light,
transcendence is my sacred right.**

2. Maha Chohan, help me see that when I am seeking to change the world or other people, I am seeking to get the world and other people to validate my separate self, my separate spirit.

Maha Chohan, your wisdom streams,
awaken all from matter's dreams.
Maha Chohan, your balance bring,
let bells of integration ring.

**O Holy Spirit, flow through me,
I am the open door for thee.
O mighty rushing stream of Light,
transcendence is my sacred right.**

3. Maha Chohan, help me see that the separate self and the ego thinks that if the entire world acknowledges the perfection of my spirit, then God must allow it into Heaven. This is the essential illusion on the path.

Maha Chohan, love's mighty call,
the prison walls are shattered all.
Maha Chohan, set all life free
through unconditionality.

O Holy Spirit, flow through me,
I am the open door for thee.
O mighty rushing stream of Light,
transcendence is my sacred right.

4. Maha Chohan, help me see that when I am so identified with and blinded by this separate spirit, I think this spirit can fool God.

Maha Chohan, intentions pure,
all life is one, I know for sure.
Maha Chohan, I am awake,
surrender all for oneness' sake.

O Holy Spirit, flow through me,
I am the open door for thee.
O mighty rushing stream of Light,
transcendence is my sacred right.

5. Maha Chohan, help me see that I think I can get God and the ascended masters, including the Chohans, to look at life through the perception filter of that spirit, but it will never happen.

Maha Chohan, help all men see,
through veils of unreality.
Maha Chohan, with single eye,
I know I am the greater "I."

O Holy Spirit, flow through me,
I am the open door for thee.
O mighty rushing stream of Light,
transcendence is my sacred right.

6. Maha Chohan, help me see that you will never acknowledge my perception filter as reality. Nor will you ever allow this separate spirit entry into the higher realms of your mystery schools and etheric retreats.

> Maha Chohan, your peace I find,
> Maitreya shows me to be kind.
> Maha Chohan, all war will cease,
> now flooding all with sacred peace.

> **O Holy Spirit, flow through me,**
> **I am the open door for thee.**
> **O mighty rushing stream of Light,**
> **transcendence is my sacred right.**

7. Maha Chohan, help me see that you are not here to raise up the separate spirit. You are not here to raise up the unreal me.

> Maha Chohan, you balance all,
> the seven rays upon my call.
> Maha Chohan, all life is free,
> transcending for eternity.

> **O Holy Spirit, flow through me,**
> **I am the open door for thee.**
> **O mighty rushing stream of Light,**
> **transcendence is my sacred right.**

8. Maha Chohan, help me see that you are here to raise up the real me. This is your task. This is your love. You have infinite and unconditional love for the real me.

Maha Chohan, your sacred Flame,
what beauty in your blessed name.
Maha Chohan, what rushing flow,
the Spirit one with life below.

**O Holy Spirit, flow through me,
I am the open door for thee.
O mighty rushing stream of Light,
transcendence is my sacred right.**

9. Maha Chohan, help me see that you also have an infinite and unconditional love for the unreal me, which is why you can see through all of its illusions. Therefore, you will not allow the separate spirits to bring their conditions into the spiritual realm, the realm of unconditionally and infinity.

Maha Chohan, your Presence here,
filling up the inner sphere.
Life is now a sacred flow,
God Wisdom we on all bestow.

**O Holy Spirit, flow through me,
I am the open door for thee.
O mighty rushing stream of Light,
transcendence is my sacred right.**

Sealing:

In the name of the Divine Mother, I fully accept that the power of these calls is used to set free the Ma-ter light, so it can outpicture the perfect vision of Christ for my own life, for all people and for the planet. In the name I AM THAT I AM, it is done! Amen.

17 | ONGOING SELF-MASTERY

The Maha Chohan I AM. And I come to give you another hint that will assist you in navigating the spiral staircase of the seven rays under the seven Chohans.

I have already talked about the fact that you are facing the journey whereby you confront and transcend the spirits you have created, or that have been created in the collective consciousness through humankind's misuse of the seven rays. Thus, what I wish to bring to your attention today is two things: First of all, I want to reinforce what I have said earlier about the very nature of the Holy Spirit, which is that it is always flowing; it is a stream. It is not a static spirit. It is an ever-flowing, ever-self-transcending Spirit that never remains the same for even a split second.

The second thing is the need to keep in mind that you are overcoming these separate spirits. And as I have said before, this will for some mean that they build a new self, a new spirit. And there is no way around this between the 48th and the 96th level of consciousness, for this is indeed your charge: to experiment with your co-creative abilities, to experiment with the seven rays, and to build a self that has some mastery of the seven rays. Nevertheless, what I would like you to keep in mind is that you are not building a self that is static. You are building a self that can flow with the Holy Spirit, the *Holy* Spirit.

Perfecting a spirit

You see, the false teachers on this earth have attempted to come up with many clever schemes for how to cause those who are the sincere spiritual seekers – those who have risen above the 48th level, those who have not gone into duality – how they can cause those to go into a blind alley that will stop their growth or even cause it to keep going down further and further into separation. And one of the main schemes they have come up with is these many subtle variations that you can create a separate self, a spirit that can actually gain entry into the spiritual realm.

You will see, when you think about this in light of what I have taught you in the previous discourses that this is, of course, the ultimate dream of the ego, of the fallen beings, and of the separate spirits. A separate spirit is by definition mortal, but it dreams of immortality. It dreams of living up to some condition whereby it becomes acceptable to God and therefore gains entry into the wedding feast with Christ.

But as Jesus said, "No man can ascend to heaven, save he who descended from heaven." The only being who can ascend to heaven is the Conscious You, and it can do so only when it sheds all of the snake skins of the separate spirits, those false serpentine spirits that slither along the ground with their subtle serpentine logic, making you think that you will become as a god who can enter heaven. Thus, you can see that the Greek gods on Mount Olympus were obviously not very high beings, given the infighting and the schemes that they came up with. This is indeed a symbol for how the fallen beings have attempted to create separate selves that they think will gain immortality. Yet nothing can enter Heaven except what came out of Heaven, which is pure awareness. So you will never be able to take these separate spirits with you, no matter how perfect they may be according to some earthly standard or another.

The false view of perfection

Do you see the problem with the separate spirit? A separate spirit may indeed grow for a time. Think about this very carefully. A separate spirit may indeed be designed to grow and to expand and to, in a sense, perfect itself. Therefore, it is perfectly possible that you come into a religion or a spiritual teaching, and now you create an ideal in your mind that if you keep applying the teaching, you will at some point have reached a state of perfection – some ultimate state – and then you will be allowed entry into heaven. Or you will reach enlightenment, or whatever the goal is defined as being.

But you see, you will not be saved, you will not be enlightened, you will not ascend, by building a stationary, perfect self. Perfection in Heaven is not the same as what most human beings see as perfection. For human beings tend to see perfection as static. For if something is perfect, well, how can it possibly improve? If it is possible to improve it, then it could not be perfect—so reasons the serpentine mind.

Yet we, who have freed ourselves from the serpentine mind, know that true perfection is flowing with the Spirit. The only ultimate state is the self-awareness at the Creator level, but you will not reach that while you are in embodiment on earth. Nor will you reach it until you have gone through the initiations of all of the spheres that are above the one in which you live right now. And so, this is not something you need to be concerned about right now; reaching the level of the Creator consciousness. For even the Creator consciousness, of course, does not stand still. For if it did stand still, why would it create the world of form out of its own Being?

You see, there is no standing still. Perfection is constant self-transcendence. This is the true definition of perfection. This is why the Holy Spirit is perfect. It does not have a goal of reaching some ultimate static state. It has a goal of continuing to transcend itself indefinitely. So it never seeks to hold on to the old, for it is always willing to shed the snake skin of the old and transcend into a new state.

This then, is what I admonish you to ponder. For there is a very fundamental difference between walking the Path of the Seven Rays with the goal that you are creating some perfect self according to a static definition of perfection, and then having the goal that you are creating a flexible self that can constantly and easily flow with the Holy Spirit in ongoing self-transcendence beyond the 96th level.

Holding on to the separate self

I have earlier talked about the death consciousness, and how there are those who come to the 96th level and will not give up the self they have created. They think they will die if they give it up, having become so identified with it. But you see, this is because they have had it as their goal to create this static self that lives up to some standard of perfection. And then, when they realize that this self they have created cannot enter Heaven – but must be allowed to die, so that they can transcend to the point where they can enter Heaven as pure awareness – well, then they become resentful.

They want to hold on to the separate self and go out and exercise power through that separate self. And that is when they begin to want to dominate others by the power they have attained on the seven rays. And this, of course, is the pride that goes before the fall. And the fall is immediate; it is instant.

So ponder this very carefully. It is necessary, as you walk the Path of the Seven Rays, to have a goal. But do not allow the false teachers of earth to trick you into defining a static goal, based on some standard that they have set up. A standard that they have designed and defined based on the consciousness of separation and the consciousness of duality that compares everything through a value judgment.

If you are striving to walk the Path of the Seven Rays in order to become better than others based on some dualistic value judgment, you will only make it harder for yourself. You may actually have a great drive to walk the path, as some students do. You may be willing to make many sacrifices in order to obtain that sense of superiority. But when it comes time to give up that self that you have created, then you are faced with the full force of the death consciousness. Because what do you now face? You face the very fact that in the collective consciousness is created this enormous conglomerate of these separate spirits, and they all do not want to die.

And so, if you have created a separate spirit as you walk the Path of the Seven Rays, you will tie in to this fear of death. And therefore, you will have to overcome the entire momentum of death in order to give up this separate self. This is, of course, possible, for when you know you are pure awareness you can give up any self, but I tell you it is very rare that students are able to do this. Far better off are those students who gave up the separate self and who learned to give up the separate self at each level of the path. So that when they come up to the 96th level, they are not faced with the entire planetary momentum of death, but only the momentum at that particular level. So again, it becomes a much smaller step, and they just effortlessly flow into it.

And they keep flowing from the 96th to the 97th to the 98th and beyond, until they are suddenly at the 144th level. And again, it is no big change to give up that self that last ghost, at the 144th level, so that you can effortlessly flow into the ascension spiral, and through the pearly gate into the ascended state. You see, it is far more difficult to give up everything all at once. It is much easier to give up a little piece at a time.

The constant fear of being wrong

And so, I wish you Godspeed on the path under the seven Chohans. I hope I have helped you set a foundation that will make it easier for you to walk this path. Truly, it is only the separate self that evaluates based on a scale of right and wrong. Do you understand that when you create a separate self out of the duality consciousness, you create a self that believes that it can only become acceptable to God by living up to a standard of perfection and by never being wrong according to that standard? Which means that this separate self lives in a constant fear of being wrong.

Do you know that there are lifestreams that come to the point where they have turned around, they do have a desire to come up higher, and they do cry out for a true teacher? Yet, when they are met by the first of the Chohans, Master MORE – or El Morya, as he has been known in the past – then they simply cannot follow his instruction. They cannot even truly see Master MORE. So they must superimpose some kind of image upon him where they often see him as a very district disciplinarian. And so, they are so afraid that this strict master with a penetrating gaze will prove them wrong that instead of embracing his teaching and his help, they seek to hide from him.

So what have we done in the past? We have given them an outer teacher, even an outer organization whereby people could maintain the belief that they were students of El Morya, but in reality they never saw the real Morya, the real MORE, for they could see him only as a fixed image. They could not see how much more he is than any fixed image that can be created by the lower consciousness.

You see, Master MORE does not judge you based on a scale of right and wrong. Master MORE has no desire to prove you wrong. Nor does he have a desire to see you prove yourself right. Master MORE, as all of the Chohans, is concerned with only one thing: that you are willing to transcend your present level of consciousness, to transcend your present sense of self, to let your present spirit die and flow into another, higher sense of self.

A dangerous level of the path

The separate spirit is created out of this standard, this dualistic standard. It has within it, within its very design, this division between right and wrong. It believes that if it is proven wrong, something terrible will happen. But if it is proven right, something good should happen. Therefore, it believes that it can even force God to accept it by proving itself right. And it seeks to prove itself right in the only way it can: by comparing itself to others based on the standard out of which is was created. So it seeks to prove itself right by proving others wrong, by putting others down. Basically, the hidden subconscious reasoning of the separate spirit is that, "If I can prove all other spirits wrong, then I must be right and God must accept *me*." But it is, of course, not so. So, do not approach the Chohans with the desire to prove yourself right. And be especially alert for the desire to prove others wrong.

But I tell you this: there is a lower point on the path where people are mostly focused on proving other people wrong and are always battling with other people. While this certainly is a lower point on the path and cannot bring you into the ascended state – cannot bring you beyond the 96th level, and cannot even, really, bring you towards the 96th level for it cannot take you that far beyond the 48th level – then it is not really the most dangerous level of the path. The most dangerous level is where you approach the 96th level, but you are still trapped in the desire to prove yourself right according to some standard.

I tell you, truly, if you look at those who are below the 48th level of consciousness, you will see that those who are at the lowest levels are not actually the ones who are, what we might say from a certain perspective, the most primitive people. They are actually the ones who are the most sophisticated, for they are the ones who are the most convinced that they are right that their standard is right.

And so, you see also that there are students who go above the 48th level and start approaching the 96th level, but they start identifying with the separate self they have created, to the point where they believe that this separate self is now right according to the standard that they have not yet given up that they have not yet seen through. And these students are the hardest to reach.

They are often the most eager students, the ones who are willing to sacrifice and work hard in order to climb to the next level. And you can, to some degree, do this between the 48th and the 96th level, for it is the level where you are seeking to attain mastery on the seven rays. And in so doing, you create that separate self that separate spirit, or at least the individual spirit, the individual self.

How a false standard is created

The students that are the hardest to reach for the Chohans, are the ones who build this unrecognized sense of pride because they think they are right. And they have not been willing to come to one of the most important insights that you come to on the path, namely that there is no standard defined on earth that can take you to heaven. For these dualistic, separate standards cannot exist in heaven.

And therefore, you are not proving yourself right in the eyes of the Chohans, for they are not in the dualistic state of consciousness. You are only proving yourself right in the eyes of the separate spirit you have created – the spirit that is based on your particular standard. Therefore, this spirit can never see anything beyond the standard. It can never see anything wrong with the standard. It can never see any of the limitations of the standard. It can never see that the standard is created by excluding certain elements of the greater picture of reality.

Let me compare this to an image with which you are familiar. You know a compass, and you know that if you are standing in the center of a compass, you can divide the circumference of the compass into 360 degrees, as you divide the circle into 360 degrees. And so, when you stand in the center of your personal compass – and you are able to see all of the 360 degrees without being particularly focused on any one of them, or without having the need to exclude any one of them – then you have reached enlightenment, then you are ready to ascend.

But you see, what happens to all of these lesser spirits is that they define a standard. And how do they define a standard? By excluding, by blocking out, some of the degrees—by labeling them as untrue, false, or evil in some way. And therefore, they create a standard that is based on excluding one or many of the 360 degrees of the circumference of what is possible to see on earth.

And when you define certain angles, certain degrees, as wrong, and therefore will not look at them, you will, by definition, have a limited, a selective, a subjective and a very biased and incomplete view of life. But beyond this, you will always be able to prove your separate self – your separate spirit – right. For you see, when you accept the very definition that certain degrees should not be looked at or are wrong, then of course you will not be able to see that the spirit, the perception filter through which you are looking at reality, is incomplete and only gives you a limited and distorted view of the totality of life.

Proving yourself "right"

Can you see that, if you are willing to exclude certain degrees on the circumference of the circle of life, then you can always prove that the self that can only encompass the remaining degrees is right? But can you also begin to see that until you can see the entire circumference of the consciousness that is possible on earth, you are not enlightened, and you are not ready for the ascension?

And how do you come to see the entire circumference? By realizing that you are the Conscious You that there is no individuality anchored in the Conscious You which makes it necessary to exclude certain degrees. And therefore, you are pure awareness. And as pure awareness, you can look at anything and everything. There is nothing you need to exclude. There is nothing you need to judge.

And when you are willing to look at any thing, then there is no thing that has power over you. For of course, when you define something as being wrong or refuse to look at it, then that which you will not look at has power over you. It defines you, for you think that if you somehow looked at it, or if you fulfilled those characteristics, you would be wrong in an ultimate sense.

So the only way to overcome the fear of being wrong is to look at exactly what is at the bottom of that fear, and realize this is just another degree on the circumference of the compass of life. And therefore, instead of focusing on a certain standard, you allow the compass needle to swing freely.

But do you not see that if you take the compass and you block out certain sections on the circumference, then the compass needle cannot rotate? And so, what are you then doing? You are actually preventing the Conscious You from doing what is its highest potential. For the highest potential of the Conscious You is to be the compass needle that always points North. It always points to the true pole star of the I AM Presence.

How else will you be like Odysseus, who navigated the treacherous waters, but still managed to find his way home? What was he doing? He was going to those points on his personal compass where he had blocked out certain degrees on the circumference. He was slaying those beasts, those spirits, those mythological creatures, and therefore he opened up the circumference, so that the compass needle could swing more freely. And when he had cleared the entire circumference, the compass needle could rotate the entire circle. And thus, after having rotated for a while, it naturally found its ideal state where it pointed directly to the North.

Using a false compass

And then, when you have a true compass that actually points North, it is not so difficult to find your way home. But when you have a false compass where the needle cannot rotate freely and thus cannot point North, how can you avoid being lost at sea? For do you not see, my beloved that when you have blockages on the circumference of the compass, the needle can only rotate so far? And then you think that because the needle has now stopped, it must be pointing North. And then you navigate based on this direction; you chart the course of your life based on this direction. But if the needle was not pointing North to begin with, how can you set a right course?

And so, what will you be moving towards? Not the pole star of being, not the pole star of your I AM Presence. You will be moving towards the very sections that you have blocked out and have refused to see. And therefore, you will be moving towards the separate spirits you have created that lie in wait to try to entrap you, like the sirens with their beguiling song. And soon you will be shipwrecked on the cliffs.

And after you have been shipwrecked enough times, you may finally come to that point where you are willing to recognize that perhaps there was something you did not see, perhaps there was something wrong with your standard—not will all these other people who did not live up to their standard.

For my point is that we of the Chohans do not want you to go on this wild journey where you only learn by being shipwrecked again and again. We want to offer you a smoother path where we direct you to what you need to look at on the circumference of your personal compass. But we help you see it ahead of time, so that you do not need to be shipwrecked on the cliffs, but can see through the initiation.

And thus, instead of your path being this abrupt journey of going from crises to crises, from shipwreck to shipwreck, your path becomes a smooth upward spiral. You ascend the spiral staircase by taking small steps at a time, and you never need to fall back down several steps and crash. Instead, you can keep going in a steady, upward movement.

This is the vision we hold for you, when you come to us and decide you are willing to enroll yourself, not in the School of Hard Knocks, but the School of the Seven Veils, the seven rays, the seven Chohans. Which of course is overseen by me, the eight Chohan, the Maha Chohan that I AM.

18 | INVOKING ONGOING SELF-MASTERY

In the name I AM THAT I AM, Jesus Christ, I call to my I AM Presence to flow through the I Will Be Presence that I AM and give this invocation with full power. I call to Jesus, Maitreya, Gautama Buddha, Sanat Kumara and the Maha Chohan to help me never stop at any point but to continue seeking self-mastery at higher levels. Help me see and surrender all patterns that block my oneness with the Maha Chohan and my oneness with my I AM Presence, including ...

[Make personal calls]

Part 1

1. Maha Chohan, help me see that the nature of the Holy Spirit is that it is always flowing. It is not a static spirit. It is an ever-self-transcending Spirit that never remains the same for even a split second.

Maha Chohan, I will to grow,
I feel the power of your flow.
Maha Chohan, the veil is rent,
creative will from heaven sent.

**O Holy Spirit, flow through me,
I am the open door for thee.
O mighty rushing stream of Light,
transcendence is my sacred right.**

2. Maha Chohan, help me see that between the 48th and the 96th level of consciousness, it is my task to experiment with my co-creative abilities and to build a self that has some mastery of the seven rays.

Maha Chohan, your wisdom streams,
awaken all from matter's dreams.
Maha Chohan, your balance bring,
let bells of integration ring.

**O Holy Spirit, flow through me,
I am the open door for thee.
O mighty rushing stream of Light,
transcendence is my sacred right.**

3. Maha Chohan, help me see that I am not building a self that is static. I am building a self that can flow with the *Holy* Spirit.

Maha Chohan, love's mighty call,
the prison walls are shattered all.
Maha Chohan, set all life free
through unconditionality.

O Holy Spirit, flow through me,
I am the open door for thee.
O mighty rushing stream of Light,
transcendence is my sacred right.

4. Maha Chohan, help me see that the false teachers want me
to go into a blind alley that will stop my growth or even cause
it to go down into separation.

Maha Chohan, intentions pure,
all life is one, I know for sure.
Maha Chohan, I am awake,
surrender all for oneness' sake.

O Holy Spirit, flow through me,
I am the open door for thee.
O mighty rushing stream of Light,
transcendence is my sacred right.

5. Maha Chohan, help me see that one of their main schemes
is the lie that I can create a separate self, a spirit, that can gain
entry into the spiritual realm.

Maha Chohan, help all men see,
through veils of unreality.
Maha Chohan, with single eye,
I know I am the greater "I."

O Holy Spirit, flow through me,
I am the open door for thee.
O mighty rushing stream of Light,
transcendence is my sacred right.

6. Maha Chohan, help me see that this is the ultimate dream of the ego, of the fallen beings and of the separate spirits.

> Maha Chohan, your peace I find,
> Maitreya shows me to be kind.
> Maha Chohan, all war will cease,
> now flooding all with sacred peace.

> **O Holy Spirit, flow through me,**
> **I am the open door for thee.**
> **O mighty rushing stream of Light,**
> **transcendence is my sacred right.**

7. Maha Chohan, help me see that a separate spirit is by definition mortal, but it dreams of immortality. It dreams of living up to some condition, whereby it becomes acceptable to God and therefore gains entry into the wedding feast with Christ.

> Maha Chohan, you balance all,
> the seven rays upon my call.
> Maha Chohan, all life is free,
> transcending for eternity.

> **O Holy Spirit, flow through me,**
> **I am the open door for thee.**
> **O mighty rushing stream of Light,**
> **transcendence is my sacred right.**

8. Maha Chohan, help me see that the only being who can ascend to heaven is the Conscious You, and it can do so only when it sheds all of the snake skins of the separate spirits, those false serpentine spirits making me think that I will become as a god who can enter heaven.

Maha Chohan, your sacred Flame,
what beauty in your blessed name.
Maha Chohan, what rushing flow,
the Spirit one with life below.

**O Holy Spirit, flow through me,
I am the open door for thee.
O mighty rushing stream of Light,
transcendence is my sacred right.**

9. Maha Chohan, help me see that the fallen beings have attempted to create separate selves that they think will gain immortality. Yet nothing can enter Heaven except what came out of Heaven, which is pure awareness.

Maha Chohan, your Presence here,
filling up the inner sphere.
Life is now a sacred flow,
God Wisdom we on all bestow.

**O Holy Spirit, flow through me,
I am the open door for thee.
O mighty rushing stream of Light,
transcendence is my sacred right.**

Part 2

1. Maha Chohan, help me see that I will never be able to take these separate spirits with me, no matter how perfect they may be according to some earthly standard. Yet a separate spirit may be designed to grow and to perfect itself.

O Jesus, blessed brother mine,
I walk the path that you outline,
a great example to us all,
I follow now your inner call.

O Jesus, let the Fire of Joy,
consume the devil's subtle ploy,
transfigured is our planet earth,
the golden age is given birth.

2. Maha Chohan, help me see that it is possible to come into a spiritual teaching and create an ideal that if I keep applying the teaching, I will at some point have reached a state of perfection and then I will be allowed entry into heaven.

O Jesus, open inner sight,
the ego wants to prove it's right,
but this I will no longer do,
I want to be all one with you.

O Jesus, let the Fire of Joy,
consume the devil's subtle ploy,
transfigured is our planet earth,
the golden age is given birth.

3. Maha Chohan, help me see that I will not be saved, I will not be enlightened, I will not ascend, by building a stationary, perfect self. Perfection in Heaven is not the same as what most human beings see as perfection.

O Jesus, I now clearly see,
the Key of Knowledge given me,

my Christ self I hereby embrace,
as you fill up my inner space.

**O Jesus, let the Fire of Joy,
consume the devil's subtle ploy,
transfigured is our planet earth,
the golden age is given birth.**

4. Maha Chohan, help me see that human beings tend to see perfection as static. For if something is perfect, how can it possibly improve? If it is possible to improve it, then it could not be perfect—according to the serpentine mind.

O Jesus, show me serpent's lie,
expose the beam in my own eye,
as Christ discernment you me give,
in oneness I forever live.

**O Jesus, let the Fire of Joy,
consume the devil's subtle ploy,
transfigured is our planet earth,
the golden age is given birth.**

5. Maha Chohan, help me see that true perfection is flowing with the Spirit. There is no standing still. Perfection is constant self-transcendence. This is the true definition of perfection.

O Jesus, I am truly meek,
and thus I turn the other cheek,
when the accuser attacks me,
I go within and merge with thee.

O Jesus, let the Fire of Joy,
consume the devil's subtle ploy,
transfigured is our planet earth,
the golden age is given birth.

6. Maha Chohan, help me see that the Holy Spirit is perfect because it does not have a goal of reaching some ultimate static state. It has a goal of continuing to transcend itself indefinitely. It never seeks to hold on to the old, for it is always willing to shed the snake skin of the old and transcend into a new state.

O Jesus, ego I let die,
surrender ev'ry earthly tie,
the dead can bury what is dead,
I choose to walk with you instead.

O Jesus, let the Fire of Joy,
consume the devil's subtle ploy,
transfigured is our planet earth,
the golden age is given birth.

7. Maha Chohan, help me see that there is a fundamental difference between walking the Path of the Seven Rays with the goal that I am creating some perfect self, and then having the goal that I am creating a flexible self that can flow with the Holy Spirit in ongoing self-transcendence.

O Jesus, help me rise above,
the devil's test through higher love,
show me separate self unreal,
my formless self you do reveal.

**O Jesus, let the Fire of Joy,
consume the devil's subtle ploy,
transfigured is our planet earth,
the golden age is given birth.**

8. Maha Chohan, help me see that it is necessary for me to have a goal. But I will not allow the false teachers to trick me into defining a static goal, based on some standard that they have set up.

O Jesus, what is that to me,
I just let go and follow thee,
with this I do pass ev'ry test,
to find with you eternal rest.

**O Jesus, let the Fire of Joy,
consume the devil's subtle ploy,
transfigured is our planet earth,
the golden age is given birth.**

9. Maha Chohan, I will not walk the Path of the Seven Rays in order to become better than others based on some dualistic value judgment.

O Jesus, fiery master mine,
my heart now melting into thine,
I love with heart and mind and soul,
the God who is my highest goal.

**O Jesus, let the Fire of Joy,
consume the devil's subtle ploy,
transfigured is our planet earth,
the golden age is given birth.**

Part 3

1. Maha Chohan, help me see that in the collective consciousness is created this enormous conglomerate of separate spirits,
and they do not want to die.

> Maitreya, I am truly meek,
> your counsel wise I humbly seek,
> your vision I so want to see,
> with you in Eden I will be.
>
> **Maitreya, kindness is the cure,**
> **in fires of kindness I am pure.**
> **Maitreya, now release the fire,**
> **that raises me forever higher.**

2. Maha Chohan, help me learn to give up the separate self at
each level of the path. So that when I come up to the 96th level,
I am not faced with the entire planetary momentum of death,
but only the momentum at that particular level.

> Maitreya, help me to return,
> to learn from you, I truly yearn,
> as oneness is all I desire
> I feel initiation's fire.
>
> **Maitreya, kindness is the cure,**
> **in fires of kindness I am pure.**
> **Maitreya, now release the fire,**
> **that raises me forever higher.**

3. Maha Chohan, help me see that when I create a separate self out of the duality consciousness, I create a self that believes that it can only become acceptable to God by living up to a standard of perfection and by never being wrong according to that standard.

> Maitreya, I hereby decide,
> from you I will no longer hide,
> expose to me the very lie
> that caused edenic self to die.

> **Maitreya, kindness is the cure,**
> **in fires of kindness I am pure.**
> **Maitreya, now release the fire,**
> **that raises me forever higher.**

4. Maha Chohan, help me see that the separate self lives in a constant fear of being wrong. Yet you do not judge me based on a scale of right and wrong. You have no desire to prove me wrong. Nor do you have a desire to see me prove myself right.

> Maitreya, blessed Guru mine,
> my heart of hearts forever thine,
> I vow that I will listen well,
> so we can break the serpent's spell.

> **Maitreya, kindness is the cure,**
> **in fires of kindness I am pure.**
> **Maitreya, now release the fire,**
> **that raises me forever higher.**

5. Maha Chohan, help me see that you are only concerned with me being willing to transcend my present level of consciousness,

to transcend my present sense of self, to let my present spirit
die and flow into another, higher sense of self.

> Maitreya, help me see the lie
> whereby the serpent broke the tie,
> the serpent now has naught in me,
> in oneness I am truly free.

> **Maitreya, kindness is the cure,**
> **in fires of kindness I am pure.**
> **Maitreya, now release the fire,**
> **that raises me forever higher.**

6. Maha Chohan, help me see that a spirit created out of this
dualistic standard has within its very design a division between
right and wrong. It believes that if it is proven wrong, something terrible will happen. But if it is proven right, something
good should happen.

> Maitreya, truth does set me free
> from falsehoods of duality,
> the fruit of knowledge I let go,
> so your true spirit I do know.

> **Maitreya, kindness is the cure,**
> **in fires of kindness I am pure.**
> **Maitreya, now release the fire,**
> **that raises me forever higher.**

7. Maha Chohan, help me see that the spirit believes that it can
force God to accept it by proving itself right. And it seeks to
prove itself right in the only way it can: by comparing itself to
others based on the standard out of which is was created. So it

seeks to prove itself right by proving others wrong, by putting others down.

> Maitreya, I submit to you,
> intentions pure, my heart is true,
> from ego I am truly free,
> as I am now all one with thee.

> **Maitreya, kindness is the cure,**
> **in fires of kindness I am pure.**
> **Maitreya, now release the fire,**
> **that raises me forever higher.**

8. Maha Chohan, help me see that the subconscious reasoning of the separate spirit is that "If I can prove all other spirits wrong, then I must be right and God must accept *me*." This is an illusion.

> Maitreya, kindness is the key,
> all shades of kindness teach to me,
> for I am now the open door,
> the Art of Kindness to restore.

> **Maitreya, kindness is the cure,**
> **in fires of kindness I am pure.**
> **Maitreya, now release the fire,**
> **that raises me forever higher.**

9. Maha Chohan, help me see that the most dangerous level of the path is where I approach the 96th level, but I am still trapped in the desire to prove myself right according to some standard.

> Maitreya, oh sweet mystery,
> immersed in your reality,
> the myst'ry school will now return,
> for this, my heart does truly burn.

> **Maitreya, kindness is the cure,**
> **in fires of kindness I am pure.**
> **Maitreya, now release the fire,**
> **that raises me forever higher.**

Part 4

1. Maha Chohan, help me see that it is difficult for you to reach students who are approaching the 96th level, but they believe that their separate self is right according to the standard that they have not given up.

> Gautama, show my mental state
> that does give rise to love and hate,
> your exposé I do endure,
> so my perception will be pure.

> **Gautama, Flame of Cosmic Peace,**
> **unruly thoughts do hereby cease,**
> **we radiate from you and me**
> **the peace to still Samsara's Sea.**

2. Maha Chohan, help me see that the students who are the hardest to reach for the Chohans, are the ones who build an unrecognized sense of pride because they think they are right.

Gautama, in your Flame of Peace,
the struggling self I now release,
the Buddha Nature I now see,
it is the core of you and me.

Gautama, Flame of Cosmic Peace,
unruly thoughts do hereby cease,
we radiate from you and me
the peace to still Samsara's Sea.

3. Maha Chohan, I am willing to come to the insight that there is no standard defined on earth that can take me to heaven. For these dualistic, separate standards cannot exist in heaven.

Gautama, I am one with thee,
Mara's demons do now flee,
your Presence like a soothing balm,
my mind and senses ever calm.

Gautama, Flame of Cosmic Peace,
unruly thoughts do hereby cease,
we radiate from you and me
the peace to still Samsara's Sea.

4. Maha Chohan, help me see that I am not proving myself right in the eyes of the Chohans, for you are not in the dualistic state of consciousness. I am only proving myself right in the eyes of the separate spirit I have created, the spirit that is based on my particular standard.

Gautama, I now take the vow,
to live in the eternal now,

with you I do transcend all time,
to live in present so sublime.

**Gautama, Flame of Cosmic Peace,
unruly thoughts do hereby cease,
we radiate from you and me
the peace to still Samsara's Sea.**

5. Maha Chohan, help me see that this spirit can never see anything beyond the standard. It can never see anything wrong with the standard. It can never see any of the limitations of the standard. It can never see that the standard is created by excluding certain elements of the greater picture of reality.

Gautama, I have no desire,
to nothing earthly I aspire,
in non-attachment I now rest,
passing Mara's subtle test.

**Gautama, Flame of Cosmic Peace,
unruly thoughts do hereby cease,
we radiate from you and me
the peace to still Samsara's Sea.**

6. Maha Chohan, help me see that the lesser spirits define a standard by excluding something. They create a standard that is based on excluding one or many of the 360 degrees of the circumference of what is possible to see on earth.

Gautama, I melt into you,
my mind is one, no longer two,
immersed in your resplendent glow,
Nirvana is all that I know.

**Gautama, Flame of Cosmic Peace,
unruly thoughts do hereby cease,
we radiate from you and me
the peace to still Samsara's Sea.**

7. Maha Chohan, help me see that when I define certain angles, certain degrees, as wrong, and therefore will not look at them, I will, by definition, have a limited, selective, subjective, biased and incomplete view of life.

Gautama, in your timeless space,
I am immersed in Cosmic Grace,
I know the God beyond all form,
to world I will no more conform.

**Gautama, Flame of Cosmic Peace,
unruly thoughts do hereby cease,
we radiate from you and me
the peace to still Samsara's Sea.**

8. Maha Chohan, help me see that I will always be able to prove my separate spirit right. For when I accept the definition that certain degrees should not be looked at or are wrong, then I will not be able to see that the spirit through which I am looking at reality gives a limited and distorted view of the totality of life.

Gautama, I am now awake,
I clearly see what is at stake,
and thus I claim my sacred right
to be on earth the Buddhic Light.

Gautama, Flame of Cosmic Peace,
unruly thoughts do hereby cease,
we radiate from you and me
the peace to still Samsara's Sea.

9. Maha Chohan, help me see that if I am willing to exclude certain degrees on the circumference of the circle of life, then I can always prove that the self that can only encompass the remaining degrees is right.

Gautama, with your thunderbolt,
we give the earth a mighty jolt,
I know that some will understand,
and join the Buddha's timeless band.

Gautama, Flame of Cosmic Peace,
unruly thoughts do hereby cease,
we radiate from you and me
the peace to still Samsara's Sea.

Part 5

1. Maha Chohan, help me recognize that until I can see the entire circumference of the consciousness that is possible on earth, I am not enlightened, and I am not ready for the ascension.

Sanat Kumara, Ruby Fire,
I seek my place in love's own choir,
with open hearts we sing your praise,
together we the earth do raise.

**Sanat Kumara, Ruby Ray,
bring to earth a higher way,
light this planet with your fire,
clothe her in a new attire.**

2. Maha Chohan, help me see that there is no individuality anchored in the Conscious You that makes it necessary to exclude certain degrees.

Sanat Kumara, Ruby Fire,
initiations I desire,
I am for you an electrode,
Shamballa is my true abode.

**Sanat Kumara, Ruby Ray,
bring to earth a higher way,
light this planet with your fire,
clothe her in a new attire.**

3. Maha Chohan, help me see that I am pure awareness. And as pure awareness, I can look at anything and everything. There is nothing I need to exclude. There is nothing I need to judge.

Sanat Kumara, Ruby Fire,
I follow path that you require,
initiate me with your love,
the open door for Holy Dove.

**Sanat Kumara, Ruby Ray,
bring to earth a higher way,
light this planet with your fire,
clothe her in a new attire.**

4. Maha Chohan, help me see that when I am willing to look at any thing, then there is no thing that has power over me.

> Sanat Kumara, Ruby Fire,
> your great example all inspire,
> with non-attachment and great mirth,
> we give the earth a true rebirth.

> **Sanat Kumara, Ruby Ray,**
> **bring to earth a higher way,**
> **light this planet with your fire,**
> **clothe her in a new attire.**

5. Maha Chohan, help me see that when I define something as being wrong or refuse to look at it, then that which I will not look at has power over me. It defines me, for I think that if I fulfilled those characteristics, I would be wrong in an ultimate sense.

> Sanat Kumara, Ruby Fire,
> you are this planet's purifier,
> consume on earth all spirits dark,
> reveal the inner Spirit Spark.

> **Sanat Kumara, Ruby Ray,**
> **bring to earth a higher way,**
> **light this planet with your fire,**
> **clothe her in a new attire.**

6. Maha Chohan, help me see that the only way to overcome the fear of being wrong is to look at what is at the bottom of that fear, and realize this is just another degree on the circumference of the compass of life. And I am not bound by it.

Sanat Kumara, Ruby Fire,
you are a cosmic amplifier,
the lower forces can't withstand,
vibrations from Venusian band.

**Sanat Kumara, Ruby Ray,
bring to earth a higher way,
light this planet with your fire,
clothe her in a new attire.**

7. Maha Chohan, help me see that the highest potential of the Conscious You is to be the compass needle that always points North. It always points to the true pole star of the I AM Presence.

Sanat Kumara, Ruby Fire,
I am on earth your magnifier,
the flow of love I do restore,
my chakras are your open door.

**Sanat Kumara, Ruby Ray,
bring to earth a higher way,
light this planet with your fire,
clothe her in a new attire.**

8. Maha Chohan, help me go to those points on my personal compass where I have blocked out certain degrees on the circumference. Help me slay those spirits and therefore open up the circumference, so that the compass needle can swing freely.

Sanat Kumara, Ruby Fire,
Venusian song the multiplier,

as we your love reverberate,
the densest minds we penetrate.

Sanat Kumara, Ruby Ray,
bring to earth a higher way,
light this planet with your fire,
clothe her in a new attire.

9. Maha Chohan, help me recognize that perhaps there is something I do not see. Help me to look at the circumference of my personal compass, so that instead of going from crises to crises, my path becomes a smooth upward spiral.

Sanat Kumara, Ruby Fire,
you are for all the sanctifier,
the earth is now a holy place,
purified by cosmic grace.

Sanat Kumara, Ruby Ray,
bring to earth a higher way,
light this planet with your fire,
clothe her in a new attire.

Sealing:

In the name of the Divine Mother, I fully accept that the power of these calls is used to set free the Ma-ter light, so it can outpicture the perfect vision of Christ for my own life, for all people and for the planet. In the name I AM THAT I AM, it is done! Amen.

19 | CO-CREATING CONSCIOUSLY

The Maha Chohan I AM. Let us summarize the message that I want to get across in this book.

The main message is, of course that you are a co-creator with your God. You are designed to co-create. And how do you co-create? You co-create because you have self-awareness. As a result of having self-awareness, you have the ability to formulate an image in your mind—an image of something that you do not experience through your physical senses and the outer consciousness. In other words, you can formulate a mental image, a mental matrix, of something that does not yet exist in physical manifestation.

The mental image you formulate will, of course, be limited by your imagination. And for many people their imagination is limited by what they see, what they experience through their physical senses and their outer mind. Nevertheless, you are a self-aware being, and you have the potential to formulate any mental image, any mental matrix that is conceivable and possible.

God has not defined any limitations for your self-awareness and your imagination. They are free, they are infinite, they are unlimited. The only thing that can limit your imagination is the limitations that you allow to be in the sphere of your consciousness.

So you co-create by formulating a mental image and then using your self-awareness to project that image upon the Ma-ter light. When that projection goes all the way through the four levels of the material universe – the identity, mental, emotional and physical – then you will co-create a physical form. The Ma-ter light will take on that physical form, and you can perceive it with your senses and outer consciousness.

Yet whenever you start the co-creative process, you are creating something. If you are creating a mental image in your identity body of who you are, it is inevitable that your self-awareness – the stream of consciousness flowing through you – will flow through that matrix. And thus, it will be projected upon the Ma-ter light in the identity realm. The same of, course, applies in the mental and emotional realms.

You cannot stop co-creating

What I need you to realize here is that you are constantly co-creating. The price you pay, so to speak, for being a self-aware co-creator is that you cannot stop co-creating because you cannot stop being conscious. Of course, you can look at planet earth and see that many people use many things, including chemical substances, to make themselves unconscious or to alter their consciousness, so that they are not really consciousness.

Nevertheless, even if you are asleep or physically unconscious, your emotional mind, mental mind, and your identity mind are not asleep or unconscious. There is always a level of your being where you hold mental images and where the stream of consciousness coming from your I AM Presence is flowing through these images, and therefore being projected upon the Ma-ter light at that level. So even if you are not co-creating a physical structure that you can detect with your senses, you are co-creating an emotional structure, a mental structure, and an identity or etheric structure.

The point I have tried to get across in this book is that all of the things that you co-create at the identity, mental, and emotional levels form what I have chosen to call spirits. And these spirits then become part of your total being, part of the lower being that many people call the soul.

Thus, when you have created such a spirit, then the light from your I AM Presence – the stream of consciousness from your I AM Presence – will stream through it, and therefore you will continually be co-creating through that spirit. This does not mean that you will be co-creating a new spirit at every moment, but it means that as the stream of your awareness flows through a particular spirit, you will be reinforcing that spirit, and thus it becomes stronger and stronger.

And so the value of having this teaching is that it makes it possible for you to do what I have explained in earlier dis-courses, namely to walk the spiritual path in a much more conscious manner. In most previous teachings that have been released on this planet, people have been given only a partial understanding of what the spiritual path is about. And there-fore, they have not had the concept I have given you that you have in the past created these spirits that these spirits have become part of your being, and that if you identify with the spirits, you cannot actually free yourself from them.

For as long as you are identified with a given spirit, your consciousness will stream through it. This will have two effects.

As the stream of your consciousness is streaming through your spirit, you cannot at the same time see the spirit as a spirit and see it from the outside. But if you do not see it, you cannot free yourself from it. At the same time as your consciousness is streaming through this spirit, your energies are tied up in the spirit, and you are reinforcing the spirit, making it more difficult for yourself to pull your consciousness away from that spirit and look at that spirit from the outside.

A spirit is not who you are

The saving grace in this scenario is what we have explained many times that the Conscious You truly has the ability to project itself anywhere it wants. This means that you can at any time project yourself outside a given spirit, or you can pull yourself away from a given spirit, so that your self-awareness is not focused in the spirit and the stream of your consciousness is not flowing through that spirit.

Now, as I tell you this, it is obvious that you still have spirits in the sphere of your being, the sphere of your consciousness. Just hearing or reading these words will not mean that you will automatically pull away from them. But what I am telling you is that by having the concept in your mind and by accepting that concept, you can take your path to an entirely new level. Once you become conscious of the fact that these spirits exist in the sphere of your consciousness, you can consciously make a decision that you will engage in the process of pulling your-self away from identification with the spirits, so that you can indeed come to see a spirit from the outside.

Now, I can assure you that if you are ready for this teaching, then you have already done this. You have been willing to look at the beam in your own eye to some degree. That means that in this lifetime, and probably also in past lifetimes, you have had incidents where you have suddenly come to see a spirit. You may not have identified it as a spirit the way I am explaining it here, but nevertheless you have suddenly shifted. You have looked at yourself and said, "I do not want to be like this anymore. I do not want to continue to repeat these old patterns anymore. I want to change. I want to be more than this."

And perhaps you are aware of having experienced this in this lifetime – where you consciously saw something – and you have probably also experienced that by consciously seeing something, seeing that it is not you, you have almost instantaneously been able to shift out of it, so that you are no longer identified with it. And of course, the essential step to rising to a higher level of the spiritual path is to come to a point where you do not identify yourself with the spirit that is the primary spirit that represents the level of consciousness you have right now.

Reinforcing a false spirit

As I have explained, there are 144 levels of consciousness on earth, and they can be seen as forming a spiral staircase where each step of consciousness is one step on the staircase. In order to rise higher on the path, you have to move from one step to another on that staircase. And the only way to move from one step to the next is to dis-identify yourself from the spirit on any given step.

So my point for this book is to give you this teaching, so that you can begin to consciously follow this path of pulling your sense of identity away from these spirits. For it is only by doing so that you will truly make progress.

I can tell you that there are millions of people on this earth, who have been spiritual people for a long time, possibility for decades or their entire lifetimes. They may have studied spiritual teachings or practiced spiritual techniques. But I can tell you that some of them have not gone through the process I have described.

There are indeed many spiritual people who have gone through the process of dis-identifying themselves from a spirit – giving up that spirit – and rising beyond it. But there are indeed quite a number of people on the spiritual path and in religious movements, who have studied a teaching, practiced a certain technique or religion, but they have not come to the point of freeing themselves from a given spirit. And thus, what has happened is very simple. Instead of transcending a certain spirit, all of the efforts they have put into their spiritual studies and practice have actually reinforced this spirit at a certain level of the spiritual path and a certain level of consciousness.

So you might see a person who, for example, found the spiritual path at the 56th level of consciousness. The person has then been practicing a certain technique diligently and has been studying spiritual teachings for perhaps many years. But the person has not actually transcended the spirit; it has not let go of that spirit of the 56th level of consciousness. What it has done instead is that it has directed its awareness through that spirit. And this means that as the person focused its awareness on the spiritual path and on studying a spiritual teaching that person has actually educated the spirit of the 56th level, so that that spirit has supposedly and seemingly become more spiritual. This has given the person the impression that he or she has progressed spiritually, but in reality it is not the person – it is not the Conscious You – that has progressed; it is only the spirit. And as I have tried to explain that spirit does not need to progress spiritually because it will never make it into Heaven.

The only thing that will make it into Heaven is the Conscious You, and you will make it into the spiritual realm only when you dis-identify yourself from any of the spirits of the physical realm or, rather, the material realm, including the identity, mental, emotional and physical.

So you see, it is possible to be on this false path for a long time and to be fooled by the false teachers – and your own ego and your own spirits – into actually thinking that you are making progress towards the ultimate goal of your spiritual search. But in reality you are not making progress at all. You, the Conscious You, are standing still, for you are still identified with a certain spirit.

Negative feelings from spirits

Now, this does not mean that you need to be discouraged and think you have wasted your efforts. For when you do dis-identify yourself from that spirit, then you can very quickly catch up to a higher level because of the efforts you made. Yet this will only happen when you dis-identify yourself from the spirit that you have educated, and you are willing to leave it behind. If you are not willing to leave it behind and let it die, then you will continue to reinforce it, and then the Conscious You that you are will not rise on the real path towards the ascension.

So then, this is indeed a serious topic that all spiritual seekers could benefit from contemplating. But again, we of the ascended masters do not want you to take anything too seriously and be burdened by it. I am not giving you this teaching to make you feel burdened. I am not giving it to make you fear that you have done something wrong or to make you feel ashamed for not having made more progress. I am giving it to you in order to help you liberate yourself from all of these feelings. For where do such feelings come from? They come from whatever spirit is in your energy field, in your mind. It is not the Conscious You that feels afraid or discouraged or ashamed or proud or superior. It can only be a spirit, and that spirit was programmed with a thought matrix of feeling this way.

Why you need a spirit for a time

One of the things we have taught consistently is that your I AM Presence sent the Conscious You into embodiment on earth because it wanted to experience the material world from the inside. And as you start the spiritual path at the 48th level, you are not yet aware that you are the Conscious You, and you are not yet able to simply be the open door – to be a clear pane of glass – without having an outer personality or individuality. So you need to have a self through which you can express yourself and integrate and interact with the physical body. And in taking on or creating this self, you are indeed creating a spirit.

This is inevitable. This is simply the process of taking incarnation. You cannot take incarnation as a new lifestream without creating one, or rather, many such spirits. This is perfectly natural and in order. But what can happen is that you can become trapped in identification with these spirits, instead of engaging in the process of letting one spirit die, ascending to the next level of consciousness, and then letting the spirit corresponding to that level die, and ascending to the next level and so on.

In other words, instead of consciously and constantly growing towards higher levels of consciousness, you are now trapped into reinforcing a certain spirit, based on the illusion that you can somehow expand or perfect that spirit, until it becomes acceptable to God. And you can thus enter the ascended state while being identified with that spirit, rather than entering the ascended state by giving up the very last ghost of any spirit in your lower being.

So you see the fundamental difference between the true inner path of self-transcendence and the false, outer path of seeking to perfect some kind of spirit that is not a self-aware spirit that descended from above, but rather a non-self-aware spirit created here below. And as I have said, this does not mean that the spirit does not have some level of consciousness, but it does not have self-awareness, and that is why it cannot consciously transcend itself. This is the central ability of the Conscious You: the ability to consciously transcend itself.

But of course, you cannot transcend your sense of self without seeing that your sense of self is just a self, a spirit that is not you. And so, the key to everything is to have this ability to pull yourself out of your current sense of self. You already have this ability, but you are not using it consciously. And this is indeed the key to taking your path to a higher level, and accelerating it beyond anything that you might have dreamt of before. So then, let me give you a few pointers.

How spirits drive world events

If you will take the teaching I have given about the existence of these many spirits on earth, you can gain a new perspective, not only on world history but on human interactions. Let me point to an obvious example. If you look at the Middle East, you will see there people who are very identified with a certain race or ethnic group. You will know that there has, for some time, been strife between Jews and Arabs. And there has been strife between various Arab groups, or between Jews and

Palestinians in the state of Israel. But if you look at history, you can see that this strife has been going on for a very, very long time. In fact, it has been going on for as long as there has been recorded history, for it is even in the Old Testament as the warring between different tribes.

So can you not see now that what has happened is that in the Middle East the people who have been warring with each other have created these collective spirits? And over thousands of years, they have fed their attention and their psycho-spiritual energy into these spirits, causing the spirits to grow stronger and stronger to the point where they are often able to completely overpower the individuality of the average person.

If you take a look at individual people who have grown up in such an environment, you will see that there are many people who actually do not have an individual life. Yes, they will have certain individual characteristics, but they are so identified with what they think is their race or their religion or their ethnic group. But in reality, what they are identified with is the collective spirit that was created a long time ago and has been reinforced for thousands of years. And their total identification with this spirit means that the spirit overpowers them to the point where they could never even dream of stepping outside of the boundaries defined by what they think is their religion or culture. Therefore, they do not even imagine that they could be anything different – that they could be anything more – than what they have been brought up to see themselves as.

And so, you can see that many of these people can spend an entire lifetime without actually doing anything that is a truly free choice that is a truly individual act. They spend their entire lifetime being so overpowered by the collective spirit that they are literally serving as a cow that is being milked for energy, and the energy goes to sustaining and reinforcing this spirit. Some of these spirits have grown so strong that they look at human beings simply as cattle that are to be milked for their energy. And that is why the spirits will agitate people's emotions, causing them to go into clashes with other groups, so that people – in their anger and hatred – feed energy to the beast, to the spirit.

Recognizing the more subtle spirits

Now, of course, I am telling you this for a very simple reason. You are not overpowered by such a collective spirit to the point where you are not able to make individual choices and take individual actions. If you had been overpowered by such a spirit – and they are, of course, found everywhere in the world – then you would not have been able to read this book. It really is that simple. And this should be an encouragement to you because it shows you that you have already discovered the process of dis-identifying yourself from a certain spirit and consciously rising above it.

How can I say this? Because, surely, you grew up in a place where there is a collective spirit. Perhaps your family members were almost fully identified with it. Perhaps most people in your town, in your country, or in your culture are completely identified with such a collective spirit. But if you had been, you would not have been a spiritual person, and you would not have been open to this book and the spiritual path.

Thus, all I am saying here is that you have gone through the process, but by becoming more conscious of it, you can greatly accelerate the process. And this is, of course, my entire purpose for this book.

Even though I say that you are not completely overpowered by the collective spirit in your area, you should not take that to mean that you are not affected by any spirit. Instead, be careful to realize a certain distinction. Because you are a spiritual person, you are not overpowered by the more common, collective spirits found on Earth. You are not completely identified with the collective spirit that dominated the culture in which you grew up.

Nevertheless, there are other collective spirits that cannot as easily be identified with certain outer characteristics, such as race, religion, ethnic group, nationality, sex and so on. They are collective spirits that have managed to hide from most people because they are not seen as spirits. And one of those spirits is what I have already described, namely the very aggressive spirit of wanting to prove other people wrong and wanting to prove yourself right. But there are many such spirits. They simply have not been recognized because they are not associated with outer, physical characteristics, but with the more subtle emotional and mental characteristics that most people are simply not aware of at this point in time.

Nevertheless, as a spiritual person, you may have well been affected by one or more of these spirits. In fact, for many people, they have become affected – or more affected – by such spirits by being involved with various spiritual groups. For there are indeed many of the spiritual, religious or New Age groups that you see today that are very much tied into a collective spirit of a certain kind. So it is indeed possible that many people have actually become more tied into a collective spirit as a result of being involved with a spiritual teaching or organization.

Yet, beyond such collective spirits, there are, of course, the individual spirits that you have created. And, of course, even though you may have transcended some of these spirits, you still have other spirits that are affecting you.

How can I say this? I can say this because you are in embodiment on earth and you are reading this book. If you did not have any spirits that were affecting you, you would have ascended, and you and I would have been meeting face to face, and I would have had no need to give you this teaching.

Freeing yourself from spirits

Do you see that there will be some spirit that you are dealing with, until the very moment, when you give up the last ghost and ascend? This is simply the reality of the spiritual path on earth. Again, there is no reason to be discouraged by it or to feel in any way afraid or shameful about it. You just accept that this is the way it is, and then you make a decision to sharpen your ability to see through these spirits as quickly as possible and thereby free yourself from them.

Now, this is, of course, a process that in a sense you cannot completely be taught. We of the Chohans can help you in many ways. We will do so in the coming books, as we have already done in previous teachings. But nevertheless, it is really a process that has an individual aspect because you are the one who must see it in your consciousness.

You can, of course, be told from the outside of a certain general spirit. You can even – if you have direct contact with a physical teacher or an ascended teacher through your intuition – you can be given a vision of how that spirit has taken on its individual form in you. And thereby, you can come to know that you are affected by a certain spirit, and you can know the characteristics of that spirit. But this is not quite the same as actually making that shift in consciousness where now you have pulled the Conscious You outside of the spirit. Now you are seeing the spirit from the outside, and you are seeing that it is not you. This is a process we can describe to you, but it really cannot be taught. It is, so to speak, built into the Conscious

You, but it is something that you must discover on your own by experiencing it. And until you experience it for the first time – fully consciously – you will not truly know what I am talking about.

Perhaps you already know what I am talking about, and perhaps you don't. But if you don't, do not be discouraged. Simply continue to ponder it and continue to use the tools that we have given and will give, so that you can move closer and closer to the point where you have diminished the magnetic pull of a certain spirit. And then the Conscious You naturally, effortlessly, and seemingly spontaneously, pulls itself out of that spirit.

Do you see what I am saying? It is natural for the Conscious You to be continuously moving, to be consciously looking at life from different perspectives. That is why you have been searching for the spiritual path. That is why you have found this book. Because the Conscious You is always looking for something different – something new – even if it does not know what it is looking for.

This is the natural aspect because, as we have said, the Conscious You is the I WILL BE aspect of your I AM Presence, the aspect that consciously says, "I will be this." But then, when it has experienced what it is like to be this, it will now say, "I will be that," and it will shift into something else in order to have that experience. And that is why it is natural for you to be identified with a certain spirit, and to experience life through the perception filter of that spirit for a time. But it is also natural for you not to remain in that spirit but to shift to a different perspective.

Forcing spirits into the open

It is only by the spirit gaining enough momentum that it can form a magnetic pull on your attention, so that it can artificially keep you focused through that spirit for any length of time. It is only by doing this that the spirit can keep you trapped at that level over a period of time. That is why you see that a spirit that is an aggressive spirit, will aggressively seek to keep you at that level. And once you begin to see this, you will actually be able to feel the aggressive force, as I imagine most of you, who will read this book, have felt it at various points in your life.

Just think back and see how easily you identified that there is something that is pulling on you that is pushing you in a certain direction that is seeking to force or manipulate or persuade you into doing something that you really do not feel is right—that you really do not feel is you. You will see that you have been exposed to this throughout your life, and you have been aware of it. So, again, simply become more conscious of this, and then see that every time you feel this aggressiveness, you know there is a spirit that is influencing you.

But instead of doing what you have been doing so far, which is running away from it, or resisting it, or perhaps even fighting it, I am asking you now to do something different. Simply say to yourself: "Ah! Here is a spirit that is hiding from me. I am going to force it to come out in the open, so that I can see it and thereby stop identifying myself with it, so that it will no longer have power over me. I am going to use the tools given to me by the Maha Chohan and the seven Chohans, so that I can flush these spirits out of their hiding places where I can see that they are not me and therefore free myself from their influence."

This is the potential you have by truly integrating the teaching that I have given in this book, and then applying it to the teachings that you will be receiving from the seven Chohans in the following books. What I am giving you here is a general insight, and I will also give you a general tool that you can use as you follow the path through the First Ray and onwards towards all of the seven rays, until you reach that 96th level of consciousness. You can, for that matter, use these insights and tools beyond the 96th level.

Spirits and the ego

Now, before I end this discourse, there is one topic I will comment on briefly. By studying this book, there is a question that might have arisen in your mind: Are the spirits I am talking about the same as the ego? What is the relationship between the ego and these spirits?

Well, this depends on your level of consciousness. If you are at the lower levels of consciousness – where you are fully identified with a certain spirit – then there is no meaningful difference between the ego and the primary spirit that is over-powering you. They are, for all practical purposes, one and the same.

However, when you transcend a certain spirit, you leave that spirit behind. When the energies that were qualified by that spirit have been fully transmuted, and when the thought matrix has been shattered by you, then that spirit is no more. It is effectively dead. Nevertheless, it would be a mistake to think that because you have overcome a certain spirit, and you are free from that spirit, you are now also free from the ego. Because the ego is not the spirit; it is not the totality of the spirit.

What I have been attempting to explain in this book is that as you walk the path up through the 144 levels of consciousness, there will be a spirit at each of those levels. Which means that when you overcome a spirit at a certain level, you will shift into seeing life through the spirit at the next level up. The challenge will be whether you will then see the need to free yourself from that spirit also? Or will you begin the cycle of reinforcing that spirit through your attention?

But nevertheless, there is a spirit, and so this means that you will not be completely free from such spirits, until you not only reach the 144th level, but actually transcend that level. And the reason for this is that in order to actually stay tied to a physical body, you need to have this kind of a spirit that can integrate with the physical body.

So what I am explaining here is something that I know will sound, perhaps, enigmatic and abstract. But you see there are a number of spirits, and when you transcend the spirit, the spirit is dead. But you are still not an ascended being, which means that you still have an ego. But we might define the ego as that which keeps you in embodiment and keeps you out of the ascended state.

The levels of ego

Now, there are other ways to define the ego, and I do not wish to go into a discussion about words and definitions. But my point is that there are levels of the ego. What many people see as the ego – what even many spiritual teachers or psychologists see as the ego – is what we might call the lower ego, the ego that is below the 48th level where it is very aggressive in seeking to control other people. Yet there is also an ego between the 48th and the 96th level, and it is the ego that is very focused on raising itself and yourself as an individual being. And then there are egos between the 96th and the 144th level that are very focused on doing something for others, raising up the whole, but still not doing this in a way that is entirely the awareness of an ascended master.

It can be difficult to realize this. Many spiritual people have indeed been able to see the lower, aggressive ego, and thought that when they did not have its tendencies anymore, they must have been free of the ego. There are even those who have come to see the individual ego, and they have thought that when they had risen above that ego, they had become free of the ego and become enlightened.

And yet, the really wise students will realize that you will not be completely free of the ego until you ascend, for there needs to be something that keeps you tied to the physical octave and a physical body. In other words, when you have no more ego, you cannot maintain yourself in a physical body; you become an ascended master.

I do not wish to go into any deeper discussion about this, as we will give other teachings as time and cycles are appropriate for this. But I would like you to take this one thing away from this discussion: instead of seeing life or the spiritual path as a process whereby you reach some ultimate stage here on earth – whether you call it enlightenment or something else – then you will shift into seeing the spiritual path as an ongoing process.

Surely, it has a goal, which we have, from the unascended perspective, defined as the ascension. But until you actually pass into the ascended realm, you are engaged in a process that requires you to constantly transcend yourself. That means transcending a certain spirit and overcoming the corresponding level of ego.

Thus, it is constructive to see yourself as not becoming ego-free until you have ascended. For this is the only way you can avoid becoming ensnared by the more subtle aspects of the ego that correspond to the higher levels of consciousness. And we would indeed like to see all of the students who recognize our teachings avoid the fate that has happened to some spiritual people, even some who have set themselves up as spiritual gurus. For they have actually risen to a high level among the 144 levels of consciousness, only to be stopped at that level because now they thought they had reached some ultimate state, from which there was no need to transcend themselves further.

My beloved, there is *always* a need for self-transcendence, for self-transcendence *is* life. Self-transcendence is the Holy Spirit. And life I AM. And the Holy Spirit, I AM. And the Maha Chohan, I AM.

A tool for dealing with spirits

The tool given for this book is relatively simple. You can make a simple prayer, silently or aloud, using your own words or the following:

Oh Maha Chohan, show me the spirit that is holding me back right now, and the decision behind it.

Oh Archangel Michael, bind that spirit, so it cannot affect myself or any part of life.

Mighty I AM Presence, shatter the thought matrix behind that spirit.

Oh Mother Mary, help me surrender myself
entirely into the River of Life.

20 | INVOKING FREEDOM FROM IDENTIFICATION WITH SPIRITS

In the name I AM THAT I AM, Jesus Christ, I call to my I AM Presence to flow through the I Will Be Presence that I AM and give this invocation with full power. I call to the Divine Director, Astrea, Shiva, Surya, Godfree, Padmasambhava and the Maha Chohan to help me pull myself away from being identified with my internal spirits. Help me see and surrender all patterns that block my oneness with the Maha Chohan and my oneness with my I AM Presence, including ...

[Make personal calls]

Part 1

1. Maha Chohan, help me see that I am designed to co-create. I have the ability to formulate an image in

my mind—an image of something that I do not experience through my physical senses and outer consciousness.

Maha Chohan, I will to grow,
I feel the power of your flow.
Maha Chohan, the veil is rent,
creative will from heaven sent.

**O Holy Spirit, flow through me,
I am the open door for thee.
O mighty rushing stream of Light,
transcendence is my sacred right.**

2. Maha Chohan, help me see that the mental image I formulate will be limited by my imagination. Yet I have the potential to formulate any mental image, any mental matrix, that is conceivable and possible.

Maha Chohan, your wisdom streams,
awaken all from matter's dreams.
Maha Chohan, your balance bring,
let bells of integration ring.

**O Holy Spirit, flow through me,
I am the open door for thee.
O mighty rushing stream of Light,
transcendence is my sacred right.**

3. Maha Chohan, help me see that God has not defined any limitations for my self-awareness and imagination. The only thing that can limit my imagination is the limitations that I allow to be in the sphere of my consciousness.

Maha Chohan, love's mighty call,
the prison walls are shattered all.
Maha Chohan, set all life free
through unconditionality.

**O Holy Spirit, flow through me,
I am the open door for thee.
O mighty rushing stream of Light,
transcendence is my sacred right.**

4. Maha Chohan, help me see that I co-create by formulating a mental image and then using my self-awareness to project that image upon the Ma-ter light. When that projection goes through the four levels of the material universe, I co-create a physical form.

Maha Chohan, intentions pure,
all life is one, I know for sure.
Maha Chohan, I am awake,
surrender all for oneness' sake.

**O Holy Spirit, flow through me,
I am the open door for thee.
O mighty rushing stream of Light,
transcendence is my sacred right.**

5. Maha Chohan, help me see that I am constantly co-creating. I cannot stop co-creating, because I cannot stop being conscious.

Maha Chohan, help all men see,
through veils of unreality.

Maha Chohan, with single eye,
I know I am the greater "I."

**O Holy Spirit, flow through me,
I am the open door for thee.
O mighty rushing stream of Light,
transcendence is my sacred right.**

6. Maha Chohan, help me see that there is always a level of my being, where I hold mental images and where the stream of consciousness coming from my I AM Presence is being projected upon the Ma-ter light.

Maha Chohan, your peace I find,
Maitreya shows me to be kind.
Maha Chohan, all war will cease,
now flooding all with sacred peace.

**O Holy Spirit, flow through me,
I am the open door for thee.
O mighty rushing stream of Light,
transcendence is my sacred right.**

7. Maha Chohan, help me see that all of the things that I co-create at the identity, mental, and emotional levels form spirits. And these spirits become part of my total being, part of my lower being.

Maha Chohan, you balance all,
the seven rays upon my call.
Maha Chohan, all life is free,
transcending for eternity.

**O Holy Spirit, flow through me,
I am the open door for thee.
O mighty rushing stream of Light,
transcendence is my sacred right.**

8. Maha Chohan, help me see that when I have created such a spirit, then the light from my I AM Presence will stream through it, and therefore I will continually be co-creating through that spirit. I will be reinforcing that spirit, and it becomes stronger and stronger.

Maha Chohan, your sacred Flame,
what beauty in your blessed name.
Maha Chohan, what rushing flow,
the Spirit one with life below.

**O Holy Spirit, flow through me,
I am the open door for thee.
O mighty rushing stream of Light,
transcendence is my sacred right.**

9. Maha Chohan, help me see that I have in the past created spirits, and these spirits have become part of my being, and if I identify with the spirits, I cannot free myself from them.

Maha Chohan, your Presence here,
filling up the inner sphere.
Life is now a sacred flow,
God Wisdom we on all bestow.

**O Holy Spirit, flow through me,
I am the open door for thee.**

**O mighty rushing stream of Light,
transcendence is my sacred right.**

Part 2

1. Maha Chohan, help me see that as the stream of my consciousness is streaming through a spirit, I cannot at the same
time see the spirit as a spirit and see it from the outside. But if
I do not see it, I cannot free myself from it.

Divine Director, I now see,
the world is unreality,
in my heart I now truly feel,
the Spirit is all that is real.

**Divine Director, send the light,
from blindness clear my inner sight,
my vision free, my vision clear,
your guidance is forever here.**

2. Maha Chohan, help me see that as my consciousness is
streaming through a spirit, my energies are tied up in the spirit,
and I am reinforcing the spirit, making it more difficult for
myself to pull my consciousness away from that spirit and look
at it from the outside.

Divine Director, vision give,
in clarity I want to live,
I now behold my plan Divine,
the plan that is uniquely mine.

Divine Director, send the light,
from blindness clear my inner sight,
my vision free, my vision clear,
your guidance is forever here.

3. Maha Chohan, help me see that the Conscious You has the ability to project itself anywhere it wants. I can at any time project myself outside a given spirit, so that my self-awareness is not focused in the spirit and the stream of my consciousness is not flowing through that spirit.

Divine Director, show in me,
the ego games, and set me free,
help me escape the ego's cage,
to help bring in the golden age.

Divine Director, send the light,
from blindness clear my inner sight,
my vision free, my vision clear,
your guidance is forever here.

4. Maha Chohan, help me take my path to an entirely new level. I consciously make the decision that I will engage in the process of pulling myself away from identification with the spirits, so that I can come to see a spirit from the outside.

Divine Director, I'm with you,
my vision one, no longer two,
as karma's veil you do disperse,
I see a whole new universe.

Divine Director, send the light,
from blindness clear my inner sight,

**my vision free, my vision clear,
your guidance is forever here.**

5. Maha Chohan, help me see that in this lifetime, and probably also in past lifetimes, I have had incidents where I came to see a spirit and I shifted.

Divine Director, I go up,
electric light now fills my cup,
consume in me all shadows old,
bestow on me a vision bold.

**Divine Director, send the light,
from blindness clear my inner sight,
my vision free, my vision clear,
your guidance is forever here.**

6. Maha Chohan, I do not want to be in my present state of consciousness anymore. I do not want to continue to repeat these old patterns. I want to change. I want to be more than this.

Divine Director, heart of gold,
my sacred labor I unfold,
o blessed Guru, I now see,
where my own plan is taking me.

**Divine Director, send the light,
from blindness clear my inner sight,
my vision free, my vision clear,
your guidance is forever here.**

7. Maha Chohan, help me consciously see the spirit and shift out of it, so that I am no longer identified with the spirit that is the primary spirit that represents the level of consciousness I have right now.

Divine Director, by your grace,
in grander scheme I find my place,
my individual flame I see,
uniqueness God has given me.

**Divine Director, send the light,
from blindness clear my inner sight,
my vision free, my vision clear,
your guidance is forever here.**

8. Maha Chohan, help me consciously follow this path of pulling my sense of identity away from these spirits. For it is only by doing so that I will truly make progress.

Divine Director, vision one,
I see that I AM God's own Sun,
with your direction so Divine,
I am now letting my light shine.

**Divine Director, send the light,
from blindness clear my inner sight,
my vision free, my vision clear,
your guidance is forever here.**

9. Maha Chohan, help me see if my study of spiritual teachings or practice of spiritual techniques have reinforced a spirit at a certain level of the path and a certain level of consciousness.

Divine Director, what a gift,
to be a part of Spirit's lift,
to raise mankind out of the night,
to bask in Spirit's loving sight.

**Divine Director, send the light,
from blindness clear my inner sight,
my vision free, my vision clear,
your guidance is forever here.**

Part 3

1. Maha Chohan, help me see if I have educated the spirit so that it has seemingly become more spiritual. Help me see if I think I have progressed spiritually, but it is not the Conscious You that has progressed; it is only the spirit.

Astrea, loving Being white,
your Presence is my pure delight,
your sword and circle white and blue,
the astral plane is cutting through.

**Astrea, come accelerate,
with purity I do vibrate,
release the fire so blue and white,
my aura filled with vibrant light.**

2. Maha Chohan, help me see that a spirit does not need to progress spiritually, because it will never make it into Heaven. The only thing that will make it into Heaven is the Conscious

You, and I will make it only when I dis-identify myself from any of my spirits.

> Astrea, calm the raging storm,
> so purity will be the norm,
> my aura filled with blue and white,
> with shining armor, like a knight.

> **Astrea, come accelerate,**
> **with purity I do vibrate,**
> **release the fire so blue and white,**
> **my aura filled with vibrant light.**

3. Maha Chohan, help me see if I have been on this false path and been fooled by the false teachers – and my own ego and my own spirits – into actually thinking that I am making progress. But in reality I am not making progress because I am still identified with a certain spirit.

> Astrea, come and cut me free,
> from every binding entity,
> let astral forces all be bound,
> true freedom I have surely found.

> **Astrea, come accelerate,**
> **with purity I do vibrate,**
> **release the fire so blue and white,**
> **my aura filled with vibrant light.**

4. Maha Chohan, help me see that when I dis-identify myself from that spirit, then I can quickly catch up to a higher level because of the efforts I made. Yet this will only happen when

I dis-identify myself from the spirit that I have educated, and I am willing to leave it behind.

> Astrea, I sincerely urge,
> from demons all, do me purge,
> consume them all and take me higher,
> I will endure your cleansing fire.

> **Astrea, come accelerate,**
> **with purity I do vibrate,**
> **release the fire so blue and white,**
> **my aura filled with vibrant light.**

5. Maha Chohan, help me see that you are not giving me this teaching to make me feel burdened. You are giving it to me in order to help me liberate myself from all of these feelings.

> Astrea, do all spirits bind,
> so that I am no longer blind,
> I see the spirit and its twin,
> the victory of Christ I win.

> **Astrea, come accelerate,**
> **with purity I do vibrate,**
> **release the fire so blue and white,**
> **my aura filled with vibrant light.**

6. Maha Chohan, help me see that such feelings come from whatever spirit is in my energy field. It is not the Conscious You that feels afraid, discouraged, ashamed, proud or superior. It can only be a spirit, and that spirit was programmed with a thought matrix of feeling this way.

Astrea, clear my every cell,
from energies of death and hell,
my body is now free to grow,
each cell emits an inner glow.

Astrea, come accelerate,
with purity I do vibrate,
release the fire so blue and white,
my aura filled with vibrant light.

7. Maha Chohan, help me see that I am the Conscious You, and I need to have a self through which I can express myself and interact with the physical body. And in taking on or creating this self, I am indeed creating a spirit.

Astrea, clear my feeling mind,
in purity my peace I find,
with higher feeling you release,
I co-create in perfect peace.

Astrea, come accelerate,
with purity I do vibrate,
release the fire so blue and white,
my aura filled with vibrant light.

8. Maha Chohan, help me see that this is inevitable, this is the process of taking incarnation. I cannot take incarnation as a new lifestream without creating such spirits. This is perfectly natural and in order.

Astrea, clear my mental realm,
my Christ self always at the helm,

I see now how to manifest,
the matrix that for all is best.

Astrea, come accelerate,
with purity I do vibrate,
release the fire so blue and white,
my aura filled with vibrant light.

9. Maha Chohan, help me engage in the process of letting one spirit die, ascending to the next level of consciousness, and then letting the spirit corresponding to that level die, and ascending to the next level and so on.

Astrea, with great clarity,
I claim a new identity,
etheric blueprint I now see,
I co-create more consciously.

Astrea, come accelerate,
with purity I do vibrate,
release the fire so blue and white,
my aura filled with vibrant light.

Part 4

1. Maha Chohan, help me see if I am trapped into reinforcing a certain spirit, based on the illusion that I can expand or perfect that spirit until it becomes acceptable to God.

O Shiva, God of Sacred Fire,
It's time to let the past expire,

I want to rise above the old,
a golden future to unfold.

O Shiva, clear the energy,
O Shiva, bring the synergy,
O Shiva, make all demons flee,
O Shiva, bring back peace to me.

2. Maha Chohan, help me see if I am trapped into thinking that I can enter the ascended state while being identified with that spirit, rather than entering the ascended state by giving up the very last ghost of any spirit in my lower being.

O Shiva, come and set me free,
from forces that do limit me,
with fire consume all that is less,
paving way for my success.

O Shiva, clear the energy,
O Shiva, bring the synergy,
O Shiva, make all demons flee,
O Shiva, bring back peace to me.

3. Maha Chohan, help me see the fundamental difference between the true inner path of self-transcendence and the false, outer path of seeking to perfect some kind of spirit, which is not a self-aware spirit that descended from above, but a non-self-aware spirit created here below.

O Shiva, Maya's veil disperse,
clear my private universe,
dispel the consciousness of death,
consume it with your Sacred Breath.

O Shiva, clear the energy,
O Shiva, bring the synergy,
O Shiva, make all demons flee,
O Shiva, bring back peace to me.

4. Maha Chohan, help me see that this does not mean that the spirit does not have some level of consciousness, but it does not have self-awareness, and that is why it cannot consciously transcend itself. This is the central ability of the Conscious You: the ability to consciously transcend itself.

O Shiva, I hereby let go,
of all attachments here below,
addictive entities consume,
the upward path I do resume.

O Shiva, clear the energy,
O Shiva, bring the synergy,
O Shiva, make all demons flee,
O Shiva, bring back peace to me.

5. Maha Chohan, help me see that I cannot transcend my sense of self without seeing that my sense of self is just a self, a spirit, that is not me.

O Shiva, I recite your name,
come banish fear and doubt and shame,
with fire expose within my mind,
what ego seeks to hide behind.

O Shiva, clear the energy,
O Shiva, bring the synergy,

O Shiva, make all demons flee,
O Shiva, bring back peace to me.

6. Maha Chohan, help me consciously use my ability to pull myself out of my current sense of self, taking my path to a higher level, and accelerating it beyond anything that I might have dreamt of before.

O Shiva, I am not afraid,
my karmic debt hereby is paid,
the past no longer owns my choice,
in breath of Shiva I rejoice.

O Shiva, clear the energy,
O Shiva, bring the synergy,
O Shiva, make all demons flee,
O Shiva, bring back peace to me.

7. Maha Chohan, help me see that I have already discovered the process of dis-identifying myself from a certain spirit and consciously rising above it. Help me become more conscious of it and accelerate the process.

O Shiva, show me spirit pairs,
that keep me trapped in their affairs,
I choose to see within my mind,
the spirits that you surely bind.

O Shiva, clear the energy,
O Shiva, bring the synergy,
O Shiva, make all demons flee,
O Shiva, bring back peace to me.

8. Maha Chohan, help me see that because I am a spiritual person, I am not overpowered by the more common collective spirits found on Earth. I am not completely identified with the collective spirit that dominated the culture in which I grew up.

> O Shiva, naked I now stand,
> my mind in freedom does expand,
> as all my ghosts I do release,
> surrender is the key to peace.

> **O Shiva, clear the energy,**
> **O Shiva, bring the synergy,**
> **O Shiva, make all demons flee,**
> **O Shiva, bring back peace to me.**

9. Maha Chohan, help me see that there are other collective spirits that cannot as easily be identified with certain outer characteristics, such as race, religion or ethnic group. These spirits have managed to hide from most people because they are not seen as spirits.

> O Shiva, all-consuming fire,
> with Parvati raise me higher,
> when I am raised your light to see,
> all men I will draw onto me.

> **O Shiva, clear the energy,**
> **O Shiva, bring the synergy,**
> **O Shiva, make all demons flee,**
> **O Shiva, bring back peace to me.**

Part 5

1. Maha Chohan, help me see that there are many such spirits, but they have not been recognized because they are not associated with physical characteristics, but with the emotional and mental characteristics that most people are not aware of.

> Surya, cosmic being bright,
> your balance is my pure delight,
> I am in orbit round God Star,
> in perfect unity we are.
>
> **Surya, banish all extremes,**
> **Surya, shatter Serpent's schemes,**
> **Surya, balance to me bring,**
> **Surya, making my heart sing.**

2. Maha Chohan, help me see if I have been affected by one or more of these spirits by being involved with various spiritual groups.

> Surya, there is more to life,
> than human conflict, war and strife,
> your balance gives me inner peace,
> all outer conflicts do now cease.
>
> **Surya, banish all extremes,**
> **Surya, shatter Serpent's schemes,**
> **Surya, balance to me bring,**
> **Surya, making my heart sing.**

3. Maha Chohan, help me see that many spiritual, religious or New Age groups are tied into a collective spirit of a certain kind. Many people have become more tied into a collective spirit as a result of being involved with a spiritual teaching or organization.

> Surya, what a wondrous sight,
> from Sirius you send the light,
> of one mind, I now call to thee,
> for your apprentice I would be.

> **Surya, banish all extremes,**
> **Surya, shatter Serpent's schemes,**
> **Surya, balance to me bring,**
> **Surya, making my heart sing.**

4. Maha Chohan, help me see that even though I have transcended some of my personal spirits, I still have other spirits that are affecting me. If I did not have any spirits, I would have ascended.

> Surya, radiate your light,
> with balance you set all things right,
> consuming energetic dross,
> my letting go is not a loss.

> **Surya, banish all extremes,**
> **Surya, shatter Serpent's schemes,**
> **Surya, balance to me bring,**
> **Surya, making my heart sing.**

5. Maha Chohan, help me see that there will be some spirit, that I am dealing with, until the moment I give up the last

ghost and ascend. This is simply the reality of the spiritual path on earth.

> Surya, your light is alive,
> for inner balance I do strive,
> the alchemy is now begun,
> my heart transformed into a sun.
>
> **Surya, banish all extremes,**
> **Surya, shatter Serpent's schemes,**
> **Surya, balance to me bring,**
> **Surya, making my heart sing.**

6. Maha Chohan, help me see that there is no reason to be discouraged by it or to feel afraid or shameful about it. I accept that this is the way it is, and I make the decision to sharpen my ability to see through these spirits as quickly as possible and thereby free myself from them.

> Surya, come enlighten me,
> duality you help me see,
> extremes they cannot pull me in,
> on Middle Way I always win.
>
> **Surya, banish all extremes,**
> **Surya, shatter Serpent's schemes,**
> **Surya, balance to me bring,**
> **Surya, making my heart sing.**

7. Maha Chohan, help me see that this is a process that has an individual aspect, because I am the one who must see it in my consciousness. I must make the shift in consciousness, where I have pulled the Conscious You outside of the spirit. I am

seeing the spirit from the outside, and I am seeing that it is not me.

> Surya, in your cosmic sphere,
> with Cuzco I your light revere,
> from your perspective o so grand,
> life finally I understand.
>
> **Surya, banish all extremes,**
> **Surya, shatter Serpent's schemes,**
> **Surya, balance to me bring,**
> **Surya, making my heart sing.**

8. Maha Chohan, help me see that this is a process that cannot be taught. It is built into the Conscious You, but it is something that I must discover on my own by experiencing it.

> Surya, show me God's design,
> I see that God is all benign,
> you calm my feeling body's storm,
> I know the God beyond all form.
>
> **Surya, banish all extremes,**
> **Surya, shatter Serpent's schemes,**
> **Surya, balance to me bring,**
> **Surya, making my heart sing.**

9. Maha Chohan, I will not be discouraged. I will continue to ponder this and continue to use the tools, so that I diminish the magnetic pull of a certain spirit. And then the Conscious You naturally, effortlessly, and seemingly spontaneously, pulls itself out of that spirit.

Surya, I come from afar,
and as you show me my home star,
I see now my internal light,
a star I am in my own right.

Surya, banish all extremes,
Surya, shatter Serpent's schemes,
Surya, balance to me bring,
Surya, making my heart sing.

Part 6

1. Maha Chohan, help me see that it is natural for the Conscious You to be continuously moving, to be consciously looking at life from different perspectives. That is why I have been searching for the spiritual path.

O Godfre, your ascension light,
leads us through the darkest night,
it is a trail that you have carved,
for all who are for freedom starved.

O Godfre, I am free to be,
one with God and one with thee,
there is no greater love I see,
than what I feel for God in me.

2. Maha Chohan, help me see that it is natural for me to be identified with a certain spirit, and to experience life through the perception filter of that spirit for a time. But it is also

natural for me not to remain in that spirit but to shift to a different perspective.

> O Godfre, I surrender all,
> as I now follow inner call.
> The providence that is Divine,
> will show me plan uniquely mine.
>
> **O Godfre, I am free to be,**
> **one with God and one with thee,**
> **there is no greater love I see,**
> **than what I feel for God in me.**

3. Maha Chohan, help me see that it is only by the spirit gaining enough momentum that it can form a magnetic pull on my attention, that the spirit can keep me trapped at that level over a period of time.

> O Godfre, show me how to be,
> from man's ambitions clearly free.
> I can of my self nothing do,
> and this I want to learn from you.
>
> **O Godfre, I am free to be,**
> **one with God and one with thee,**
> **there is no greater love I see,**
> **than what I feel for God in me.**

4. Maha Chohan, help me see that an aggressive spirit will aggressively seek to keep me at that level. Help me feel the aggressive force that is pulling on me, that is pushing me in a certain direction.

O Godfre, I would know your flame,
so I will never be the same.
I want to grow forever more,
and help God's kingdom to restore.

**O Godfre, I am free to be,
one with God and one with thee,
there is no greater love I see,
than what I feel for God in me.**

5. Maha Chohan, help me become more conscious of this, and know that every time I feel this aggressiveness, there is a spirit that is influencing me.

O Godfre, help me now to see,
complete surrender is the key.
All problems can be solved by me,
when I surrender all to thee.

**O Godfre, I am free to be,
one with God and one with thee,
there is no greater love I see,
than what I feel for God in me.**

6. Maha Chohan, help me see that instead of running away from it, resisting it or fighting it, I now say: "Here is a spirit that is hiding from me. I am going to force it to come out in the open, so that I can see it and thereby stop identifying myself with it, so that it will no longer have power over me.

O Godfre, for your flame I call,
a great example to us all.

You stand so firm in time of need,
so we can move with true God-speed.

**O Godfre, I am free to be,
one with God and one with thee,
there is no greater love I see,
than what I feel for God in me.**

7. Maha Chohan, I am going to use the tools given to me, so that I can flush these spirits out of their hiding places, where I can see that they are not me and therefore free myself from their influence.

O Godfre, I would know your mind,
to see the secret you did find.
of when to do and when to stop,
so I am always going up.

**O Godfre, I am free to be,
one with God and one with thee,
there is no greater love I see,
than what I feel for God in me.**

8. Maha Chohan, help me see that at the lower levels of consciousness, there is no meaningful difference between the ego and the primary spirit that is overpowering people.

O Godfre, you are always free,
for you obedience is the key,
we go beyond all human flaw,
by following the greater law.

**O Godfre, I am free to be,
one with God and one with thee,
there is no greater love I see,
than what I feel for God in me.**

9. Maha Chohan, help me see that it is a mistake to think that because I have overcome a certain spirit, and I am free from that spirit, I am now also free from the ego. Because the ego is not the spirit; it is not the totality of the spirit.

O Godfre, light is shining clear,
the mighty I AM Presence near,
I go with you beyond the fray,
to set example in my day.

**O Godfre, I am free to be,
one with God and one with thee,
there is no greater love I see,
than what I feel for God in me.**

Part 7

1. Maha Chohan, help me see that as I overcome a spirit at a certain level, I will shift into seeing life through the spirit at the next level up. The challenge will be whether I will see the need to free myself from that spirit also or begin the cycle of reinforcing that spirit through my attention.

I see how my senses can only deceive,
for nothing they tell me, I fully believe.

Behind all appearances is only light,
they only seem real to our limited sight.

O Padmasambhava, in your Flame of Peace,
all human opinions I hereby release.
I see now the ultimate truth you reveal,
earth is an appearance, where nothing is real.

2. Maha Chohan, help me see that there are a number of spirits, and when I transcend a spirit, the spirit is dead. But I am still not an ascended being, which means that I still have an ego. The ego is what keeps me in embodiment and keeps me out of the ascended state.

My mind and my senses are only a tool,
and I am determined to not be a fool.
My personal self, is no more who I am,
the earthly identity is but a scam.

O Padmasambhava, in your Flame of Peace,
all human opinions I hereby release.
I see now the ultimate truth you reveal,
earth is an appearance, where nothing is real.

3. Maha Chohan, help me see that there are levels of the ego. I will not be completely free of the ego until I ascend, for there needs to be something that keeps me tied to the physical octave. When I have no more ego, I cannot maintain myself in a physical body.

From sense-based perception I want to be free,
clear my inner sight, so I truly can see.

My human opinions, they do make me blind,
with neutral awareness, new visions I find.

**O Padmasambhava, in your Flame of Peace,
all human opinions I hereby release.
I see now the ultimate truth you reveal,
earth is an appearance, where nothing is real.**

4. Maha Chohan, help me see that I will not become ego-free until I have ascended. Help me avoid becoming ensnared by the more subtle aspects of the ego that correspond to the higher levels of consciousness and can cause me to become stuck at that level.

A self is what makes an opinion seem real,
it projects there's a problem, with which I must deal.
I will not be free, till I see through this lie,
and say to the self: I am letting you die.

**O Padmasambhava, in your Flame of Peace,
all human opinions I hereby release.
I see now the ultimate truth you reveal,
earth is an appearance, where nothing is real.**

5. Maha Chohan, help me see that there is *always* a need for self-transcendence, for self-transcendence *is* life. Self-transcendence is the Holy Spirit.

Through human opinions, I simply can't see,
the higher perspective—Christ reality,
When the self dualistic, I truly let die,
the Christ mind does open, up my inner eye.

> **O Padmasambhava, in your Flame of Peace,**
> **all human opinions I hereby release.**
> **I see now the ultimate truth you reveal,**
> **earth is an appearance, where nothing is real.**

6. Oh Maha Chohan, show me the spirit that is holding me back right now, and the decision behind it.

> O Padmasambhava, the world has gone mad,
> as dualistic thinking, defines good and bad.
> The judgment of Christ, upon forces so dark,
> rekindle in people, our spiritual spark.

> **O Padmasambhava, in your Flame of Peace,**
> **all human opinions I hereby release.**
> **I see now the ultimate truth you reveal,**
> **earth is an appearance, where nothing is real.**

7. Oh Archangel Michael, bind that spirit, so it cannot affect myself or any part of life.

> O Padmasambhava, set all people free,
> from mindset so epic, from duality.
> Cut all people free from the serpentine lie,
> so that to Christ Jesus, we all can draw nigh.

> **O Padmasambhava, in your Flame of Peace,**
> **all human opinions I hereby release.**
> **I see now the ultimate truth you reveal,**
> **earth is an appearance, where nothing is real.**

8. Oh Mighty I AM Presence, shatter the thought matrix behind that spirit.

The serpentine lie, says that what we now see,
is all that our lives, on this planet can be.
Yet with the Christ mind, we can see there is
more,
the earth will be brighter than ever before.

O Padmasambhava, in your Flame of Peace,
all human opinions I hereby release.
I see now the ultimate truth you reveal,
earth is an appearance, where nothing is real.

9. Oh Mother Mary, help me surrender myself entirely into
the River of Life.

Saint Germain has the plans, for a bright Golden
Age,
to receive them, our minds must be free from the
cage,
O Padmasambhava, with your Flame of Peace,
the vision of Oneness, to all you release.

O Padmasambhava, in your Flame of Peace,
all human opinions I hereby release.
I see now the ultimate truth you reveal,
earth is an appearance, where nothing is real.

Sealing:

In the name of the Divine Mother, I fully accept that the
power of these calls is used to set free the Ma-ter light, so it
can outpicture the perfect vision of Christ for my own life, for

all people and for the planet. In the name I AM THAT I AM, it is done! Amen.

DECREE TO THE MAHA CHOHAN

In the name I AM THAT I AM, Jesus Christ, I call to my I Will Be Presence to flow through my being and give these decrees with full power. I call to beloved Maha Chohan and the seven Chohans to release flood tides of light, to consume all blocks and attachments that prevent me from flowing with the River of Life and transcending myself daily, including…

[Make personal calls]

1. Maha Chohan, I will to grow,
I feel the power of your flow.
Maha Chohan, the veil is rent,
creative will from heaven sent.

**O Holy Spirit, flow through me,
I am the open door for thee.
O mighty rushing stream of Light,
transcendence is my sacred right.**

2. Maha Chohan, your wisdom streams,
awaken all from matter's dreams.
Maha Chohan, your balance bring,
let bells of integration ring.

**O Holy Spirit, flow through me,
I am the open door for thee.
O mighty rushing stream of Light,
transcendence is my sacred right.**

3. Maha Chohan, love's mighty call,
the prison walls are shattered all.
Maha Chohan, set all life free
through unconditionality.

**O Holy Spirit, flow through me,
I am the open door for thee.
O mighty rushing stream of Light,
transcendence is my sacred right.**

4. Maha Chohan, intentions pure,
all life is one, I know for sure.
Maha Chohan, I am awake,
surrender all for oneness' sake.

**O Holy Spirit, flow through me,
I am the open door for thee.
O mighty rushing stream of Light,
transcendence is my sacred right.**

5. Maha Chohan, help all men see,
through veils of unreality.

Maha Chohan, with single eye,
I know I am the greater "I."

**O Holy Spirit, flow through me,
I am the open door for thee.
O mighty rushing stream of Light,
transcendence is my sacred right.**

6. Maha Chohan, your peace I find,
Maitreya shows me to be kind.
Maha Chohan, all war will cease,
now flooding all with sacred peace.

**O Holy Spirit, flow through me,
I am the open door for thee.
O mighty rushing stream of Light,
transcendence is my sacred right.**

7. Maha Chohan, you balance all,
the seven rays upon my call.
Maha Chohan, all life is free,
transcending for eternity.

**O Holy Spirit, flow through me,
I am the open door for thee.
O mighty rushing stream of Light,
transcendence is my sacred right.**

8. Maha Chohan, your sacred Flame,
what beauty in your blessed name.
Maha Chohan, what rushing flow,
the Spirit one with life below.

**O Holy Spirit, flow through me,
I am the open door for thee.
O mighty rushing stream of Light,
transcendence is my sacred right.**

9. Maha Chohan, your Presence here,
filling up the inner sphere.
Life is now a sacred flow,
God Wisdom we on all bestow.

**O Holy Spirit, flow through me,
I am the open door for thee.
O mighty rushing stream of Light,
transcendence is my sacred right.**

Sealing:

In the name of the Divine Mother, I fully accept that the power of these calls is used to set free the Ma-ter light, so it can outpicture the perfect vision of Christ for my own life, for all people and for the planet. In the name I AM THAT I AM, it is done! Amen.